▲.The American
Diabetes Association®

The American
Dietetic Association

FAMILY
COOKBOOK
Volume II

Revised Edition

The American Diabetes Association is the nation's leading voluntary health agency in the field of diabetes, with 55 state affiliates and more than 800 chapters across the country.

The American Dietetic Association is the nation's largest group of nutrition professionals, with more than 50,000 members.

Other books by the authors:

The American Diabetes Association
The American Dietetic Association
    Family Cookbook, Volume I (Rev. Ed.)

The American Diabetes Association
The American Dietetic Association
    Family Cookbook, Volume III
    With Microwave Adaptations

American Diabetes Association
    Holiday Cookbook
Betty Wedman, M.S., R.D.

▲ The American Diabetes Association®

The American Dietetic Association

FAMILY COOKBOOK

Volume II

Revised Edition

Illustrated by Lauren Rosen

PRENTICE HALL PRESS

New York   London   Toronto   Sydney   Tokyo

Published in 1987 by Prentice Hall Press
A Division of Simon & Schuster Inc.
Gulf + Western Building
One Gulf + Western Plaza
New York, NY 10023

PRENTICE HALL PRESS is a trademark of Simon & Schuster, Inc.

Originally published in 1984 by Prentice-Hall, Inc.

LC No. 87-42674

ISBN 0-13-003955-1

Manufactured in the United States of America

10 9 8 7 6 5 4 3 2

ACKNOWLEDGMENTS

The American Diabetes Association and The American Dietetic Association gratefully acknowledge the contributions made by:

Cookbook Advisory Committee

Marion Franz, R.D.
Georgia Kimmel, R.D.
Joy Kirkpatrick, R.D.
Madelyn Wheeler, R.D.
Judith Wylie-Rosett, Ed.D., R.D. (Chair)

Cookbook Computer Services

Indiana University Computing Facilities
Patricia S. Ours, R.D.
Lawrence A. Wheeler, Ph.D., M.D.

Contributors

Nutritional Needs Through Life's Stages

Margaret Bogle, R.D.
Sue Brady, R.D.
Judith Ernst, R.D.
Karyl Rickard, Ph.D., R.D.

On Fighting Fat II: Keeping Primed

  Marjan Schneider, M.S.W., A.C.S.W.

Exercise: Nutrition's Important Partner

  Peter J. Spiers, M.S. (Exercise Physiologist)

Introducing Tofu and Recipe for Scrambled Tofu

  Naoko Owaki Robinson, founder, House of Kenko, Center
    for Optimal Health and Oriental Studies

Chapters adapted from *Diabetes Forecast* magazine

  Nirmala Auerbach, R.D.
  Barbara Burgess, R.D.
  Marion Franz, R.D.
  Kathy McFarland
  Beth Naylor, R.D.
  F. Xavier Pi-Sunyer, M.D.
  Dorothea Sims
  Janice M. Whitfield, R.D.
  Judy Wylie-Rosett, Ed.D., R.D.

Recipe Development

  Alice Bachrach, R.D.
  Peggy Brown
  Alice Knight
  Frances H. Lee, R.D., Coordinator
  Lavoyce McCurdy
  Ruth Strickland, R.D.
  All the friends of the Associations, including *Diabetes
    Forecast* subscribers, who contributed recipes

Several recipes in this collection are reprinted or adapted from the Indiana University School of Medicine's Collection of Recipes, Department of Nutrition and Dietetics, Bloomington, printing, 1983; and from *Cooking to Stay in Shape*, by Marion Franz, Betsy Kerr Hedding,and Gayle Leitch.

In addition to the recipes submitted by individuals for testing and use in this collection, several were reprinted directly or adapted from the following sources:

Collection of Recipes of the Department of Nutrition and Dietetics, Indiana University School of Medicine, H. Bernice Boucher, M.S., R.D., editor, Indianapolis, IN, scheduled for publication in 1984.

Cooking to Stay in Shape, *by Marion Franz, Betsy Kerr Hedding and Gayle Leitch, SHAPE, Inc., Minnetonka, MN, 1983.*

An Apple a Day, *Volume 2, Loma Linda University School of Medicine Women's Auxiliary to the Alumni Association, Typecraft, Inc., Pasadena, CA, 1983.*

Nutritious and Delicious, *the Greater Cincinnati Dietetic Association and the Greater Cincinnati Nutrition Council, Joerger-Vetter Printing, Cincinnati, OH, 1982.*

Manuscript Production

> Mary M. Astarita
> Barbara Burgess, R.D., Coordinator
> Robert P. Lundy
> Ricki Rusting, Coordinator
> Caroline Stevens

☐ CONTENTS

☐ FOREWORD

Volume II of the *Family Cookbook* was prepared to complement the first *Family Cookbook*, which was extremely well received. This book, like the first, is directed to anyone with diabetes as well as to others who care about their health.

In addition to giving you more than 200 new recipes, Volume II includes a nutrition guide that elaborates on many of the topics in the first volume and responds to reader requests for added information. For instance, chapters in Volume II deal with fiber, emotional aspects of dieting, and the various nutritional needs through life's stages. Moreover, up-to-the-minute information on diabetes is included, such as a discussion of the glycemic index (a new concept in meal planning), as well as a review of current dietary strategies for managing type I (insulin-dependent) and type II (non-insulin-dependent) diabetes.

We are proud of this new volume of the *Family Cookbook* and sincerely hope it will assist you to live more comfortably with diabetes until a cure or prevention can be found.

> Karl E. Sussman, M.D.
> President, American
> Diabetes Association

The American Dietetic Association is again pleased to collaborate with the American Diabetes Association in the preparation of the second volume of the *Family Cookbook*. Recipes in this collection were developed consistent with the nutritional guidelines formulated by nutrition experts and health and government agencies for decreasing dietary risk factors associated with diabetes and other chronic diseases.

Health-conscious persons will not only find delightful, nutritious, and economical recipes but information on fitness and food management needed by individuals taking more responsibility for their own health. This volume expands on information in Volume I and offers new features, including a chapter on exercise, a walking program, a chapter on emotional considerations of weight control, information on tofu and its use in meal planning, an update on fiber, and advice on how to decrease sugar, calories, and fat in family meal preparation. As with Volume I of the *Family Cookbook*, families with a diabetic member, as well as individuals and families in pursuit of a healthier lifestyle, will find this to be an indispensable book, one that dietitians and physicians will happily recommend.

The American Dietetic Association enthusiastically presents this second volume of the *Family Cookbook* and acknowledges the contribution of the Advisory Committee of Registered Dietitians, The American Dietetic Association Publications Committee, and the many Registered Dietitians who assisted in preparation of the manuscript and reviewed the material for publication.

Kathleen Zolber, Ph.D., R.D.,
President,
The American Dietetic Association

☐ LOCATING THE ASSOCIATIONS

NATIONAL OFFICES

American Diabetes Association
1660 Duke Street
Alexandria, Virginia 22314
(703) 549-1500

The American Dietetic Association
430 North Michigan Avenue
Chicago, Illinois 60611
(312) 280-5000

AFFILIATE ASSOCIATIONS
OF THE AMERICAN DIABETES ASSOCIATION

Alabama Affiliate, Inc.
904 Bob Wallace Avenue
Suite 222
Huntsville, AL 35801
(205) 533-5775 or (205) 533-5776

Alaska Affiliate, Inc.
201 E. Third Avenue
Suite 301
Anchorage, AK 99501
(907) 276-3607

Arizona Affiliate, Inc.
7337 North Nineteenth Avenue
Room 404
Phoenix, AZ 85021
(602) 995-1515

Arkansas Affiliate, Inc.
Tanglewood Shopping Center
7509 Cantrell Road
Suite 227
Little Rock, AR 72207
(501) 666-6345

Northern California Affiliate, Inc.
2550 Ninth Street
Suite 114
Berkeley, CA 94710
(415) 644-0920

Southern California Affiliate, Inc.
3460 Wilshire Boulevard
Suite 900
Los Angeles, CA 90010
(213) 381-3689

Colorado Affiliate, Inc.
2450 South Downing Street
Denver, CO 80210
(303) 778-7556

Connecticut Affiliate, Inc.
40 South St.
P.O. Box 10160
Elmwood, CT 06110
(203) 249-9942 or 1 (800) 842-6323

Delaware Affiliate, Inc.
2713 Lancaster Avenue
Wilmington, DE 19805
(302) 656-0030

Washington, D.C Area
   Affiliate, Inc.
1819 H Street, N.W.
Suite 1200
Washington, DC 20006
(202) 331-8303

Florida Affiliate, Inc.
P.O. Box 19745 (mailing address)
Orlando, FL 32814
3101 Maguire Blvd.
   (street address)
Suite 288
Orlando, FL 32803
(305) 894-6664

Georgia Affiliate, Inc.
3783 Presidential Parkway
Suite 102
Atlanta, GA 30340
(404) 454-8401

Hawaii Affiliate, Inc.
510 South Beretania Street
Honolulu, HI 96813
(808) 521-5677

Idaho Affiliate, Inc.
1528 Vista
Boise, ID 83705
(208) 342-2774

Downstate Illinois Affiliate, Inc.
965 North Water Street
Decatur, IL 62523
(217) 422-8228

Northern Illinois Affiliate, Inc.
6 North Michigan Avenue
Suite 1202
Chicago, IL 60602
(312) 346-1805

Indiana Affiliate, Inc.
222 South Downey Avenue
Suite 320
Indianapolis, IN 46219
(317) 352-9226

Iowa Affiliate, Inc.
888 Tenth Street
Marion, IA 52302
(319) 373-0530

Kansas Affiliate, Inc.
3210 E. Douglas
Wichita, KS 67208
(316) 681-6091

Kentucky Affiliate, Inc.
P.O. Box 345 (mailing address)
Frankfort, KY 40602
306 West Main (street address)
Suite #513
Frankfort, KY 40602
(502) 223-2971

Louisiana Affiliate, Inc.
9420 Lindale Avenue
Suite B
Baton Rouge, LA 70815
(504) 927-7732

Maine Affiliate, Inc.
59 Northport Avenue
Belfast, ME 04915
(207) 338-5132

Maryland Affiliate, Inc.
3701 Old Court Road
Suite 19
Baltimore, MD 21208
(301) 486-5516

Massachusetts Affiliate, Inc.
190 North Main Street
Natick, MA 01760
(617) 655-6900

Michigan Affiliate, Inc.
The Clausen Bldg. North Unit
23100 Providence Drive
Suite 475
Southfield, MI 48075
(313) 552-0480

Minnesota Affiliate, Inc.
3005 Ottawa Avenue, South
Minneapolis, MN 55416
(612) 920-6796

Mississippi Affiliate, Inc.
10 Lakeland Circle
Jackson, MS 39216
(601) 981-9511

Greater St. Louis Affiliate, Inc.
1790 South Brentwood Boulevard
St. Louis, MO 63144
(314) 968-3196

Heart of America Affiliate, Inc.
9201 Ward Parkway
Suite 300
Kansas City, MO 64114
(816) 361-3361

Missouri Regional Affiliate, Inc.
P.O. Box 11 (mailing address)
811 Cherry (street address)
Suite 304
Columbia, MO 65201
(314) 443-8611

Montana Affiliate, Inc.
Box 2411 (mailing address)
Great Falls, MT 59403
600 Central Plaza (street address)
Suite 304
Great Falls, MT 59401
(406) 761-0908

Nebraska Affiliate, Inc.
7377 Pacific
Suite 216A
Omaha, NE 68114
(402) 391-1251

Nevada Affiliate, Inc.
4550 East Charleston Boulevard
Las Vegas, NV 89104
(702) 459-7099

New Hampshire Affiliate, Inc.
P.O. Box 595 (mailing address)
Manchester, NH 03105
104 Middle Street
   (mailing address)
Manchester, NH 03101
(603) 627-9579

New Jersey Affiliate, Inc.
P.O. Box 6423 (mailing address)
312 North Adamsville Rd.
   (street address)
Bridgewater, NJ 08807
(201) 725-7878

New Mexico Affiliate, Inc.
525 San Pedro, N.E.
Suite 101
Albuquerque, NM 87108
(505) 266-5716

New York Diabetes Affiliate, Inc.
505 Eighth Avenue
New York, NY 10018
(212) 947-9707

New York State Affiliate, Inc.
P.O. Box 1037 (mailing address)
Syracuse, NY 13201
113 East Willow Street
   (street address)
Syracuse, NY 13202
(315) 472-9111

North Carolina Affiliate, Inc.
2315-A Sunset Avenue
Rocky Mount, NC 27801
(919) 937-4121

North Dakota Affiliate, Inc.
P.O. Box 234 (mailing address)
Grand Forks, ND 58206-0234
101 North Third Street
   (street address)
Suite 502
Grand Forks, ND 58201
(701) 746-4427

Ohio Affiliate, Inc.
1855 Fountain Square Court
Suite 310
Columbus, OH 43224-1360
(614) 263-2330

Oklahoma Affiliate, Inc.
Warren Professional Building
6465 South Yale Avenue
Suite 423
Tulsa, OK 74136
(918) 492-3839 or 1 (800) 722-5448

Oregon Affiliate, Inc.
3607 S.W. Corbett Street
Portland, OR 97201
(503) 228-0849

Greater Philadelphia Affiliate,
Inc.
21 South Fifth Street
The Bourse
Suite 570
Philadelphia, PA 19106
(215) 627-7718

Western Pennsylvania Affiliate,
Inc.
4617 Winthrop Street
Pittsburgh, PA 15213
(412) 682-3392

Mid-Pennsylvania Affiliate, Inc.
2045 Westgate Drive
Suite B-1
Bethlehem, PA 18017
(215) 867-6660

Rhode Island Affiliate, Inc.
4 Fallon Avenue
Providence, RI 02908
(401) 331-0099

South Carolina Affiliate, Inc.
2838 Devine Street
Columbia, SC 29205
(803) 799-4246

South Dakota Affiliate, Inc.
P.O. Box 659
Sioux Falls, SD 57101
(605) 335-7670

Tennessee Affiliate, Inc.
1701 Twenty-first Avenue, South
Room 403
Nashville, TN 37212
(615) 298-9919

Texas Affiliate, Inc.
8140 North Mopac
Building 1
Suite 130
Austin, TX 78759
(512) 343-6981

Utah Affiliate, Inc.
564 East 300 South
Salt Lake City, UT 84102
(801) 363-3024

Vermont Affiliate, Inc.
217 Church Street
Burlington, VT 05401
(802) 862-3882

Virginia Affiliate, Inc.
404 Eighth Street, N.E.
Suite C
Charlottesville, VA 22901
(804) 293-4953

Washington Affiliate, Inc.
3201 Fremont Avenue North
Seattle, WA 98103
(206) 632-4576

West Virginia Affiliate, Inc.
Professional Building
1036 Quarrier Street
Room 404
Charleston, WV 25301
(304) 346-6418 or 1 (800) 642-3055

Wisconsin Affiliate, Inc.
10721 West Capitol Drive
Milwaukee, WI 53222
(414) 464-9395

Wyoming Affiliate, Inc.
2908 Kelly Drive
Cheyenne, WY 82001
(307) 638-3578

AFFILIATE ASSOCIATIONS
OF THE AMERICAN DIETETIC ASSOCIATION

The American Dietetic Association has state associations in each state and district associations in many areas. Your local American Diabetes Association can provide you with the address of the Dietetic Association nearest you. Or you can get the address through the national office of the The American Dietetic Association.

☐ INTRODUCTION

If you want everyone in your family to enjoy the same menu at meals . . . if you want to make delicious yet healthy dishes with ease . . . if you want to learn more about eating to promote health and prevent diet-related diseases . . . if you want to learn more about the dietary side of diabetes care . . . this book is for you.

Volume II of the American Diabetes Association/The American Dietetic Association *Family Cookbook* builds on Volume I, yet can also stand alone. The content of Volume II is entirely new. It does the following:

- ☐ Adds more than 200 delicious, economical, and nutritious recipes formulated according to healthful criteria and taste tests.
- ☐ Addresses the special dietary dilemmas of people who take insulin.
- ☐ Offers in-depth advice on weight control for the many individuals (diabetic or not) who are overweight, taking into account the *emotional* as well as behavioral side of the fight against fat.
- ☐ Encourages you to exercise and gives you tips for doing it safely.
- ☐ Includes great ideas for meal planning, with advice on how to add zest to your creations while reducing calories.
- ☐ Suggests practical ways to cut kitchen costs.
- ☐ Gives you an update on fiber and the "glycemic index" and includes the fiber content in one serving of each recipe as well as an array of high-fiber recipes.
- ☐ Helps you to handle such special activities as wildernesss camping, canoeing, and hiking.
- ☐ Adds ethnic recipes and "exchanges."

In addition, the elements that made Volume I so popular are here. Like the first cookbook, this one is meant for the whole family, so the recipes usually yield four to six servings. However, many also include directions for making two servings. Moreover, along with fiber content, all receipes are once again accompanied by a listing of the grams of protein, fat, and carbohydrate, the calories, and the milligrams of sodium, potassium, and cholesterol in a single serving. The exchange values are also listed for those of you who plan your meals on the basis of The American Diabetes Association/The American Dietetic Association's *Exchange Lists for Meal Planning*. In general, the recipes are in keeping with the national dietary guidelines aimed at helping all Americans reduce their risk of chronic disease. These guidelines are very similar to those of the American Diabetes Association and other health agencies and suggest reducing the total amount of fat eaten, particularly saturated fat and cholesterol, decreasing the amount of sugar and salt consumed, and increasing the amount of unrefined carbohydrates eaten (especially those with fiber), as well as controlling calories. The majority of the recipes, therefore, are limited in fat, saturated fat, and cholesterol, and are low in sugar and salt.

Volume I is an excellent introduction to the principles of good nutrition. It describes the basic food groups and explains the logic behind meal planning for the general population and for people who have diabetes. Volume II reviews that information briefly and emphasizes the practical side of living with diabetes without giving up good food. We want you to be happy with your meals because if you are, chances are good that you'll eat right and be a lot healthier, too.

FAMILY
COOKBOOK
Volume II

1 □ NUTRITION AND GOOD HEALTH

Good nutrition is essential to good health whether one has diabetes or not. But what exactly is meant by good nutrition? Simply put, it means maintaining an adequate supply of the materials the body needs for growth, tissue repair, and normal life functioning. These vital materials, or nutrients, may be classified as follows:

> Proteins
> Carbohydrates
> Fats
> Vitamins
> Minerals
> Water

The foods we eat provide us with these nutrients in a wide variety of forms. Through the processes of digestion, absorption, and metabolism, the foods are broken down chemically, and nutrients are taken into the bloodstream and moved from the blood into cells for storage or for immediate use as energy. Whatever the body cannot use is excreted as waste.

Some foods are better suppliers of certain nutrients than are others. Fish, for example, is relatively high in protein, whereas whole grain breads are a good source of carbohydrates, and nuts contain a large percentage of fat. To achieve the goal of good nutrition, therefore, you need to select a wide variety of foods. With a well-balanced diet, you can ensure that you get the right

1

amount and variety of the essential nutrients. (For more information, see Volume I, Chapter 1, "The Basics of Good Nutrition.")

DIET AND DISEASE PREVENTION

Good nutrition is one of the most valuable forms of preventive medicine. Many aspects of our health are beyond our control. For example, our genetic makeup may leave us susceptible to certain chronic diseases. But diet and exercise are two crucial areas in which we can directly and positively influence our long-term well-being.

The consequence of failing to eat a balanced diet may be serious health problems, particularly if too much of the wrong kind of food is eaten over a long period of time and if poor diet is combined with inactivity. Overeating of foods high in calories, fat, salt, and sugar, for instance, may contribute in varying measures to heart disease, high blood pressure, obesity, stroke, diabetes, and, possibly, some forms of cancer. Prolonged alcohol abuse has been definitely linked to cirrhosis of the liver and to other health-threatening disorders. These and other food-related problems often start in youth. They may be difficult to cure once they are under way, so it is important to recognize them and, when possible, prevent them early.

Furthermore, the foods we eat affect more than our general physical health and risk of developing certain diseases. Current research suggests that mood, sleep patterns, appetite, and a host of other psychological and emotional functions may be influenced, at least in part, by dietary factors. This is because the nutrients obtained from food make up the chemical substances that control these processes in the brain.

Good nutrition is vital to the development of learning and motor skills in very young children; nutritional imbalances can contribute to behavior problems and poor concentration in school-age youngsters. Healthy eating also becomes especially important for maintaining brain power in older people. Often, the apparent symptoms of senility in the elderly are actually the cumulative results of malnutrition. Fortunately, in cases where physical damage to the brain has not occurred, many of these symptoms are reversible.

BALANCE IS THE KEY

The "balanced" diet you want for yourself and your family should:

☐ Furnish sufficient amounts of the various essential nutrients.

☐ Avoid excesses of certain nutrients that increase the risk of diet-related diseases.

☐ Provide sources of calories, or energy, needed to maintain an appropriate weight and activity level.

To plan well-balanced meals, be sure to select foods from each of the four major food groups:

☐ *Fruits and Vegetables.* These provide: vitamin A (deep yellow or dark green vegetables), vitamin C (citrus, berries, tomatoes), potassium, B vitamins, iron, calcium, carbohydrates, and fiber.

☐ *Whole Grain Cereals and Breads.* For: B vitamins, iron, vitamin E, carbohydrates, and fiber.

☐ *Dairy Products.* For: calcium, protein, riboflavin, vitamins A and D (if fortified), and vitamin B_{12}.

☐ *Meats, Fish, Poultry, Eggs, Dried Beans, Peas, and Nuts.* For: protein, B vitamins, iron, and zinc.

If you follow the exchange-type meal plan recommended by the American Diabetes Association, you will notice that you are told to choose foods from six, rather than four, food groups. In actuality, you are choosing foods from similar groups; the Exchange Lists simply divide the groups into like foods for more specificity.

The lists are titled: Starch/Bread, Meat, Vegetable, Fruit, Milk, and Fat.

HOW THE GROUPS COMPARE

BASIC 4	EXCHANGE LISTS
1. Fruits and Vegetables	Fruit
	Vegetable
	Starch/Bread
2. Breads	Starch/Bread
3. Dairy Products	Milk
4. Meats	Meat (subdivided by fat content; also includes fish, poultry, cheese, eggs, and peanut butter)
	Fat (derived from Meat and Milk groups; also includes such fatty items as nuts, oils, and salad dressings)

Work out the specific amounts you need from each food group with your doctor, dietitian, or diet counselor. Individual nutritional needs may vary according to age and activity level, among other factors. (Chapter 3 provides a description of some of these considerations at different stages of life.) However, the basic principle of a balanced diet for good health is a sound one and applies to everyone.

Finally, you should be able to have a well-balanced meal plan and meet all your nutritional requirements with ordinary food. Special supplements of food products, vitamins, and minerals are rarely needed. (Menstruating women who lose a lot of blood each month, however, may need additional iron to make up for the iron losses in the blood.) No scientific evidence shows that such supplements offer any significant improvement on a regular, well-balanced food plan. In some instances, very large quantities of certain vitamin supplements may have harmful side effects or may interfere with the absorption of other vital nutrients.

NUTRITIONAL GUIDELINES

The following seven basic nutritional guidelines were designed by nutrition experts for the federal government to promote healthful eating and to reduce the risk of food-related diseases in the general population. They are also consistent with the current recommended principles for the nutritional management of diabetes. They are appropriate for the whole family—small children and adolescents, as well as adults.

1. EAT A VARIETY OF FOODS. Variety is the spice of life, it is said; but when it comes to good nutrition, variety is essential. There are up to fifty known nutrients that the body needs to stay healthy, and no single food contains them all. The wider the variety of foods in your diet, the less likely you are to develop either a deficiency or an excess of any single nutrient. Variety also reduces the likelihood of exposure to large amounts of contaminants in any single food.

Choosing foods from each of the four major groups will help insure variety in your daily diet. However, people often forget that variety *within* the food groups is also important. If you reach for the green beans every night for vegetables, you are denying yourself and your family the nutrients present in butternut squash or corn. If orange juice and grapefruit are your only source of fruit, you are missing out on the nutritional advantages in tomato juice, grapes, and mangos. Naturally, season, location, and cost will determine the availability of some foods. Nevertheless, in this country you almost always have a range of choices wide enough to please any palate and meet all nutritional needs. Don't shortchange yourself.

Choosing a variety of food sources is crucial with respect to protein, in particular. Proteins are made of amino acids, which are important to growth in children and to tissue building and repair in everyone. Animal protein sources have different amino-acid patterns than plant-protein sources. Animal sources provide "complete" proteins (all the needed amino-acid combinations), while plant proteins do not. When choosing animal sources, emphasize *lean* items. Also, learn how to combine vegetables and starches so that you get the right pairings of amino acids even when you don't eat meat. (See Chapter 15.)

2. ADJUST CALORIE INTAKE AND EXERCISE FOR PROPER WEIGHT. Calories* are the basic units of measurement of energy taken in and used up by the body. When calories "in" exceed calories "out," the body stores the excess for future use. In other words, when the food you eat provides more calories than your body needs, unused calories are converted to fat—the body's main storage depot for energy—and you gain weight.

To lose one pound of body fat, you must cut back 3,500 calories from your food intake. Exercise of any kind will also help to use up these calories. And it may be beneficial to reduce your intake of fat. The body gets its energy (calories) from four sources: protein, carbohydrate, fat, and alcohol. Measure for measure, fat contains about twice as many calories as carbohydrate or protein. This is why fat has to be monitored even more carefully than the other calorie-suppliers when losing weight. (For more specifics on weight control, see Chapters 5, 6, 7, and 8 in this volume.)

3. LIMIT FATS AND CONSUMPTION OF HIGH-FAT FOODS. Fatty foods are more than just a weight-control problem. Excess fat—particularly saturated fats and cholesterol—may contribute to heart disease. And certain kinds of cancer may also be linked to fat intake. The average American gets 40 to 50 percent of his or her total calories from foods high in fat. Most dietitians recommend that this be reduced to 30 to 35 percent, except for infants, who need more. (Check with your pediatrician.)

Reducing fat consumption may be difficult because much of the fat content of many foods is hidden. The following list classifies selected common foods by fat content:

*The word *calorie,* as used here, is actually a shortened version of the term kilocalorie, which is used in science to describe the amount of energy in foods. Technically, however, a calorie (small "c") is 1,000 times smaller than a kilocalorie.

FAT CALORIES IN RELATION TO TOTAL CALORIES

More than 90% fat	Bacon, mayonnaise, butter, margarine, salad and cooking oils, lard, cream, baking chocolate, vegetable shortening, olives.
80–90%	Sausages, most salad dressings, corned beef, cream cheese, unsweetened coconut, walnuts, pecans, sesame seeds, avocados.
65–80%	Potato chips, dry-roasted peanuts, ham, frankfurters, American cheese, Swiss cheese, Cheddar cheese, sunflower seeds, cashews, peanut butter.
50–65%	Broiled beef, loin steak, roasted leg of lamb.
35–50%	Most cookies, crackers, cakes, donuts, round steak, lean ground beef, whole milk.
20–35%	2 percent milk, low-fat yogurt.
10–20%	Roasted chicken (without skin), broiled fish.
Negligible amount	Skim milk, dry cereal, dry cottage cheese, beans, baked or broiled potatoes, most breads, rice, pasta, fruits, vegetables (except avocados and olives).

Source: *Basic Nutrition Facts,* Michigan Department of Public Health, Lansing, Michigan, 1980.

Fat consumption can be reduced by making informed food choices, eating smaller portions, trimming fat before cooking, cooking with low-fat methods, and eating more dried peas and beans, grain products, fruits, vegetables, low-fat dairy products, and low-fat meats. (See Volume I of the *Family Cookbook* for discussion of fat subclasses and cholesterol, and their relationship to atherosclerosis.)

4. INCREASE INTAKE OF UNREFINED CARBOHY-DRATES AND LIMIT INTAKE OF REFINED CARBOHYDRATES. Gram for gram, all carbohydrates contain the same number of calories, but different sources of carbohydrates will vary in overall nutritional value. Biochemically, carbohydrates are subdivided into three groups: the term "sugar" or "simple" carbohydrate is usually applied to "monosaccharides" (which have one sugar group per molecule) and "disaccharides" (which have two sugars per molecule). The term "complex" carbohydrates usually refers to "polysaccharides" (which have many sugar groups per molecule).

Complex carbohydrates are found primarily in legumes (beans and peas), grain products, and vegetables, while simple carbohydrates are found naturally in fruit and milk. Complex carbohydrates and foods with naturally occurring simple carbohydrates are each important sources of many essential nutrients, such as vitamins, minerals, and fiber. When carbohydrates are processed or "refined" into commercial sugar and other sweeteners, however, they are left with calories but very little else in the way of nutritional value. This is why the calories in refined carbohydrates are often called "empty" or "naked."

5. INCREASE CONSUMPTION OF FIBER-RICH FOODS. Fiber, or roughage, as our grandparents called it, is the portion of plants that the human body cannot readily digest. Rich sources of fiber include complex or unrefined carbohydrates such as fresh vegetables and fruits, whole grains, beans, peas, and nuts. Fiber comes in several forms and there is some evidence that different fibers may have different effects in the body. (See Chapter 10 called "Fiber: What's In It for You?")

6. REDUCE INTAKE OF SODIUM. Sodium, like saturated fat, may be associated with health problems, notably high blood pressure. The primary source of sodium in the American diet is table salt, which is about 40 percent sodium. (One teaspoon of

salt weighs 5 grams and has about 2,000 milligrams of sodium.) Relatively large amounts of sodium also enter our diet through convenience foods of all kinds. Foods that are salty to the taste— bacon or pickles, for example—may well contain high levels of sodium, but taste alone is not always an accurate indicator. Commercial soups, peanut butters, and salad dressings are a few of the many common foods that frequently have substantial amounts of sodium.

It takes a little effort at first to adjust to a reduced-salt diet, but it can be done. In fact, many people find that they don't enjoy very salty foods after they get used to cutting back.

Because of public concern about salt consumption, food manufacturers commonly print the sodium content of their products on the package label. In addition, several food companies have developed tasty new low-sodium lines. However, many canned goods still contain high sodium levels, so, it is a good idea to rinse these foods under tap water for a full minute before cooking or serving.

7. USE ALCOHOL SPARINGLY, IF AT ALL. Alcohol is high in calories and has almost no nutritional value. Therefore, if weight reduction is an issue, even light drinkers should consider cutting back on those empty calories. The general rule is: If you do drink, do so in moderation at all times. One or two drinks daily appears to cause no harm in most adults. Pregnant women, however, should avoid alcohol to be on the safe side. People with diabetes should consult their physicians about alcohol use; they may have to observe special restrictions concerning times for drinking and amounts consumed. (See Volume I, Chapter 11: "Alcohol and Diabetes.")

2 □ NUTRITION AND DIABETES

Role of Diet in Treatment . . .
Goals of Diet Therapy . . .
The "Glycemic Index"

The dietary recommendations of the American Diabetes Association are very similar to the general nutrition guidelines outlined in Chapter 1, but they take into account the special concerns of people who have diabetes. To understand the Association's recommendations, you may first need to review the definition and causes of diabetes.

"Diabetes" is a disorder characterized by the body's failure to properly convert the fuel derived from food into energy for the body's cells. This processing difficulty causes high blood-glucose levels. Untreated, diabetes can cause such immediate problems as fatigue and excessive hunger, thirst, and urination. Over the long term, it also damages nerves and blood vessels, sometimes leading to such serious health problems as blindness, kidney failure, gangrene (with possible foot and leg amputations), and heart disease.

Broadly speaking, diabetes develops when a person has too little insulin for the body's needs. Insulin, a hormone produced in the pancreas, has many roles, but one of its major ones is to help body cells use blood glucose (sugar). Glucose, which is formed when food (especially carbohydrate) is digested, is a fuel for the body much as gasoline is a fuel for cars. If the fuel is in the tank but can't feed the engine properly, the car won't run very smoothly. Similarly, if the body doesn't have enough insulin or can't use it efficiently, the glucose stays in the blood and the starved body cells won't run very smoothly, either.

TYPE I
(INSULIN-DEPENDENT)
DIABETES

People with insulin-dependent diabetes mellitus (also known as IDDM or type I) produce essentially no insulin. As a result, they need daily injections of insulin to survive. Insulin lowers blood-glucose levels and would cause *low* blood glucose if the user did not eat enough food. Therefore, people with type I diabetes have to eat enough food to avoid low blood glucose, but not so much food as to overcome the insulin and send blood glucose soaring. This is quite a balancing act, because food and insulin are not the only factors that affect blood-glucose levels; exercise, for instance, generally lowers blood glucose, and stress (either emotional or physical) can raise it. This kind of diabetes used to be called juvenile-onset diabetes because it typically develops during childhood or adolescence, although it can occur later, too. About 10 percent of all people with diabetes have type I.

TYPE II
(NON-INSULIN-DEPENDENT)
DIABETES

People who have non-insulin-dependent diabetes mellitus (also known as NIDDM or type II) produce insulin. In fact, they may have a normal amount or even higher-than-normal amounts, but the insulin is not as effective as it should be, a problem referred to as *insulin resistance*. (That is, cells don't respond as they should to insulin's messages. As a researcher once put it, "The cells are like children who are busy playing. Their mom can yell at them all she likes, but they aren't listening.") Insulin resistance is largely due to excess body fat, which is common in people with type II diabetes. This form of diabetes, formerly called maturity-onset diabetes, usually develops after age 40.

About 90 percent of people with diabetes have type II, and 80 percent of them are overweight at the time of diagnosis. Being too fat seems to make people resistant to insulin whether or not they have diabetes, and losing weight often causes a remarkable improvement. Therefore, weight loss and maintenance of ideal weight is the major goal of therapy in type II diabetes in the overweight. Exercise also helps the body to use its insulin and to lower blood-glucose levels, so most doctors recommend a combination of caloric limitation and regular exercise. Some people with type II diabetes take insulin or pills for controlling blood glucose when their weight-loss and exercise program does not control blood glucose acceptably. People who are treated with insulin, and some people who are treated with pills, need to eat food at prescribed times. But those whose diabetes is managed by diet and exercise alone are not prone to low blood glucose. Therefore, it is not as important for them to eat on a rigid schedule.

A small number of people with type II diabetes are of normal or near-normal weight when they develop this condition. These people, too, can often benefit from losing a few pounds, especially if they are pushing the high end of normal. However, not everyone needs to reduce. Some of these people also need insulin therapy.

If you are relatively thin and have type II diabetes, you may find that frequent small feedings are better than three big meals a day. Smaller meals allow the body to use its insulin most efficiently because they do not make heavy demands on the pancreas for insulin. Fiber-rich and whole foods as well as regular exercise are also recommended to help reduce blood-glucose fluctuation.

YOUR GOALS

No matter what kind of diabetes you have, the following are the goals of diet therapy:

□ Improve overall health through optimal nutrition.

□ Provide for normal growth in children.

□ Achieve and/or maintain a body weight appropriate for height.

□ Maintain blood glucose at as close to normal levels as possible.

□ Prevent or delay heart, kidney, eye, nerve, and other complications associated with diabetes. (Much research suggests that keeping blood-glucose levels at or near the normal range may prevent or delay long-term complications.)

To achieve these goals, the American Diabetes Association recommends the following guidelines in addition to the ones outlined in Chapter 1:

□ Pay particular attention to caloric intake—excess calories cause high blood-glucose levels and obesity.

□ Increase your intake of fiber-rich complex carbohydrates. Limit your intake of highly refined carbohydrates and sugars. In addition to being low in vitamins and other nutrients, these sugary foods cause a rapid and high rise in blood glucose.

□ Follow an individualized meal plan that suits your lifestyle. Work with a dietitian familiar with diabetes to develop the plan. (See Chapter 15 for advice on finding a dietitian.) Generally, dietitians will suggest a meal plan in which about 55 to 60 percent of calories come from carbohydrate, mostly unrefined carbohydrates (dried beans and peas, whole-grain cereals and breads, vegetables, fruit); 12 to 20 percent from protein; and less than 30 percent from fat, mainly vegetable fat. A mimeographed meal plan given to you without discussion is *not* adequate. Many dietitians also recommend that you follow a meal plan based on the *Exchange Lists for Meal Planning,* a joint publication of the American Diabetes Association and The American Dietetic Association. (See Appendix 1, page 412.)

MEAL PLANNING OF TOMORROW: A GLYCEMIC INDEX?

In the future, meal planning may be more precise than it is today. It has long been believed that simple carbohydrates (sugars) cause the greatest rise in blood-glucose levels, while complex carbohydrates (which also often contain fiber) cause a less dramatic blood-glucose rise. However, some complex carbohydrates don't seem to fit the mold. They act more like sugars—at least in some studies.

Because of such findings, nutritional researchers are continuing to evaluate the need for a "glycemic index" for diabetic meal planning. Such an index could, theoretically, rate individual foods on their effects on blood-glucose levels, and you could then choose your foods based on their rating.

However, research is still conflicting. More studies are needed to see if a standardized index could be used by people with diabetes. After all, the effect of a given food depends not only on the food itself, but on how it is prepared, when it is eaten, what else is eaten with it, when the last meal was eaten and what it contained, and finally, who is eating it, since people can respond differently to the same foods. Particularly in people with type I diabetes, the amount of insulin in the body makes a big difference in how high the blood glucose rises after eating.

Until questions raised by this research are answered, continue to favor foods high in complex carbohydrate and low in sugar and follow the other recommendations of your dietitian and in Volumes I and II of the *Family Cookbook*. (Also, you can see how *your* body responds to different foods by testing your blood after eating them.)

Of course, knowing what you should do to eat properly and doing it are two different things. After describing the ways that nutritional needs are influenced by age, the next several chapters will give you practical advice on how to cope with diet dilemmas of insulin use and, for the overweight, on how to lose weight . . . and keep it off.

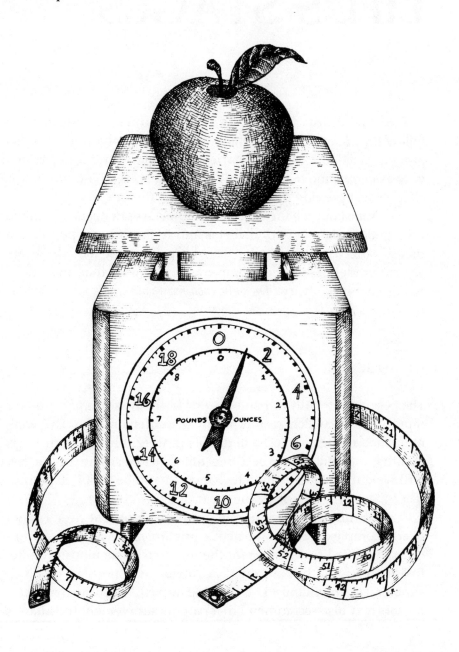

3 □ NUTRITION NEEDS THROUGH LIFE'S STAGES

The general nutrition principles outlined so far are important to follow throughout life. But there is no denying that the amounts of foods needed and the obstacles to getting nutrient needs met vary as people move through different life stages. Therefore, this chapter will provide details about those differences.

Note: For each life stage listed, the nutrient needs described refer both to people with diabetes and to the general population unless otherwise specified. Also, keep in mind that these are *general* guidelines based on average size and that individual requirements will vary. *The only good meal plan is one that is tailored to individual needs.*

INFANCY

The period from birth through the first birthday is one of extremely rapid growth, which results in great nutrient needs. The well-nourished infant, in fact, will double in weight by age four to six months and will likely be three times heavier than his or her birthweight by 12 months. The baby will also be about 50 percent taller than birth height by one year of age.

Fortunately, meeting the newborn's nutrient needs is not overly complex. The infant needs primarily human milk or formula (modified cow's milk) for the first four to six months of life. Infants receiving human milk, however, may need to be given supplements of vitamin D beginning at birth. In some instances, doctors may also recommend that parents supplement the infant's diet with fluoride if the substance is not being supplied by another source, such as drinking water.

At four to six months, parents can begin giving the baby solid food in amounts recommended by the doctor, particularly foods that are good sources of iron, such as iron-fortified cereals. For some breast-fed babies it may be desirable to give a supplement with an additional source of energy (calories).

Of course, parents should also continue with milk and formula feedings. Strained vegetables and fruits may also be given as early as 6 months. When introducing new foods, parents should begin with a small amount and continue offering the food to the child for three days.

Parents should introduce finger foods and foods of different textures (such as strained carrots with carrot bits in it) at six to eight months, the sensitive period for learning to chew.

The diabetic infant will have essentially the same needs as the nondiabetic infant, but parents may want to wait until the six-month mark to introduce solid foods. At that time, the baby's insulin dose and/or the timing of injections may need to be adjusted to cover the foods. The best approach is to discuss the individual needs of the baby with your doctor and diet counselor.

As with older insulin users, the diabetic infant needs to have insulin action matched by food. This often means that whoever is doing the feeding will need to gently awaken the baby to keep feedings regular. To be sure that the baby has enough glucose in the blood yet does not develop excessively high blood glucose, parents of diabetic infants usually give the child frequent, small feedings.

As the diabetic child starts to develop a feeding pattern that more closely approximates three meals plus snacks, the doctor may recommend covering some of the meals with added insulin (Regular). When in doubt about the baby's need for food or insulin, parents can test the baby's blood-glucose level by using a heelprick instead of a fingerprick. Blood-testing is especially useful for the parent who is wondering whether the baby's crankiness is due to low blood glucose or merely to being a baby!

TODDLERS (Preschool)

The period of one to six years is one of slower growth than before and of increasing physical activity. As the growth rate slows, the child's appetite will decrease. Children are good judges of the *amount* of food they need, but it is up to the parent to provide the right *kind* of food. Children are born without food prejudice. Their eating patterns are learned. Children who taste new foods each time they are served learn to know and enjoy a wide variety of foods. But introduce only one new food at a meal, perhaps along with a favorite food.

The nutritional needs of the diabetic toddler are no different than those of the nondiabetic, except that the parent of the diabetic child will be more concerned about timing and amounts of food because of the need to match insulin action. For the child who is cared for by a baby sitter, nursery school, or day-care facility, the caretaker should be instructed about the warning signs and treatment of insulin reactions and should be made aware of the child's food needs.

In general, depending on activity levels, the caloric needs of children one to six years old can be estimated using the following rule of thumb:

1000 calories for the first year, plus,
100 calories for each additional year thereafter
    until about 10 years of age

EXAMPLE:

3-year old:	1000	1st year
	200	Years 2 and 3
	1200	Total
5-year old:	1000	1st year
	400	Years 2, 3, 4, and 5
	1400	Total

The bulk of the calories should come from complex carbohydrates, protein, and milk (for calcium and other nutrients), and from good sources of Vitamins C and A and iron. (See table of vitamins and minerals at the end of this chapter for sources and Appendix I for the nutrient and caloric values for food.)

For protein, it is best to emphasize animal proteins (meats, fish, poultry, milk), because they provide the amino acids essential for growth. For variety, vegetable proteins can be combined with small amounts of animal protein (such as milk and cereal) or specific vegetable-vegetable combinations can be formed that together will be as effective as animal proteins. (Discuss options with a dietitian and also see Chapter 15, page 390.)

Iron-rich foods are particularly important at this stage of life to help prevent iron-deficiency anemia, a common result of a child's narrow food intake and reduced appetite. A child who insists on having mostly milk or bread and resists other foods would be a good candidate for this form of anemia.

Of course, children will have "off days" when they are irritable and refuse to eat what you serve. They also go through whimsical phases of alternately liking and disliking certain foods, even rejecting ones they once adored. If you are a parent, try to avoid making a big issue over the child's refusal to eat a given food. If rejecting foods get attention, food dislikes may become permanent, or, worse, the child may use eating as an arena for getting attention.

Children—both diabetic and nondiabetic—in this stage of the life cycle can't hold very much food in the stomach at one time, and they also have short attention spans, both of which contribute to the need for frequent small feedings (four to six) rather than the traditional adult three meals a day. These feedings are important for providing nutrients and should be wholesome rather than sugary even if the child is nondiabetic. Offer the child foods that are easily chewed and swallowed because, at least in the early toddler stage, chewing skills are just developing. Give meats, cheeses, or vegetables that are tender and cut into bite-sized pieces. Snacks high in unrefined carbohydrates and protein (such as crackers with either peanut butter or cheese) are excellent for any child, diabetic or not.

For diabetic children, eating at regular times is generally considered to be critical. Parents should, therefore, be firm and matter-of-fact about the need to eat on time, just as they are firm about insulin injections.

SUGGESTED SNACKS AND
FINGER FOODS FOR LITTLE PEOPLE*
(See *Exchange Lists for Meal Planning*
for exchange equivalents, in Appendix I)

Fruits
Apple wedges
Banana slices
Berries
Fresh peach wedges
Fresh pear wedges
Fresh pineapple sticks
Grapefruit sections (seeded)
Grapes
Melon cubes or balls
Orange sections (seeded)
Pitted plums
Tangerine sections

Breads/Cereals
Cold cereals
Toast fingers
Whole-grain crackers

Milk Products
Milk
Yogurt
Puddings made with milk

Vegetables
Cabbage wedges
Carrot sticks
Cauliflowerets
Celery sticks**
Cherry tomatoes
Cucumber slices
Green pepper sticks
Tomato wedges
Turnip sticks
Zucchini or summer squash
   strips

Meats
Cheese cubes
Cooked meat cubes
Hard-cooked eggs
Small sandwiches
   (quartered)

*Adapted from "A Planning Guide for Food Service in Child Care Centers," USDA, FNS-64, Food and Nutrition Service, Washington, D.C., revised 1976.
**May be stuffed with cheese or peanut butter.

SCHOOL AGE AND PREADOLESCENCE

The ages of seven to ten are periods of varying individual growth rates. The caloric needs of children in this age group vary greatly and are influenced by age, body size, and physical activity. Having enough calories is important for the body to be able to effectively use the protein from food for growth. Seven- to ten-year-olds commonly consume from 1,650 to 3,300 calories a day. Thus, a child in the middle of the age range would need about 2,400 calories, the midpoint of the calorie range.

Because this preadolescent stage is one of storing nutrients for the growth spurt of adolescence, some children might become slightly chunky, only to slim down suddenly in the next stage. Again, four to five small meals, or meals plus snacks, are recommended. Children at this age are just beginning to "go with the group," so that if one child dislikes (or likes) a food, he or she may influence others. The best way to combat negativity is to be a good "role model" and eat the foods you want your child to eat. Often the child will imitate adults he or she loves.

The preadolescent person with diabetes may choose to test his or her emerging independence by refusing to eat on schedule and by rejecting previously accepted foods. This can result in insulin reactions. Try to avoid turning mealtime into battle time. Allowing the young diabetic person to develop a list of three to four foods that don't have to be eaten (while all others must) may help to reduce food-related conflict.

Regularity of meals and a matter-of-fact approach may be helpful in reducing potential conflict. Since children with diabetes, like nondiabetic children, are influenced by TV commercials and peers, they may start asking for sugary foods. Allowing limited choices occasionally, such as among cereals that have limited amounts of sugar, may suffice. Some families save sweets for before-exercise snacks. Giving the child food choices can also be used to start teaching the child some of the information he or she will need when taking on some responsibility for self-care.

Preferences for single food items over a period of time are

also common during this stage and will generally pass. This phase might create some problems for the diabetic child if overreliance on the favored food starts to play havoc with diabetes control. A parent's best bet may be to learn how to work the food into the diet to some extent, and to explain to the child that the food is only allowable if other nutrient needs are also met.

As school terms (and gym classes) come and go and the child spends more time in activities with friends, his or her insulin and food schedules may have to be adjusted to adapt to activity-level changes. In addition to discussing insulin dose and timing changes with the doctor as your child's schedule changes, parents will need to give the child guidance in handling insulin reactions solo. When you feel he or she is ready, you can give the child food to carry for use as needed.

Note that the treatment plan—insulin, food, and activity— should promote normal growth in the child. If your child seems unusually short, this may indicate that a change is needed in insulin dose and/or in the amount of food being eaten.

SUGGESTIONS FOR HANDLING THE EASTER CANDY BASKET, TREATS AT HALLOWEEN, AND GRANDPARENTS' GIFTS FOR CHILDREN

EASTER
- ☐ Use small gifts other than food in Easter basket.
- ☐ Use sugar-free gum or bubble gum.
- ☐ If candy is necessary, use dietetic hard candies.

HALLOWEEN
- ☐ Go trick-or-treating and give candy to a child who is ill and cannot go.
- ☐ Give candy to children in the hospital.
- ☐ Collect for UNICEF.
- ☐ Divide treats with friends, brothers, and sisters.
- ☐ Take treats to school for children in class.

GRANDPARENTS
□ Ask them to bring treats other than food: clothes, books, small toys.
□ Set quotas in advance if food is to be used as a gift.

ADOLESCENCE (TEEN YEARS)

In the first three stages of the life cycle, the sex of the person makes no difference to recommendations for caloric intake. In the adolescent years, however, sex differences alter the rate of growth and the nutrient needs. The growth spurt of adolescence begins for girls at ages 9 to 10 and for boys at ages 11 to 13. The spurt for boys is more intense and lasts longer than for girls, and boys typically need more calories. (The body composition of males and females begin to differ considerably, too, with girls having a greater percentage of fat compared to muscle, and boys having a greater percentage of muscle.) Common caloric ranges for boys and girls follow. Keep in mind that, in general, children at the younger end of the age range need fewer calories than children at the older end of the range. The exception may be girls ages 15 to 18; sometimes the oldest ones need the fewest calories, in part because they have reached their adult heights. Calorie requirements, however, will also be influenced by body size and activity levels; the greater these are, the more calories the child is likely to need.

Boys ages 11 to 14 tend to require about 2,000 to 3,700 calories a day, with 12- to 13-year-olds needing about 2,700 calories (the midpoint of the calorie range). Boys 15 to 18 years old have a range of 2,100 to 3,900 calories, with the 16- to 17-year-olds requiring about 2,800 calories.

Girls have a somewhat lower caloric requirement. Girls aged 11 to 14 need about 1,500 to 3,000 calories, with 12- to 13-year-olds needing about 2,200 calories. The older girls, 15 to 18 years old, need about 1,200 to 3,000 calories, with the 16- to 17-year-olds needing about 2,100 calories.

Iron-rich foods are very important for adolescent boys and

girls. Boys need iron for their developing muscles and rapidly expanding blood volume. Girls need it because once they begin menstruating they lose blood each month. The iron in meats is used better by the body than iron of plant origin, although eating foods rich in vitamin C (such as citrus fruits or tomatoes) will enhance the availability of vegetable iron when sources of non-meat iron and vitamin C are eaten together.

During this period, the adolescent becomes responsible for his or her own food intake. No longer is the child fed, but rather eats according to what food is available and what foods friends are eating. Snacking, or eating many small meals, is a common pattern for this age group. To help the teenager eat right, parents can keep nutritious, ready-to-eat foods available at all times. (Teenagers are notorious for grabbing food rather than taking the time to go through preparations.) Also, parents will want to encourage the teenager to eat a variety of foods.

Adolescent boys generally eat larger quantities of food than do girls and for that reason may come closer to meeting their nutrient needs. Girls tend to be especially conscious of weight control and may diet unwisely. They should be taught to eat a variety of low-calorie foods to meet their energy and growth needs without gaining a lot of weight.

Teenagers with diabetes may benefit from meeting with a dietitian and a doctor who can help them to set up a weight-loss plan, if desired, or work on adding more variety (including portions of pizza, or even 'burgers and fries if it's important to them) into the meal plan. Some teenagers will benefit from the reminder that more food can be eaten if exercise follows it. Also, discussing the pros and cons of alcohol use with a dietitian may help the teenagers to make wiser choices at parties and to take appropriate precautions if they decide to drink beer or wine. Counseling from someone who understands their need to be like their friends, but who can also help to motivate them to attend to diabetes, may help to prevent some of the teenage rebellion common at this stage. Maintaining some flexibility may also help to prevent binges on sweets that are common during the teen years.

As the teens hit puberty and their bodies change, they may need to have their treatment plans changed once again. Girls may find that they have difficulty managing diabetes during their menstrual cycle because hormones make blood-glucose levels erratic. Self-monitoring of blood glucose (which is more precise than urine testing) can be especially useful during adolescence. Seeing how blood-glucose levels change in response to meals and exercise (and stress) and learning how to adjust food and exercise and, in some instances, insulin in response to blood-glucose changes can help to improve diabetes control.

SNACKS FOR SCHOOLAGERS AND TEENAGERS

STARCH/BREAD
Bread (plain, toasted with margarine)
Sandwiches (with meat or cheese or vegetable fillings)
Crackers (plain, with meat or cheese toppings)
Rolls (with margarine, meat or cheese spreads)
Waffles, pancakes, biscuits
Cereal (dry, with milk, with fruit)
Popcorn (plain, with margarine)
Pizza—toppings provide sources from other groups

MEAT
Meat, fish, peanut butter sandwiches
Chicken, ham, tuna salad (on crackers, vegetables)
Peanut butter (with raw vegetables, raw fruits)
Cheese (cubes, sticks, slices, dips, spreads)
Cottage cheese (plain, with fruit added)

FRUITS AND VEGETABLES
Fruits
Fresh whole fruit (apples, oranges, bananas, pears, peaches, plums, grapefruits, melons, grapes, watermelon, pineapple)

Fruit juice (as a beverage, as an ice)
Fresh fruit added to yogurt, cottage cheese, milkshakes
Fruit on top of waffles, pancakes, biscuits, cereal

Vegetables
Raw vegetables (plain, with cheese dips, peanut butter)
   (cauliflower, broccoli, green pepper, zucchini, carrots,
   celery, turnips, cucumbers, radishes)
Vegetable juice (tomato, carrot)

MILK
Milk (whole, 2%, skim, buttermilk)
Milkshakes (with fruit, ice milk, or just crushed ice to make
   thick)
Yogurt (plain, with fresh fruit, frozen)

FATS
Nuts (peanuts, mixed); olives

FREE SNACKS
Sugar-free carbonated beverages or packaged drink mixes
   (plain or frozen as in ice)
Gelatin (prepared with sugar substitutes, flavorings)
Raw vegetables (½ cup or less)—(lettuce, green pepper,
   cauliflower, broccoli, celery, pickles, cucumbers,
   radishes)

EARLY AND MIDDLE ADULT YEARS

The adult years mark the end of growth and the beginning of a
rather stable period as far as nutrient needs are concerned. Recommendations for adults are different for males and females,
primarily because of differences in body size and composition.
Only in the case of iron do females have a greater need than males
because of their monthly blood losses (menstruation). Just as in
other periods of life, lifestyle (active or inactive) will have an
impact on caloric needs. Weight control continues to be a concern

to women and may become a concern to more men when they suddenly notice a new arrival in their lives: the pot belly.

Males ages 19 to 50 generally need about 2,300 to 3,300 calories a day, and females of the same age generally need about 1,600 to 2,500 calories. Men need more protein than women because men are generally bigger.

In adults with diabetes, the daily schedule has usually become more routine because of work and family responsibilities, which makes meal planning easier. Although food habits are well established by the adult years, changes can still be made to improve nutrient intake, manage weight, promote good health, and prevent chronic diseases or manage diabetes. You may be somewhat set in your ways, but human beings have a remarkable capacity for change.

Two important aspects of the adult years that have an impact only on the nutrient needs of women are pregnancy and breast feeding (lactation). The pregnant woman needs to take in about 300 calories extra a day and considerably more protein, and the woman who is breast feeding needs about 500 calories more than her prepregnancy meal plan and less protein than when she was pregnant but more than she needed prior to the pregnancy. The diabetic woman will follow a meal plan much like the non-diabetic woman except, of course, that the diabetic woman will need to pay close attention to blood-glucose levels before *conceiving* and throughout her pregnancy to protect the baby.

LATER ADULT YEARS (ELDERLY)

The adult years were described as a period of stability. The later years are characterized by a great deal of individual variation in body functioning and activity. Generally, however, a person's metabolism slows down and physical activity, sensitivity to taste, and vigor decrease. At the same time, the proportion of fat compared with muscle increases and so does susceptibility to disease. Good nutrition during these years may help to alter the timing, rate, and severity of these processes.

Little nutrition research has been conducted on this older age group and is sorely needed; we are, after all, an aging nation. (A few decades from now, the elderly will make up a much larger proportion of the total population than they do today.) However, one thing is clear: since older people eat less, each calorie eaten must contribute to nutrient requirements. The elderly, in particular, need to eat wholesome foods.

While more research is awaited, a common recommendation for calorie intake in the later adult years is about 2,000 to 2,800 calories for men ages 51 to 75, and 1,650 to 2,450 calories for men older than 76. For women ages 51 to 75, an intake of about 1,400 to 2,200 calories should be adequate, and women older than that should have about 1,200 to 2,000 calories.

Unfortunately, meeting nutrient needs during later life often becomes increasingly difficult, because of such factors as:

1. *Lack of motivation.* Many elderly people live alone and are not motivated to prepare food for themselves. (Group feeding is known to improve food intake for many when it is available, even if it's just once a day.)
2. *Lack of transportation, money, or cooking facilities.*
3. *Poor food habits* that are resistant to change.
4. *Environmental changes* that force different (worse) eating patterns, such as having to move from a rural setting with a garden food supply into a city where only convenience food is easily available.
5. *The presence of chronic illness,* which can reduce appetite and alter taste.
6. *Physical disabilities,* such as missing teeth, poor eyesight, impairment of memory, or confusion.
7. *Isolation.*

Inadequate nutrient intake may lead to irritability, moodiness, depression, and other symptoms that are commonly considered a "natural" part of aging but are not necessarily unavoidable. If elderly people can be encouraged to eat an adequate diet with a variety of foods, they may be able to stay healthy and vigorous and minimize health problems.

For elderly people with diabetes who take pills or insulin—as many do—it is crucial to eat regularly and to have enough food to avoid low blood sugar. If you have an elderly relative with diabetes who lives alone and seems to have trouble in this area, you may need to arrange for home health services. (Contact a dietitian or diet counselor or your local health department for information.)

VITAMINS, MINERALS—AND YOU*

WHY YOU NEED THEM	FOODS THAT SUPPLY THEM
VITAMIN C (Ascorbic Acid): Helps hold body cells together and strengthens walls of blood cells. Helps in wound healing. Helps body to build bones and teeth. Helps in absorption and use of iron.	Cantaloupe, grapefruit, oranges, strawberries, broccoli, cabbage, tomatoes, green leafy vegetables, and fresh potatoes.
THIAMINE (B₁): Helps body cells obtain energy from food. Helps keep nerves in healthy condition. Promotes good appetite and digestion.	Whole-grain and enriched breads and cereals, potatoes, organ meats, pork, other meats, poultry and fish, nuts, milk, green vegetables, dried peas, and beans.
RIBOFLAVIN (B₂): Helps cells use oxygen to release energy from food. Helps keep eyes healthy. Helps keep skin around mouth and nose healthy.	Milk, liver, kidney, heart, lean meat, eggs, green leafy vegetables, enriched and whole-grain breads and cereals.

NIACIN: Helps the cells of the body use oxygen to produce energy. Maintains health of skin, tongue, digestive tract, and nervous system.

Liver, poultry, fish, lean meat, peanuts and peanut butter, beans and peas, and whole-grain and enriched breads and cereals.

VITAMIN B_{12}: Helps with normal functioning of all body cells. Necessary for formation of red blood cells.

Foods of animal origin (such as liver, other organ meats, fish, meat, eggs, shellfish, milk, cottage cheese and other milk products, except butter).

VITAMIN A: Helps keeps eyes healthy and able to adjust to dim light. Keeps skin healthy. Helps keep lining of mouth, nose, throat, and digestive tract healthy and resistant to infection. Promotes growth.

Liver; dark green and deep-yellow vegetables such as broccoli, collards, and other dark-green leafy vegetables; carrots, pumpkin; sweet potatoes; winter squash; tomatoes; green pepper; apricots; cantaloupe; strawberries; papaya; watermelon; butter; and fortified margarine.

VITAMIN D: Promotes growth and lays down minerals for bones and teeth.

Egg yolk, butter, fortified margarine, fortified milk, fatty fish, and liver. Vitamin D is produced in the skin with the stimulus of sunlight.

VITAMIN E: Helps other vitamins and unsaturated fatty acids perform their special functions in the body.

Fats and polyunsaturated oils of vegetable products, safflower oil. Meats and green vegetables contain small amounts. Whole-grain cereals and peanuts.

IRON: Combines with protein to make hemoglobin, the red substance of blood that carries oxygen from the lungs to muscles, brain, and other cells of the body. Helps cells use oxygen. Prevents anemia.

Liver, kidney, heart, oysters, lean meat, egg yolk, dried beans, dried peas, dark-green leafy vegetables, dried fruit, parts of whole-grain and enriched bread and cereals, and prune juice.

CALCIUM: Builds bones and teeth. Helps blood to clot. Helps nerves, muscles, and heart to function properly.

Milk: fortified skim, low-fat, whole, buttermilk, yogurt; cheeses made from skim or partially skim milk (such as mozzarella), whole-milk cheese (such as Cheddar); leafy vegetables, such as collards, dandelion, kale, mustard, and turnip greens.

MAGNESIUM: Activates various enzymes. Aids in erergy production and utilization, contraction of nerves and muscles, and building tissue.

Bananas, whole-grain cereals, dried beans, milk, most dark-green vegetables, meat, nuts, peanuts and peanut butter.

ZINC: Is a constituent of the hormone insulin. Activates various enzymes. Aids in growth, wound healing, taste acuity, and prevention of anemia.

Whole grains, dried beans and peas, nuts, shellfish (particularly oysters), meat, cheese, and cocoa.

SODIUM: Is a key element in regulation of body water and of acid-base balance in the body.

Naturally occurs in most foods, broth, gelatin dessert, table salt, baking soda, and most processed foods.

POTASSIUM: Is a component of lean body tissue. Contributes to growth and muscle strength. Helps regulate body water and acid-base balance. Helps maintain neuromuscular function.

Meats, milk, fruits (especially citrus fruits), bananas, dried dates, cantaloupe, apricots, tomato juice, potatoes, and dark-green leafy vegetables.

*From the book, *The American Diabetes Association/The American Dietetic Association Family Cookbook,* © 1980 by The American Diabetes Association/The American Dietetic Association. Published by Prentice-Hall, Inc., Englewood Cliffs, New Jersey 07632.

4 □ DIET DILEMMAS OF INSULIN USERS

People who take insulin to treat their diabetes have special dietary concerns. The first consideration is, of course, *what* to eat. For this, a careful daily meal plan should be worked up with the help of their physician and dietitian or diet counselor. (See Appendix I for more information on meal plans.) Insulin users also have to pay close attention to the timing of their meals and snacks, and they must be prepared to adjust their diets to compensate for insulin reactions, unusual activity, delayed meals, and illness.

TIMING OF MEALS AND SNACKS. When you take insulin, you have to coordinate the size and scheduling of your meals with the time of your injections. This is to insure a proper balance of the foods you eat with the amount of insulin you receive and the exercise you get. Food raises blood-glucose levels, and insulin and exercise (if diabetes is under control) lower it. Generally speaking, you should eat at regular times and plan meals and snacks to coincide with the greatest insulin activity (see chart).

For example, if you use rapid-acting insulin (Regular) you should eat a half hour after your insulin injection, and if you use an intermediate-acting (such as *NPH* or lente) insulin, you may need a midafternoon snack to cover the peak insulin action. A bedtime snack is used to cover the action of insulin during the night.

In the past, most insulin users ate three meals a day and snacks at midmorning, midafternoon, and bedtime. Today, more

INSULIN ACTION

RAPID ACTING (onset 1/2–4 hours, peak action 1–5 hours duration 5–16 hours)

Humulin Regular

Novolin R (Regular)
   (formerly Actrapid Human)

Velosulin (Regular)

Purified Pork S (Semilente)
   (formerly Semitard)

Iletin I Regular

Regular

Iletin I Semilente

Semilente

INTERMEDIATE ACTING (onset 1–4 hours, peak action 4–12 hours, duration 16–28 hours)

Humulin L

Humulin NPH

Insulatard + (NPH)

Novolin L (Lente)
   (formerly Monotard Human)

Novolin N (NPH)

Iletin II Lente

Iletin II NPH

Iletin II Lente

Iletin II NPH

Insulatard (NPH)

Purified Pork Lente
   (formerly Monotard)

Purified Pork N (NPH)
   formerly Protaphane)

Iletin I Lente

Iletin I NPH

NPH

LONG ACTING (onset 4–6 hours, peak action 14–24 hours, duration 36 hours)

Iletin II PZI

Iletin II PZI

Purified Beef U (Ultralente)
   (formerly Ultratard)

Iletin I PZI

Iletin I Ultralente

Ultralente

MIXTURES

Mixtard + 30%
   (30% Regular, 70% NPH)

Source: From *Diabetes Forecast* 39 (3): 1986.

flexibility may be allowed, depending on the timing and number of injections and the type and amount of insulin you use. See your doctor and/or diet counselor for more details on adding flexibility to your life.

INSULIN REACTIONS. These are always a threat for the person with type I diabetes. When you feel a reaction coming on, test your blood glucose to see if it is, indeed, low. If blood testing is not practical, treat yourself as if you were having a reaction. For low blood glucose, take about 15 grams of carbohydrate, such as 1 tablespoon of honey or corn syrup, 2 tablespoons of raisins, ½ cup fruit juice or a *non*dietetic soft drink, or indicated portion of a packaged product for insulin reactions (for example, three glucose tablets). Usually, symptoms will go away within twenty minutes. Retest blood glucose at that point. If symptoms persist, treat again. Carbohydrate eaten to treat insulin reactions that occur at other than meal times generally does not need to be subtracted from the carbohydrate allowance in your meal plan.

EXERCISE. Physical activity burns calories and uses up some glucose for energy. A certain amount of regular exercise is accounted for in your daily meal plan. If you engage in additional exercise, however, you may need to eat a snack before you start or else risk an insulin reaction.

How much extra should you eat before exercising? For light activity, such as walking a half mile at a modest pace, you should not need any additional food. For moderate exercise, such as playing golf without a cart, you may need 10 to 15 grams of carbohydrate for each hour of exercise planned. Eat this snack just before you begin. For vigorous exercise, such as roller skating or running, you may need as much as 20 to 30 grams of carbohydrate for each hour of anticipated activity. After strenuous exercise, it may be necessary to eat again, because the body may have used up the carbohydrate stored in liver and muscle cells during especially heavy workouts, and it needs to be replaced. Remember, these are *rough* guidelines. You may need more or less food, depending on your blood-glucose level, your usual activity level, and past experience. Testing before unplanned exercise is always wise.

Crackers, bread sticks, and fruit are good sources of on-the-spot carbohydrate before exercising. One small apple or pear, for example, will give you 10 grams of carbohydrate. This food is *not counted* toward your meal plan allotment if it is eaten to cover extra exercise; the additional calories should be burned off by the extra exercise.

Although eating carbohydrates as described above is the most common way to compensate for the calories burned in exercise, alternative approaches are available. Consult your dietitian for more details.

DELAYED MEALS. For the times you cannot eat on schedule, 15 to 30 grams of carbohydrates should prevent low blood glucose for one to two hours. Again, crackers or bread sticks are good sources; you can carry them in your pocket or keep some in the glove compartment of your car. (Three graham crackers, for instance, would give you about 15 grams of carbohydrate.) In this case *deduct the amount you eat as a snack* from the total carbohydrate in your delayed meal.

ILLNESS. Many illnesses cause a lack of appetite. And when you eat less, your tendency might be to decrease your insulin. Nevertheless, you *must* take insulin to avoid ketoacidosis if you have insulin-dependent diabetes. In fact, the stress of illness may elevate your blood glucose even when you are eating very little, and you may actually have to *increase* your insulin dose. Additionally, if you take insulin, you must also take in calories to avoid reactions. To be sure you are eating enough, have at least 50 to 75 grams of carbohydrate during every six to eight hours, or the amount your doctor recommends. If you are nauseated, try sipping sweetened ginger ale or soup or eating ice cream or custard.

During illness, test your blood for glucose and urine for ketones, even if you do not normally use these tests. Blood-glucose monitoring combined with multiple injections of Regular insulin (or with an insulin pump if you normally use one) can give you a bit of flexibility in choosing meal and snack times. This is because you will not have to worry about covering long-acting insulin if you don't use any. (For more advice on handling illness, see Volume I, Chapter 13.)

5 □ ON FIGHTING FAT I: WHY LIMIT CALORIES?

Losing weight and keeping it off is a challenge that is little understood by people who are "naturally thin." Unfortunately, nobody can give you a magic key to weight control. But three kinds of information can help you achieve your weight goal:

- □ *An explanation of the biological side of weight loss,* so that you will understand the reasons for restricting calories. It's hard to do something well if you don't understand the logic behind it.
- □ *Practical advice* about steps you can take to make your next effort at weight control more successful.
- □ *A glimpse of the feelings expressed by many people who have type II* diabetes and are struggling to control their weight. Their responses may help you feel less alone.

This chapter deals with the biological side of losing weight. It answers some of the basic questions people have before embarking on a weight-loss program:

- □ What are the benefits of being at your suggested weight and what are the risks of being overweight?
- □ How do you know whether you are too fat?
- □ What happens in the body when you restrict calories?

□   What kind of diet will allow you to lose weight without jeopardizing your health?

□   Once you have lost weight, how do you keep it off?

WHY LOSE WEIGHT?

A prominent researcher, the late Dr. Kelly West, wrote:

Being fat has some advantages, but these are outweighed by major disadvantages. Hard chairs are less uncomfortable for those who are generously padded. Because fat is less dense than muscle or bone, folks with extra fat are particularly good floaters. When obese people go out in the cold, their blankets of fat keep them warmer. Also, obese people are full of calories, so . . . they tolerate prolonged famine well.

On the other hand, fat people move around less comfortably, are hotter in summer, and are often considered less attractive. What's worse, they suffer more and die earlier than slender people. Although fat people are often free of medical difficulties during the first years of obesity, after one or two decades of excess weight, more and more problems appear. Overweight people have more pain in their backs, knees, and hips. They have more gall bladder operations and more lung trouble . . . And, for people more than 40 percent overweight, death rates are three times as high as for people of normal weight.

Obesity (having too much fat) also plays a major role in *causing* diabetes and makes *controlling* diabetes difficult. When you are too fat, your body's insulin works less effectively, because the body's cells "resist" acting on its messages. In addition, the pancreas has to work harder to keep the fat person supplied with enough insulin and sometimes is not up to the task. Losing weight (and fat!) helps the body to use its insulin more effectively and also gives the pancreas a break. In fact, people with type II diabetes who lose enough weight and exercise regularly can often stop taking insulin or diabetes pills, if they get a doctor's approval, of course.

AM I TOO FAT?

Now that you know about the risks of being too heavy, you may be wondering if *your* "baby fat" is excessive enough to cause trouble. (*Note*: It is the excess of fat that causes body cells to "resist" insulin, not extra weight per se. But with the exception of some extremely muscular people, most people who are over-weight tend to have too much fat.) Doctors have some very precise methods of measuring fat, including underwater weighing and the use of a device called a caliper, which measures skinfold thickness. In most cases, these tools are not really necessary. To see if you need to shed some pounds, try these simple methods:

THE PINCH TEST. Using your thumb and forefinger, pinch a fold of skin on the back of your upper arm. If the fold is more than an inch thick, you are probably too fat.

THE RULER TEST. Lying on your back, place a 12-inch ruler on your stomach pointing from head to toe. If the ends of the ruler fail to touch your body, you should probably lose weight.

THE BELT TEST. (For men.) Wrap a belt around your middle and note where the notch is. Now place the belt around your chest. If you're wider at the waist than at the chest, you're carrying more fat on your body than you need.

Of course, just weighing yourself and comparing the results to the generally accepted weights for your height and build should give a pretty good idea of where you stand. If you are 20 percent or more heavier than the norm for your height, weight, and sex, you would generally be classified as obese. Use this formula to estimate the suggested weight for your height.

DESIRABLE BODY WEIGHT

Women:	100 pounds for the first five feet, 5 pounds for each additional inch
Men:	106 pounds for the first five feet, 6 pounds for each additional inch.

Add 10 percent for large body frame; subtract 10 percent for small body frame.

In general, your weight should fall within a range of 10 percent above or below the accepted weight for your height. (That is, if the appropriate weight for your height is 115, you could weigh between 103 and 127 and be within the normal range.)

YOU ARE WHAT YOU EAT

What has to happen for the fat to flee? Essentially, you have to take in fewer calories than the body needs each day. When you don't provide it with enough energy (calories), the body turns to its stores of fat and breaks them down. In this way, the body gets the fuel it needs and you lose fat . . . and weight.

Of course, if you take in *more* calories than you burn off, the body *stores* the excess as fat for future use. Popular storage depots are just beneath the skin of the waist, stomach, thighs, and upper arms.

To find out how many calories your body needs for weight maintenance, and how many calories to eat each day in order to lose weight, talk to your doctor or dietitian. Your health advisors will give you an individualized set of guidelines, taking into account your activity level, size, sex, and the energy your body needs to maintain its involuntary processes ("basal metabolism"), such as breathing and keeping a normal temperature. Your basal caloric needs are usually highest up to the ages of 19 to 22. After that, basal requirements shift down, with a marked drop at around age 50. Also, as you age, the percentage of body fat (compared to muscle) tends to increase.

For normal adults, basal metabolism uses about 1,300 to 1,700 calories a day. The remainder of your daily calorie supply is used to give you energy for your regular physical activities. The more active you are, the more calories you can have while maintaining your weight. See the chart called "Estimated Caloric Requirements Reflecting Effects of Physical Activity" to get an idea of how many calories you need to sustain your desired weight at any given activity level. But remember, this is just a general guide.

For an example of how to use the chart, let's say your appropriate weight is 120 pounds. To maintain that weight despite

ESTIMATED CALORIC REQUIREMENTS REFLECTING EFFECTS OF PHYSICAL ACTIVITY

Calories per pound of desirable body weight		Level of activity
Up to Age 55	*Older than 55*	
10	9	*Basal* (resting: little or no activity)
12	11	*Sedentary* (usual activity; activities that burn 25–80 calories per hour, such as most done seated or standing, including auto and truck driving, office work, light housework, standing, croquet)
15	14	*Moderate** (activities that burn 150–300 calories per hour; such as carpentry, plastering, weeding, hoeing, scrubbing floors, shopping with a heavy load, cycling, tennis, walking 3–5 miles per hour, rowing with two oars)
18–20	17–19	*Very active** (activities that burn 300+ calories per hour, such as working with a pick and shovel, playing basketball or football, swimming, climbing, skiing, walking up stairs)

*To consider yourself to be moderately or very active, you must participate in activities like the ones listed for an average of at least two hours each day.

having little exercise (being sedentary), you would need about 12 calories × 120, or 1,440 calories a day. If you wanted to eat more, you would have to increase your activity level.

For weight *loss*, you have to cut back 3,500 calories from your "maintenance" food intake to lose one pound of body fat. For example, let's say that 2,000 calories a day keeps your weight fairly constant. To eliminate 3,500 calories—and one pound—in a week, you would have to reduce your calories by 500 a day. This would leave you with a daily intake allowance of 1,500 calories. If you were to add exercise to this weight-loss plan, you would lose that pound more quickly or would lose more weight in one week. (Unfortunately, brain-work doesn't count as calorie-burning exercise!)

WHAT KIND OF DIET?

For a long time, researchers have sought the safest and easiest method for losing weight and keeping it off, but so far no single "right way" has emerged. Some determined people can lose weight slowly but steadily with only a modest reduction in calories. Others need a brief, dramatic cutback to begin. Everyone, however, needs a lifelong commitment to healthful eating habits. Otherwise, weight loss is likely to be temporary.

"Easy" weight-loss schemes will not help you to keep weight off because they do not change your basic eating habits. Fad diets that exclude certain types of food may deprive the body of needed nutrients; they are nutritionally unsound and may be hazardous to your health.

The best results usually come from a balanced low-calorie diet (following the principle of Chapters I and II) combined with planned exercise. Better than diet alone, diet plus exercise gets rid of more fat and builds attractive muscles in place of fat. Because muscle cells need more food than fat cells, your maintenance diet can also be more generous when you are physically fit.

If you want a realistic weight-loss and exercise program

that will help you to change your habits, contact your dietitian or diet counselor. Also get a thorough check-up from your physician before starting.

People who have type I diabetes will have to be especially careful as they switch to a weight-loss meal plan. They will need to work with a dietitian and doctor to be sure that insulin is reduced if necessary and that the low-calorie diet adequately covers the insulin injected.

The weight-loss program suggested to you will probably be fairly low in fat. This is because fat is the most calorie-dense of all the nutrients, with more than twice the calories of an equal measure of protein or carbohydrate. (See the following chart.)

The meal plan will also include foods you like because it will make your commitment easier to keep. High-fiber foods, such as whole-grain cereals and uncooked fruits and vegetables with edible seeds and skins, are valuable because they provide bulk that helps to satisfy hunger. Also, the fiber in these foods needs to be chewed, and chewing is one of the pleasures of eating.

CALORIES IN 1 GRAM
OF EACH NUTRIENT

NUTRIENT	CALORIES PER GRAM (28 gm = 1 oz)
Carbohydrate (CHO)	4
Protein (PRO)	4
Fat	9
Alcohol	7
Vitamins	0
Minerals	0
Water	0

CONSOLIDATING YOUR LOSSES

When you have finally reached your goal and brought your weight down to where you want it, you will need a long-term meal plan to help you keep it there. If you remember that proper weight and better health go hand in hand, sticking to this plan will be easier.

As with weight loss, no one formula for weight maintenance works for everyone. For most people, including those with non-insulin-dependent diabetes, a gradual increase in carbohydrate, protein, and fat intake is desirable after reaching the suggested weight range. But if you reach the upper limit of that range, you will have to reduce calories once again. If maintenance is difficult, consult a dietitian or other diet counselor.

SUMMING UP

Especially when you have a weight-related disorder, such as type II diabetes, the earlier you lose weight the better. Of course, there is no guarantee that the improvements that come from weight-loss and exercise will be permanent. However, chances are good that if you lose enough weight *and keep it off*, the benefits of your hard work will stick.

6 □ ON FIGHTING FAT II: KEEPING PRIMED

As Chapter 5 indicates, a nutritionally balanced, low-caloric meal plan is a safe and effective way to lose weight if you follow the plan consistently. But that's a big "if." Setting up a weight-loss plan is easy compared to following it day in, day out. Yes, the market is filled with diet books claiming to be the last word on easy weight control and personal happiness. But don't believe them! Many overlook the hidden factors (such as emotions) that can contribute to weight problems, and even if the diet "works," the success is usually fleeting.

A crucial element in successful weight loss is mental preparation. This, combined with practical strategies for resisting temptations—especially the temptation to go back to your old way of eating—raises your odds for success.

It's best to think in terms of long-term weight control rather than a "diet." Going on a diet indicates that some day you will also be going off it. You may be willing to follow someone else's dictates for a while, but the time will come when you rebel and insist on making your own choices again. This is the time when many a diet falls apart and the weight you lose comes right back. It is not uncommon for people to end a diet and then become even heavier than before.

To develop a new way of eating that frees you from the feast-and-famine cycle (yo-yo dieting), you will need a plan that balances all of your food-related needs: emotional as well as nutritional. Most overweight people have an intense desire to regain control over their bodies and their lives. Balance in your diet and also *in your life* should help to strengthen your sense of control and allow you to persist in your efforts at taking weight off and keeping it off.

Such internal balance does not grow out of a spur-of-the-moment resolution, based on a chance remark or embarrassing situation. Rather, it takes careful introspection as well as planning. Achieving balance also takes motivation, which can only come from within. Slimming down for the beach audience each summer is something you do to impress others; the pounds may come off in June, but they will be back on by October. If you are to make any lasting progress, you will have to decide that it is worth doing for *yourself*, and you will have to set your mind to working on change.

KNOW YOURSELF

A new pattern of eating, if it is to work, must be one you will be able to live with indefinitely. It must be one that is tailored to your style and your needs, not your neighbor's. The first and most important step, therefore, is to understand just what your own nature is. This entails a conscious (and sometimes painful) effort to see yourself as you really are, to observe your present and past eating patterns and your personal and family eating history, including the *emotional* interactions involving food. Once you are able consciously to recognize and *understand* the origins of your eating habits and food-related behavior, you will be better able to come up with a plan to improve, or replace, them with a more positive and healthy approach.

You can start your self-examination by asking yourself what food really means to you emotionally. Is it a means of comfort when you are angry? Upset? Scared? Lonely? Or is it a drug—an ongoing pacifier, or antidepressant? Do you handle strong feelings by swallowing them, along with forkfuls of food? Is food one of your few real joys? There is something in many of us that delights in the forbidden, such as stealing from the cookie jar. If you recognize yourself in any of these questions, you'll have an idea of where your work has to begin. You'll know what emotions are likely to trigger overeating unless you are prepared with other outlets.

You may also gain a better *physiological* understanding of your problem by observing when and how you overeat. When you get "the munchies," what foods, in particular, give you comfort? For some people, certain types of food cause most of their weight troubles. If you can isolate these problem foods, you will have a big advantage when trying to develop an effective meal plan. For example, there are people who can easily follow almost any diet regimen until they have sugar, even a small amount. Then their self-control evaporates. Other people may be thrown off the track by caffeine or chocolate. And some find that they are unable to control weight without first controlling salt intake.

Another aid to self-awareness is to examine your weight changes over time. Take a piece of graph paper and chart your weight since early adolescence. Where are the sharp gains and losses? Do they correspond to significant life events? With severe emotional stress, such as death of a loved one, some people may eat more and gain weight, while others may eat less and lose weight. Positive events—marriage, birth of a child, a promotion— can also be stressful and affect eating habits. Many women put on a layer of fat with each pregnancy, going from light to medium to heavy in three pregnancies. Other women find that staying at home with young children may result in a sharp increase in weight. Retirement or reducing one's workload can also be associated with weight gain. If you know how life changes have affected your weight in the past, you may be able to exercise better control in the future. When stressful events arise, you can recognize—and resist—that impulse to reach for the refrigerator door. There are other means of comfort besides food. Start searching for them.

In family therapy, counselors often ask people to look back further still—to recall what mealtime was like in their childhood, because the habits established early in life are the most powerful and long-lasting. Some people remember mealtime as an ordeal, because parents chose that time to interrogate and criticize. Others feel that eating was the one thing their family had in common, and that food was their sole shared pleasure. Or the mother may have taken it as a personal rejection if her children refused any food. Some families never ate together, and it was a lonely time.

Much can be learned by observing our extended families as well. Many of us are but one or two generations removed from our immigrant predecessors, whose attitudes toward food may have been formed under conditions of scarcity. To them, a layer of fat may have been a sign of health and security, even a status symbol of sorts; being thin may have been indicative of illness. These attitudes may well have been reproduced in our families and in ourselves. Understanding their history will help us to realize that such fears of going without need no longer trouble us today. By looking into your family's and your past, you can begin to evaluate whether old habits that once served a purpose are useful to you today.

LEARNING TO SAVOR YOUR FOOD

Along with introspection you can take other steps to build new habits. It may sound paradoxical, but if you can learn to truly enjoy your food, to concentrate on and savor the act of eating itself, you will probably get more satisfaction while eating less. If, for example, you gulp your food, not only do you need larger quantities before your appetite is satiated, you also miss out on the pleasure of tasting each individual bite. To remedy this, try learning to chew very slowly and carefully. Chewing to the pace of a metronome set to its lowest count may help.

Another solution to mouth-stuffing is to make sure you eat only when you are with others. Even better, place a large mirror in front of yourself when eating alone, and watch closely. Try to eat as calmly and gracefully in front of yourself as you do in front of others. If you don't treat yourself with deference, no one else will.

Make a commitment to yourself not to eat standing up, and never to eat (standing or sitting) at the refrigerator. Some people kid themselves into believing that leftovers have fewer calories. Not so! Don't eat while doing something else (watching TV or reading); with your mind on the book or picture, you won't realize how much you have swallowed.

It takes time to learn to permit yourself to enjoy food. In time, you can eat less and enjoy it more. Ask someone who is permanently slim. (For more behavioral tips, see Chapter 8, on binge eating.)

KEEPING IT UP

To maintain your commitment to your weight-control program, you need to work on accepting yourself. A new way of eating, if it is to be successful, must be predicated upon a new feeling about yourself.

Accepting yourself means acknowledging both your hidden capabilities (your intelligence, generosity, sense of humor, and . . .) and your human limitations.

It also means that there are times for strict dieting, but also times to let up and take a breather. Otherwise, incessant and inflexible demands on yourself for constant perfection may jeopardize the entire enterprise.

For example, you may be one of the many people for whom Christmas is a lonely time of the year. To force yourself to diet rigidly at that point is cruel and unusual punishment; furthermore, it just won't work. If you recognize this, and if you are *not* diabetic, you may be able to compensate by dieting carefully in the preceding month (from the end of the Thanksgiving feast until Christmas Eve). You will then have balanced out your inevitable five-pound gain of the week just prior to the New Year. If you have diabetes, you unfortunately cannot abandon your meal plan safely. However, you *can* talk with your diet counselor and get an alternative meal plan for the holidays.

There may be other times in the year, month, or even day that you have to accept some vulnerability. Remember that there is a vast difference between maintaining and gaining; sometimes, simply holding steady may be progress enough.

Also, although the scale can be a useful reminder of your progress as well as your need to redouble your efforts, don't let it punish you inordinately. There are ways to measure progress other than the scale. We tend to endow the scale with unreasonable powers, allowing it to determine our self-worth. Scales unfortunately register in black and white, leaving no room for mitigating explanations. If only their data could be softened with messages: "You've gained half a pound, but that always happens when you're premenstrual." Or: "You've taken off two pounds overnight. But don't be too quick to celebrate. Saunas will do that every time (dehydration). And drinking water will undo it."

Instead of weighing yourself, you can weigh and measure the foods you eat and keep track in a regular food diary. In this way, you can chart your progress without risking the occasional (but devastating) disapproval of the scale. Or you can use a tape measure or the fit of your clothes as your indicators. At the start of your weight-loss program, choose a favorite dress or pair of well-fitting pants and then try them on at weekly intervals. You'll know how well you are doing by the bagginess of the outfit. When friends and family ask you the inevitable question: "How much have you lost?" give your answer in inches or sizes and save pressure on yourself.

UNDERSTAND THE INFLUENCE OF OTHERS

It is great to have a friend or family member with whom you can share your struggle, who will congratulate you on your progress and offer encouragement when you slip. Just be careful to choose a "cheerleader" who is not too judgmental. If your supporter makes you feel humiliated or depressed, it defeats the purpose. Also beware of relying on people who have a hidden wish to keep you fat. (Sometimes a spouse or friend unconsciously wants you to be heavy.) These people may choose fat spouses or friends because, on some level, it makes them feel more secure. Or they may choose slim mates and then go about fattening them up to fill some kind of inner need.

In the final analysis, however, we are responsible for our own choices and our own fates. It is *our* decision whether or not we are going to let someone else's pastries or pasta determine how we look and feel next week.

Once again, the motivation to lose weight has to be internal. If you have attained some balance within yourself, you will not be so easily tempted by others, nor will you look to others to save you from yourself.

HAVE REALISTIC EXPECTATIONS

If someone were to ask you how you would climb a tall mountain, you would likely answer "very slowly." Probably you would not attempt to climb straight up either; the task would be too hard, and you would quickly become so exhausted that you might have to give up the effort. Similarly, there is no reason to diet as if you were climbing a tall mountain in one day.

Sometimes the circular route is fastest, even if it doesn't seem so at first. Of course, at various plateaus on the mountain you might be tempted to gaze up and dwell on all you have left to accomplish, filling yourself with fear and self-doubt. But if you are a wise traveler, you will re-energize yourself by thinking about the distance you *have already climbed* and about your budding faith in your ability to continue. And you will make steady progress.

Speaking of plateaus, they're very common in people who are working on weight loss. Sometimes you just stop losing weight for a while despite your efforts. Now is not the time to give up. Try on an old pair of slacks and savor the progress you have made. Should you stay at your plateau for a long time, remind yourself that maintaining your slimmed-down weight is indeed progress. You may not have lost more weight, but neither did you fall headlong off your plateau! You have the strength to stick with your weight-control program despite having no obvious reward from the scale for your trouble.

As you embark on your lifelong weight-control plan, keep in mind that losing weight won't change your life in the magical way promised in magazine ads. In fact, getting used to your new, thinner self can be downright disconcerting at first. Just as adolescents feel awkward about their rapidly changing bodies, adults may experience confusion or new vulnerability along with their newly reduced dimensions. People may not recognize you; they may even say disparaging things about your old self (of whom you may have been rather fond). Women may find that men are beginning to make remarks they have never heard directed at them before, and it may seem threatening. There is really no way to know what the changes will be like in advance and to expect the world to adhere to an imagined scenario is to ask for disappointment.

It may be difficult to accept that losing weight will not solve all your problems. But it may be necessary to separate weight-related problems from your old conflicts in order to prevent recurrent relapses of old eating habits. One young man, for example, pudgy since childhood, had always blamed his extra girth for his failure with the opposite sex. But, in actuality, he had developed a needley, porcupiny personality that was much more distancing than his overweight appearance. He finally lost weight—grumpily, in fact—and began woman-hunting with a vengeance. After a year he was no closer to a relationship than he had ever been. He then went from his boyish teddy-bear pudge to true obesity, never acknowledging that it was his manner and not his baby fat that kept the world at bay. Focusing on weight, in other words, can be a form of tunnel vision that shuts out other aspects of ourselves in need of growth and change.

The idea that slim people were born that way and maintain their weight effortlessly is another self-defeating fairy tale. True, there are a few fortunate souls for whom food never presents a problem. Most people, however, *choose* to be the way they are. They have developed an inner control mechanism that helps them to eat more slowly or to be more careful between meals.

When you are finally fully ready to begin a serious weight-control program, keep in mind that you are not alone. As the next chapter will demonstrate, many people travel the same path that you are considering. It can be a great help to find others who are headed in the same direction and who share many of your fears and anxieties. The next chapter is based on experiences of people who have diabetes, but many of the feelings expressed are common to anyone who is overweight.

7 □ ON FIGHTING FAT III: COPING WITH FEELINGS

The combination of diabetes, obesity, and the stress of having to change daily habits can produce anxiety, loneliness, fear, guilt, anger, and depression. Such feelings can take the joy out of life, tarnish a person's self-esteem, and dampen one's interest in diabetes control. It is difficult to succeed at anything—even taking care of yourself—if you do not feel well and if you doubt your value as a person.

This chapter is based on a series of discussions among people with non-insulin-dependent diabetes who are struggling with weight control. Their personal feelings, along with comments by health care professionals specializing in diabetes treatment, are offered here to let you know that you are not alone and to encourage you to hang in there. Try not to let your negative moods get in the way of taking care of your body. If they begin to, you may want to consider sharing your feelings with others who understand. Research has shown that talking about feelings can be an effective form of self-help.

"SO ALONE"

I feel so alone . . . No one's interested in my problem. I just seem to get in everyone's way.

Loneliness is a common feeling among people with either type of diabetes. People who have insulin-dependent (type I) diabetes

55

feel "different" from the rest of the world because they take injections. They also feel that it is unfair that they have to spend so much of their time and energy calculating balances of food, exercise, and insulin. "If I only had to worry about my diet," they often say, "life would be so simple!"

But for overweight people with type II diabetes, losing weight and staying on a meal plan is far from simple. Knowing that other (thin) people think diet control is easy makes them feel isolated and angry. Overweight people have to fight constantly against their hunger, habits, and perhaps an inherited tendency to gain weight. Yet, they are not often praised for their efforts. In fact, they may have to deal with friends and family members who invite them to eat "forbidden" foods and then blame their obesity on self-indulgence. Add to this the fear of developing complications and/or type I diabetes, and you have a heavy emotional burden.

"THEN I FEEL GUILTY"

Sometimes, I make three trips to the candy machine and fight off the urge each time. But then, on the fourth trip, I give in. It's as if the food talks to me, saying, "Come and eat me. I won't hurt your diet just this once."

It's like alcoholism. If I'm invited to a party, my first thought is, "What will be served?" All day long, on or off my diet, I think about food. My hunger has nothing to do with appetite, and I can't tell when I'm full.

I do all right when no one else is home. The trouble is, if anyone offers me a bite, I get a shovel to taste it with, and then I feel guilty.

Research has shown that hunger has both physical and psychological elements and that the balance between them varies with the individual and his or her circumstances. In other words, intense food cravings are not necessarily "all in your head."

Feeling guilty for constantly craving food, or for giving in to cravings, is a waste of time and energy. It would be far better to use that energy to transform your guilt into determination, and to use your time to work on developing your coping skills. Keep in mind that many other people with your problem have learned to distinguish between just wanting to eat and really needing nourishment.

PLATEAUS

I had lost 20 of my 30 extra pounds, and everything was going great, when all of a sudden my progress just stopped. I wasn't eating anything more, and I was doing my exercises, but some days I even seemed to be gaining weight. After a few weeks of this, I got so discouraged that I started straying from my meal plan every now and then.

Some people are slow to lose weight or become stuck at plateaus even if they never succumb to temptation. Not only do they find this frustrating, but they may also be unfairly accused of weakness or lack of will power. Health professionals have come to realize, however, that the scales alone cannot always reflect the tremendous effort people make to lose weight. If you find yourself at a discouraging plateau, don't hesitate to seek help. Overweight people with diabetes need lifelong support just as much as those dependent on insulin do.

Actually, plateaus in weight loss are relatively common. There are three main reasons for these standstills:

First, when a person loses a great deal of weight, the body starts to behave as if it were semistarved. It slows down its "machinery" to conserve energy and, as a result, burns fewer calories than usual. This, in turn, hampers further weight loss.

Second, to compensate for its reduced bulk, the body may conserve more than usual amounts of fluid for future use. In particular, the kidneys retain salt and water. Eventually, however, as you continue to lose fat, the kidneys release the fluid and the pointer on the scale moves downward once again.

Third, exercise replaces fat with muscle tissue, and muscle weighs more than fat. Nevertheless, muscle development is a good sign, indicating that your body's fat level is declining and that you are becoming more fit.

FAMILY UPSETS:
AN OBSTACLE TO CHANGE

. . . and she said, "Mom, can't you please taste just a tiny piece of this apple pie?"

Temptations offered by those you love can be the most painful to resist. In fact, it is not unusual to get subtle discouraging signals from the people you counted on most for support. The diagnosis of diabetes—or the renewed determination to control it through weight loss—can threaten other family members in surprising ways. They may not like the changes!

There are no easy prescriptions for helping family members to adapt to changing behavior and responsibility. But openly acknowledging the feelings and conflicts can be an important first step. Often, family members are not even aware that they are being discouraging.

FEAR OF LOSING
FRIENDS: ANOTHER HURDLE

So much of socializing seems to revolve around eating. I always feel like the odd man out when my friends get together.

Taking control of diabetes involves some difficult trade-offs. But if you feel left out of socializing, consider taking the offensive. Many of your friends and co-workers may also want to lose weight and get in shape. Form a mutual support group, with its own meals and activities. You'll be helping them and easing your own loneliness at the same time.

For those who aren't ready to change, consider making non-food dates—go to a museum or play tennis. Or, meet for a drink and have a glass of sparkling water with a twist. Or, invite friends to your place, where you can control what's served.

IMAGE PROBLEMS:
STILL ANOTHER ROADBLOCK

I always saw myself as the food provider in the family. Now that I have to limit what I eat and keep out of the kitchen more, I'm not sure just who I am.

How you picture yourself and your role in life can have a big effect on eating behavior and weight. For example, women in our society today are under great pressure to play several different roles: assertive and successful at business, attractive and yet unthreatening to men, nurturing at home. Some people find these contradictions too much to bear and may subconsciously gain weight or stay heavy to avoid competing for certain kinds of work or for love relationships.

Of course, women are not the only ones who suffer from image problems. Some men may fear losing weight because they will become smaller and, therefore, somehow less masculine.

MOTIVATION

You have to understand what diabetes is really doing to your body, otherwise you won't watch your blood and urine, do your tests, and stay on your diet.

If I go off my diet, at first I think of myself as a no-good person. But if I write it down, somehow, admitting what I've done lessens the guilt. I face up to it and am able to see that my overall effort is really not bad. Then I'm ready to try again.

Truly, motivation is a subtle and individual process. Many people have found that the turning point in their decision to lose weight came when their health professionals sat them down and explained what diabetes could do to them. Others have noted that seeing consistent, near-normal results in blood-glucose tests serves as an incentive to keep on controlling weight.

Maintaining one's motivation can be quite a challenge. In fact, people have to recharge their batteries, so to speak, over and over throughout their lives. Losing motivation does not imply failure if you make an effort to recapture your energy.

Feeling well is the best motivator of all. Yet even success has its pitfalls. If losing weight makes you relax your vigilance, you may find yourself slipping back into old eating habits. Eternal vigilance is the price that has to be paid for good health in both types of diabetes.

CARING AND SHARING

I'm going to be fighting this battle for the rest of my life . . . please keep the caring coming!

It is important both for people with diabetes and for health professionals to recognize the unique qualities of each human being. We each have our own happiness and stress, frustration and accomplishment, loneliness, illness, and health. We all need constantly to re-examine our own progress and motivation and to understand and respect the difficulties that other people face. We need to search out those who succeed and learn from them, and, just as important, we have a responsibility to pass on our own strengths and knowledge to others in need.

Throughout the country, there are already groups set up for people who have diabetes who want to share their feelings and help each other build up strength and confidence. To find out if a group exists in your area, contact your American Diabetes Association affiliate, listed on pages xv-xx.

8 □ HELP FOR COMPULSIVE BINGERS

Almost everyone has gone on an eating binge at one time or another. But for tens of thousands, binge-eating is more than an occasional fall from grace. It is a bewildering and tormenting part of their everyday lives—a compulsion, like alcoholism, and equally hard to conquer.

A compulsive binger is one who feels powerless over food and, as one eating disorder expert puts it, "eats anything that is not nailed down as often as several times a day." Once a binge gets started, it may go on and on and can total thousands of calories.

No one knows just how many compulsive bingers there are in either the general or the diabetic population, in part because people who binge heavily often do so "in the closet" and are too embarrassed to admit it. "I have done this for so long," says one woman, "that I have become a professional at hiding it."

Researchers also have few hard answers to the question of what causes binging. They have observed, however, that many people who binge in this way seem to have particular difficulty handling stress and react by binge-eating, in part because food is so easily available as an outlet for anxiety. There are indications that at least some people who have diabetes binge in response to feelings of deprivation.

The short-term physical consequences of binging—bloat, pain, and so on—can be uncomfortable for anyone, but they spell double trouble for people who have diabetes.

In the aftermath of a binge, people who are not diabetic may feel pretty ill and disgusted. But people with diabetes also have to contend with elevated blood glucose and its effects, such as excessive thirst and constant trips to the bathroom to urinate. Insulin users who try to treat themselves with extra insulin often find that even a large dose can't restore blood-glucose control and can actually disrupt it by causing a severe insulin reaction, which, in turn, sometimes leads to yet another binge (because of hunger and eating to treat the reaction).

Those are just the short-term effects. In the long run, compulsive bingers leave themselves open to increased risks for high blood pressure, heart disease, and other disorders if they become obese as a result of chronic binge-eating. And people with diabetes also run an increased risk of developing diabetic complications if frequent binges lead to chronically uncontrolled diabetes.

BINGE-PURGE CYCLE IS DEADLY

An apparently growing number of people—primarily slender college-aged women as well as athletes and models—try to "undo" their binges and avoid weight gain by coupling their binges with purges. They either cause themselves to vomit, or they take large amounts of diuretics (water pills) and/or laxatives. People who engage in binge-purge behaviors regularly are commonly said to have "bulimia," although, technically, several criteria need to be met and a person may be diagnosed bulimic even if he or she does not purge. The number of people who binge and purge is unknown, but it is clear that at least some people with diabetes are among their numbers.

For anyone, such behavior can be devastating if done regularly. Chronic vomiting, for example, can cause serious damage to the liver, kidneys, esophagus, and teeth. Abuse of laxatives and diuretics can disrupt the normal functioning of the intestinal tract. Purging can also upset the chemical balance in the body and seriously reduce potassium, a loss that can cause severe dehydration and muscle weakness and, in extreme cases, disturbed heart function and even death.

In people with diabetes, a major loss of potassium can also play havoc with an already disturbed metabolism. And vomiting and dehydration added to already poor diabetes control can push a person toward a diabetic coma.

"WHAT SHOULD I DO?":
A QUESTION WITH NO EASY ANSWERS

"You can advise a person not to smoke," says a doctor, "but you can't tell a person not to eat." Treatment for binge-eating has to teach people to cope with almost constant temptation.

Occasional bingers in good health can try some of the self-help tips listed later in this chapter before turning to professional assistance. They may also find help through such reputable diet groups as Weight Watchers. In addition, many people benefit from attending meetings of Overeaters Anonymous (OA), a free self-help group modeled on Alcoholics Anonymous. In many cities, group meetings are available daily, and chapters everywhere offer access to a network of people to call for support when the going gets rough. (Local chapters of OA are listed in the white pages of your phone book.)

However, people who binge frequently and seemingly uncontrollably—or who binge and purge—need professional help, preferably behavior therapy and psychotherapy. This is because compulsive behavior can be extremely difficult to correct on one's own. (See the resource list at the end of this chapter for help in locating professionals.)

By pinpointing the situations and feelings that trigger and reinforce binge-eating, and by making plans to defuse them, behavior therapy can sometimes bring about relatively rapid changes in these habits. And by unearthing and dealing with emotions that encourage binge-eating and/or purging, psycho-therapy can help to ensure that these behavior changes are lasting. Other important resources include a diet counselor and, partic-ularly with diabetes, a physician who can monitor any medical problems.

Fortunately, people usually do not have to shop around for several specialists. Once a doctor or therapist familiar with eating disorders is found, he or she can steer the person to other needed resources.

Even with professional help, neither binging nor purging can be shut off like a light switch, and many people with these problems in their past consider themselves to be much like recovered alcoholics. Those bingers who gain control over their eating habits report, however, that giving up the momentary "high" of their binges is well worth the sacrifice.

HELP YOURSELF

To stop binge-eating, you first need the determination to stop. Then, you need some aids to help you avoid taking the "one little bite" that leads to all the rest. The following approaches have helped some people, although none can substitute for the therapy needed by compulsive bingers.

- □ *Keep a log of your food intake* and how you feel before, during, and after binges. This can help you pinpoint why you binge, so you can develop strategies for avoiding eating sprees.
- □ *Keep binge foods out of the house:* Don't buy them yourself, and ask your family to do the same and to avoid eating those foods in front of you.
- □ *Don't skip meals:* You'll get too hungry to control yourself. Resolve to eat only at the table, never standing up or serving yourself from the container.
- □ *Set up a support system:* Have a list of people you can call when cravings begin to overpower you. Decide on your menu in advance and commit yourself to just those foods and portions by announcing your intentions to your companion.
- □ *Stop and think:* Before you grab food, ask yourself, "Am I

really hungry?" Think about how you will feel after the binge.

□ *Put it off:* Tell yourself you can have the food if you really need it—later. Often the craving will pass.

□ *Do something . . . anything:* Take a walk. Draw a bath. Jog. Wash the car. Put on music and dance! Have a list of activities you enjoy ready in advance. Exercise (in moderation) has saved many a binger.

□ *Be on your own side:* For one woman who gained control over binging, the crucial realization came when, "I finally understood that if the diabetic in the family were someone else, I'd do anything to see that the person had a proper diet."

□ *Change your thinking about food:* Instead of bemoaning the items you cannot eat, think about the foods you *can* have. Find permissible foods (perhaps a favorite fruit) that will feel like a treat whenever you have it. If you hate your meal plan or always feel hungry, perhaps your dietitian can suggest changes to make the diet more appealing to you.

□ *Eat one portion of a food you enjoy:* Do this when you absolutely must have *something*. But don't choose a food that will lead to an uncontrolled binge. Eat slowly, savoring every bite so you'll feel satisfied. Make a list of problem foods—decide which ones you should avoid and which ones you can learn to eat in limited quantities.

□ *Be prepared:* Keep cut-up raw vegetables in the refrigerator. And there's always popcorn—three cups cooked with no oil in a hot-air popper are only 80 calories, one Starch/Bread exchange.

□ *Become involved in activities that make you feel good about yourself:* Feeling good often reduces the need to overeat.

□ *If you're a teen with diabetes and you binge to rebel and feel normal, consider the words of one of your peers:* "I finally realized that I was so busy worrying about being normal that

I was making myself a real pig! Once I came to my senses, I realized that nowadays teens are worried about *not* eating so much."

☐ *See your doctor:* If you have diabetes, perpetual hunger is sometimes a sign that your treatment plan needs adjustment.

☐ *Don't be a perfectionist:* For many people, the urge to binge never goes away completely. To think you will never slip is unrealistic and sets you up for failure. If you slip up, do not give up. Forgive yourself and start over.

RESOURCES FOR COMPULSIVE BINGERS

GROUPS FOR PEOPLE WITH BULIMIA

ANAD (Anorexia Nervosa and Associated Disorders), Box 7, Highland Park, IL 60035. (312) 831-3438.

AABA (American Anorexia Bulimia Association), 133 Cedar Lane, Teaneck, NJ 07666. (201) 836-1800.

Both groups offer information on bulimia and have names of health professionals concerned with eating disorders.

EATING DISORDER CLINICS
To find a reputable clinic near you, call the psychology or community-relations department of a local university hospital or medical center.

OTHER
Consult the yellow pages of your phone book for local weight-control programs and get the approval of your dietitian or diet counselor before joining any organization with a diet plan of its own. Your affiliate of the American Diabetes Association may also be able to provide information about community resources.

9 □ EXERCISE: NUTRITION'S IMPORTANT PARTNER

Everyone today seems to be joining an exercise class or fitness club. But not everyone knows exactly what physical fitness is, why it is important, and the best way to achieve it.

Physical fitness is a state of high-level well-being: your body becomes more efficient, and both your endurance and your ability to cope with stress increase as well. On the cellular level, regular, reasonably strenuous exercise (such as jogging) improves the body's ability to transport and use the nutrients and oxygen that our 75 trillion cells need to perform their complex tasks. Exercise also helps to improve the tone, size, and endurance of muscles, and may, along with good nutrition, help to prevent certain disorders, such as heart and blood-vessel disease, high blood pressure, degenerative joint disease, obesity, and type II diabetes. Exercise can strengthen the lungs, heart, and circulatory system while making their work easier. It can also enhance joint flexibility, reduce levels of certain blood fats, and improve the body's ability to use its insulin.

If you are already overweight, regular exercise can help you to lose weight. It does this in part by increasing your *basal metabolic rate* (BMR), the rate at which your body burns fuel (calories) for energy. When you are on a low-calorie diet for a long time, your metabolism eventually adapts to fewer calories and burns them more frugally, so you stop losing weight or lose it more slowly. Speeding up your BMR through exercise helps to keep the needle on the scale moving down.

One way to lose weight is to continue to eat your usual amount of calories while exercising more. For example, a 200-pound person who maintains the same diet but adds a brisk walk of 1½ miles to each day's activity will lose 10 to 14 pounds per year. But your best bet is to increase exercise *and* cut back on calories, because you will lose weight even faster.

If you are overweight *and* diabetic, exercise can benefit you in two ways. By helping you to lose weight, it should help to improve diabetes control. In addition, because exercise helps the body to use its insulin and overcome insulin resistance—and therefore to handle its blood glucose more efficiently—it helps to keep blood glucose levels down. In fact, exercise enhances glucose use by the body for several hours—and sometimes for more than a day—after a workout. This prolonged effect is one reason why regular exercise is highly recommended for most people with diabetes *as long as the precautions outlined later in this chapter are followed.*

(*Note:* Certain people should *not* exercise unless under close medical guidance. Among these are people who have very high fasting levels of blood glucose. When diabetes is so out of control, exercise can make the situation worse. In addition, individuals who have had diabetes for many years or who have diabetic complications may need to avoid some exercises. If you are one of these people, see your doctor for advice.)

NO TIME TO EXERCISE?

Just as a car engine needs a regular maintenance program and performs better tuned than untuned, your body needs regular care, too. Fortunately it is a lot less expensive to keep the body tuned! But it does take work. Physical fitness is not something you can gain by wishing for it. You have to invest energy and time.

Before you say that you cannot make these investments,

consider this perspective: A seven-day week has 168 hours, or a little over 10,000 minutes. To become physically fit, you have to invest only *90 minutes per week of vigorous exercise.* That's just 1 percent of the total time available to you in a week. (Did you know that you spend about a third of your week sleeping?)

PRELIMINARY CONSIDERATIONS

Before starting any exercise routine, see your doctor. Discuss your exercise goals with him or her and get a thorough medical examination. If you are over 40, you should probably get an exercise stress, or tolerance, test. This test consists of taking an electrocardiogram to record the heart's activity during exercise (usually on a treadmill or a stationary bicycle). It not only provides a good basis for rating your overall fitness but can also indicate the presence of heart disease, high blood pressure, poor circulation, and other chronic conditions. These basic precautions apply to diabetic and nondiabetic individuals alike.

Once you've received your physician's medical approval to exercise, the next step is mental preparation. If you are out of shape, you have to realize that your body did not get so soft and tired overnight, or in just the last couple of weeks or months. Nor are the changes necessarily due to aging. They are caused, in large part, by your body's adaptation to a sedentary lifestyle.

The fact is that most Americans get little vigorous exercise at work or during leisure hours. Today, only a few jobs (i.e., lumberjacking) require real physical exertion. People usually ride in cars or buses rather than walk, take elevators instead of stairs, and sit at home watching television during much of their free time. Recreational activities such as golf with a cart may be enjoyable, but offer little in the way of physical conditioning. Similarly, spot toning exercises may firm up flab and improve muscle tone in specific areas, but they do not affect overall fitness.

The transition from a sedentary lifestyle to one that includes frequent and demanding exercise should be carried out gradually. Don't expect instant results; it took time to get this far out of shape, and it's going to take time to get back in. Accept from the outset that it may take months before you reap any lasting benefits. In fact, regular physical training is a lifelong project. If you stick to your program, however, you will probably start to notice a difference in the way you *feel*—more energy, less fatigue, better sleep—within a few weeks.

CHOOSING YOUR EXERCISE: AEROBIC VS. ANAEROBIC

The best exercise for weight loss and all-around conditioning— and for improving blood glucose control in people with diabetes— is called "aerobic" exercise. The word aerobic is of Greek origin and means "to use or be in the presence of oxygen." Aerobic exercise improves the body's ability to transport and process oxygen and, by so doing, builds strength and endurance in the muscle cells. The regular contraction of the muscles in aerobic exercise assists blood circulation and, since the heart itself is a muscle, the entire blood-pumping system is strengthened.

Aerobic activities are rhythmic and continuous, meaning that you should be able to perform them for at least three minutes without experiencing *extreme* fatigue and breathlessness. They also involve large muscle groups, which makes them sufficiently strenuous to increase the heart rate as you do them. Walking, jogging, swimming, dancing, and cycling are some good examples of aerobic exercise.

On the other hand, there are many forms of strenuous exercise that *do not* increase the body's capacity to handle oxygen. These *anaerobic* exercises require bursts of exertion so intense that the muscles are actually deprived of sufficient oxygen. Such extreme exertion can be sustained for only brief periods of time.

Examples of pure anaerobic activities include weight-lifting, sprinting, shot-putting, and high jump. Activities such as basketball, soccer, and middle-distance running events combine elements of both aerobic and anaerobic exercise.

GETTING STARTED

You need at least 20 minutes of moderately vigorous exercise to get a proper aerobic workout. But that doesn't mean that you just put on your exercise outfit and start right in. Each exercise session should be preceded by at least 10 to 15 minutes of warming-up, and followed by an equivalent cooling-down period.

A good warm-up should start with long, slow stretching exercises, which will improve flexibility in the muscles and joints and help to prevent pulls, strains, and sprains. It may also include some light calisthenics to get the heart pumping, and thus, pre-pare the body for the more vigorous activity to follow. In cold weather, a longer warm-up period may be necessary. People whose muscles are normally tight, or who are prone to muscle or bone injuries, may also want to spend more time on their warm-ups.

The cooling-down, or slow-down, period after exercise should be like the warm-up in reverse; again, the purpose is to help your body to adjust to the change in activity level. Stretching the muscles after strenuous exercise will also aid in preventing spasms and charley horse, and will reduce the soreness and stiff-ness that often develops overnight.

For most beginners, 20 minutes of continuous aerobic activity will probably be too much. So, to gradually improve your endurance, you can start off by exercising in work-rest intervals. For example, if jogging is your "thing" you can try a jog-walk routine: 10 sets of 2-minute jogs, each followed by a minute of easy walking. Or, if you are a cyclist, you can pedal hard for two minutes, then coast for a minute, and repeat until you have com-pleted 10 intervals. In this way, you will have gotten in your 20 minutes of aerobic exercise without overextending yourself. And as your aerobic capacity improves, you can gradually remove the rest periods until you are able to exercise for 20 minutes (or more) without a break.

HOW MUCH?

To get the most out of your exercise routine, work out at least three, and at most five, times a week. Try to work up to about 30 to 45 minutes per session.

If you are looking for an aerobic-exercise program that will help you to lose weight, keep in mind that burning calories is more a function of duration than of speed. In other words, the total caloric cost of performing a given task—say, jogging for a half hour—is about the same whether the pace is fast or slow. *It is the length of time* spent at the activity that counts most; increasing or decreasing the speed has little effect on total energy expended. Thus, an aerobic activity that can be performed continuously for an extended period will burn calories and reduce fat, while an all-out anaerobic effect will be too brief to use up a significant number of calories.

HOW MUCH IS TOO MUCH?

Your heart rate, taken sporadically (such as every five minutes) during the aerobic part of your exercise session, is a good indicator of whether or not you are getting the desired training effect from your aerobics program. (You can find out your heart rate by calculating the number of heart beats per minute. A simple way to do this is to find the pulse on your wrist, count the beats in a ten-second interval, and multiply by six.) Find out from your doctor what your "target heart rate" is. This is your safety range, and it varies from person to person according to age, weight, and normal level of activity.

If your heart rate during exercise is in the target range, it means that you are probably getting a good, safe workout. If it is below the target range, you may need to work a little harder; if it is above, you could be overdoing it. Other ways to tell when it is time to ease off are: extreme breathlessness, to the degree that you cannot speak while exercising; extreme muscle weakness or heavy, tired, and burning muscles; lightheadedness; and nausea.

Note that in certain circumstances measuring the heart rate will not be useful. If you have autonomic neuropathy or if you take medicines called beta blockers (such as Inderal) for blood-pressure control or heart disease, measuring your pulse will not warn you that you are overdoing it. Ask your physician or exercise physiologist how to monitor yourself.

To find an organized exercise program run by a true authority on physical fitness, ask your doctor; a member of the physical education department of the local high school, community college, or university; or a program planner at your local "Y" to point you in the right direction. While some neighborhood spas and health clubs might be excellent, others are not.

EXERCISE AND DIABETES

People with diabetes should be aware of the special precautions they may have to take to ensure a sound, safe, and effective exercise regimen. Here are the answers to some common questions about diabetes and exercise:

QUESTION: What is the best time of day for a diabetic individual to exercise?

ANSWER: People who do *not* take insulin can usually exercise whenever they like, although people who are treated with diabetes pills should avoid exercising on an empty stomach.

For insulin users, the best time to exercise is generally one to three hours after a meal, unless insulin is peaking during that time. Be very careful about vigorous exercise before meals (when blood glucose may be falling) or when insulin is likely to be peaking, because you are most likely to have an insulin reaction at those times. For example, in a person who takes a mixed dose of Regular and NPH insulin at 7 A.M., the insulin will peak at about

10 A.M. and 3 P.M. These would probably be poor choices of exercise times. If you must exercise then, be sure to cover yourself with a snack (see next questions for details).

QUESTION: What tests are needed before I exercise?

ANSWER: People with type I diabetes should perform blood-glucose and urine-ketone tests before exercise. The glucose level will give you an idea of whether or not you need the extra pre-exercise snack, and whether blood glucose is too high for safe exercising. The ketone test lets you know if you have enough insulin available to safely exercise.

(Ketones are substances formed when the body breaks down fat, which it does when it lacks insulin. If they appear in the urine *before* you exercise, ketones generally mean that you do not have enough insulin available to exercise safely and that you need to get your diabetes in better control before working out. Unless you have enough insulin in your blood, exercise will not help your body to use its glucose, anyway.)

However, you generally do not have to worry about ketones that appear *after* exercise; this can occur even in nondiabetic individuals. If ketones persist for more than a day, though, contact your doctor.

QUESTION: Should I eat before exercise?

ANSWER: People who do not take insulin generally do not need an extra snack before exercise.

For people who take insulin, it is generally advisable to have an extra snack of carbohydrate *before* you exercise unless a blood test indicates that your glucose is elevated. Have 10 to 30 grams of carbohydrate (depending on the activity, your blood-glucose level, and your past experience) within 15 to 30 minutes before you start each hour of vigorous activity. A small apple or banana or a half cup of juice has about 15 grams of carbohydrate. A snack is particularly important if you must exercise at times when your blood sugar is likely to be at its lowest.

Once exercise becomes a part of your lifestyle and you have worked out insulin and meal-plan adjustments with your health professionals, you will probably have to add very few calories to your usual meal plan unless the training is unusually long or intense.

QUESTION: Do I need to change insulin doses on the day I exercise?

ANSWER: At the start of an exercise training program this is often important. Check with your physician or diabetes specialist concerning changes in insulin dosages. After a few weeks, when your body has adjusted to your new routine, you may not need to make continual changes. In the adjustment period, however, you may have some fluctuations in blood glucose, possibly leading to more reactions than usual.

QUESTION: Where should I inject my insulin?

ANSWER: The injection site may be important because the pumping effect of nearby muscles being exercised tends to move insulin rapidly into the bloodstream, and thus generally increases the risk of an insulin reaction. Therefore, it's usually advisable to use an abdominal injection site before leg exercises, such as running or bicycling. Conversely, when the arms are heavily exercised as in rowing or canoeing, the thigh might be an ideal injection site.

QUESTION: During prolonged exercise, should I cut my insulin dose or eat more food?

ANSWER: For activities lasting over a full day, such as hiking, skiing, canoeing, or biking trips, the insulin dose will usually have to be reduced. In addition, a light snack of 10 to 50 grams of long-acting carbohydrate, such as crackers, bread, or granola, eaten every 20 minutes to an hour for the duration of the activity may help to prevent an insulin reaction. You might also combine the carbohydrate with some meat to delay the carbohydrate's absorption into the bloodstream. It is important to consult your physician prior to altering your insulin dosage.

QUESTION: Do I need to exercise every day to keep blood sugar under control?

ANSWER: A good recommendation is to exercise at least four days a week. Most people with diabetes find that an every-other-day schedule allows for adequate control with little need to adjust the insulin dose. On the days you don't exercise strenuously, you can engage in milder activities such as walking or non-demanding recreational sports. The benefits of proper exercise in controlling blood glucose may last for up to a full day; however, more than two to four days without training often results in increased insulin requirements for people with insulin-dependent diabetes.

ENJOY

One other word of advice: in choosing your exercise program, whatever it is, make sure that it consists of activities you enjoy. Exercising for good health is hard work—but it should also be fun. If it isn't, you aren't likely to keep it up for long. Since the most important part of any exercise routine is sticking to it, pick a program you can at least learn to live with. If jogging bores you, there's always cycling or swimming or, weather permitting, cross-country skiing. If you don't like exercising alone, you may want to consider an aerobic dance class. And for people who just wouldn't feel comfortable participating in any of these activities, the walking program detailed below may be the most pleasant and natural introduction to healthful exercise.

WHY NOT WALK?

Walking is man's best medicine, according to the ancient Greek physician Hippocrates. His statement is as true today as it was in his day when walking was the primary means of transportation.

It's safe. Nearly everyone can do it. You don't need lessons. It doesn't cost a lot. You can do it anywhere, anytime. And, you can start as soon as your doctor gives the word.

According to "Walking for Exercise and Pleasure," a Blue Shield pamphlet, you should strike out at a steady clip that is brisk enough to get your heart beating faster and your lungs working harder. Hold your head erect and keep your back straight and abdomen flat. Point your toes straight ahead and let your arms swing loosely at your sides. Land on the heel of the foot and roll forward to drive off the ball of the foot. Be sure not to walk only on the ball of the foot or in a flat-footed style, as this may cause fatigue and soreness. Take long, easy strides, but don't strain yourself.

Of course, before you begin any exercise program, including a walking program, discuss any precautions with your doctor. Generally, however, a minimum of twenty minutes and a maximum of one hour of walking are recommended. If your pace is too tiring, or too easy, reduce or lengthen your walking time accordingly. Try to fit in at least three walking sessions per week. As your fitness level and staying power increases, set a swifter pace and walk longer distances. The more you walk, the more efficient your exercise program will be. Eventually, you may want to progress to more strenuous activities as well.

Adequate footwear is usually the only special equipment

walking requires. Lighter trail and hiking boots, or casual shoes with heavy rubber or crepe soles, are suitable. Shoes should fit well around the heel with plenty of room at the toes. Make sure your shoes are comfortable and provide support and don't cause blisters or calluses. Consult your podiatrist or the doctor who treats your diabetes before choosing a pair of walking shoes, in case you need special adaptations in your shoes.

Walking generates a lot of body heat, so keep this in mind when dressing for your workout. On hot days, the lighter the better. Cotton is a good choice; it absorbs perspiration and lets excess moisture evaporate. On wet days, choose shoes made of leather or nylon because they shed water better. When it's colder outside, dress in layers. Several thin layers of clothing will help insulate you better than a single thick layer. In addition, you can peel off clothes as you warm up. Wear cotton or silk next to your skin, wool on the outside. A nylon windbreaker over your layers provides the best insulation, as seasoned runners have learned. Don't forget mittens or knit gloves, and always wear a hat on cold and damp days.

THE FIRST STEP

Walking can be as easy as opening up the front door and stepping outside. For some people, however, following a specially designed program is the best way to get motivated. (See the following chart.) Be sure to do plenty of stretching warmup exercises to increase flexibility before you walk. If you have been an exercise dropout in the past, take heart—walking has a low dropout rate! No matter what your age or condition, it's an activity that can make you healthier and happier.

**PICK UP THE PACE:
TRY RACEWALKING**

If walking is too slow, and jogging or running too strenuous, consider racewalking—a cross between the two. Racewalking

A STEP-BY-STEP WALKING PROGRAM

If you find a particular week's pattern of exercise tiring, repeat it before going on to the next pattern. You do not have to complete the program in 12 weeks. Remember to do stretching warmup exercises before the walking warmup. Check with your doctor before beginning this program.

	WARMUP (Slow walking)	EXERCISE (Brisk walking)	COOL DOWN (Slow walking)	TOTAL TIME
WEEK 1				
Session A	5 min.	5 min.	5 min.	15 min.
Session B	5 min.	5 min.	5 min.	15 min.
Session C	5 min.	5 min.	5 min.	15 min.
Continue with at least three exercise sessions during each week.				
WEEK 2 (each session)	5 min.	7 min.	5 min.	17 min.
WEEK 3 "	5 min.	9 min.	5 min.	19 min.
WEEK 4 "	5 min.	11 min.	5 min.	21 min.
WEEK 5 "	5 min.	13 min.	5 min.	23 min.
WEEK 6 "	5 min.	15 min.	5 min.	25 min.
WEEK 7 "	5 min.	18 min.	5 min.	28 min.
WEEK 8 "	5 min.	20 min.	5 min.	30 min.
WEEK 9 "	5 min.	23 min.	5 min.	33 min.
WEEK 10 "	5 min.	26 min.	5 min.	36 min.
WEEK 11 "	5 min.	28 min.	5 min.	38 min.
WEEK 12 "	5 min.	30 min.	5 min.	40 min.

Designed by the National Heart, Lung, and Blood Institute. Reprinted from the publication, "Exercise and Your Heart."

resembles accelerated "street walking," with more emphasis on the pumping action of the arms. As you stride, the back leg remains straight, and foot contact is maintained with the ground at all times. To aid the forward motion, the arms are bent at right angles and are pumped back and forth. Regular racewalking can give your heart and lungs a good workout without making your feet, ankles, and knees take a beating. Many people are finding it a great way to get fit and stay that way. As with any strenuous exercise, be sure to discuss precautions and proper footwear with your doctor before beginning.

Racewalking burns about as many calories per mile as plain fast walking and doesn't require any special equipment other than a good pair of shoes and clothing that suits the weather. However, you may need a qualified instructor or experienced racewalker to teach you the proper technique. The athletic department of your local high school or college may be able to help. Or, to find a racewalking clinic in your area, write to the New York Walker's Club, Box M, Livingston Manor, NY 12758. (914) 439-5155. (Include a self-addressed, stamped envelope.)

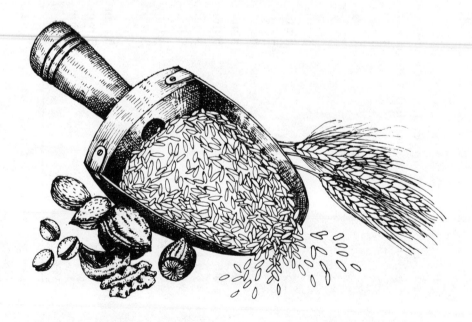

10 □ FIBER: WHAT'S IN IT FOR YOU?

Fiber, the undigestible part of plants, comes in several forms. Some fibers, such as cellulose, make up cell walls and help the plant to hold a firm shape. These are "water-insoluble," or "unfermentable," fibers. That is, bacteria in the digestive tract do not break them down, and they tend to maintain their structure throughout the digestive process. Wheat bran and whole grains, for example, contain such insoluble fibers.

Other forms of fiber repair injuries to the plant. Among these fibers are gums, pectins, and mucilages, which are "water-soluble," or "fermentable." That is, they do not retain their structure but become gummy or gel-like in the digestive tract. These fibers are found in fruits and legumes (dried* beans and peas). The differences are worth noting because some evidence suggests that soluble and insoluble fibers have different effects in the body and may well prove to differ in their impact on blood-glucose and blood-lipid (fat) levels. For instance, it seems that soluble fibers (such as dried beans) may be better for keeping blood glucose down right after a meal.

In reading food charts, you have probably seen fiber referred to as *crude, dietary,* or *total.* These terms all refer to laboratory measurement techniques rather than to the chemical makeup of the fiber. *Crude* fiber is measured in an old-fashioned way and tends to underestimate the fiber content. If you see the

---

*Dried beans and peas are ones you soak before cooking. Canned versions may be acceptable but choose carefully; they may be prepared with salt, sugar, and oil.

other terms, you can usually assume that the fiber has been measured by a newer technique that gives higher values, ones more
representative of the amount of matter that goes undigested in
the human body. However, no measurement approach used today
is considered to be the definitive one.

HOW DOES FIBER AFFECT BLOOD GLUCOSE?

As physicians in India suggested 2,000 years ago, high-fiber diets
seem capable of improving blood-glucose control, although how
fiber does that is still not completely clear. Researchers have several theories, however. One way for overweight people to improve
blood-glucose control is to lose weight, and substituting high-
fiber carbohydrates for high-fat foods seems to help in this effort.
For instance, a plate of high-fiber foods (such as fresh vegetables)
is quite filling yet relatively low in calories, assuming you steer
clear of sauces, cheese toppings, and the like. Many high-fiber
foods (think brown rice or broccoli) are low calorie because, in
addition to having a lot of indigestible matter (which provides no
calories), they are high in carbohydrate and water and low in fat.
(Water, as you know, is calorie-free. Carbohydrate has four calories per gram, in contrast to fat, which has nine.)

In addition to helping control blood glucose by helping
you to lose weight, fiber seems to improve control by slowing the
rate at which glucose is absorbed into the blood from the intestines. As a result, the blood-glucose rise after eating is less rapid
and less high than it might have been. In several studies, when
fiber was eaten along with sugar, the sugar was absorbed more
slowly than usual, and the blood-glucose rise was not as high.

Researchers do not know exactly how fiber slows absorption. But one mechanism seems to be that it somehow slows the
emptying of the stomach and the movement of food through the
upper digestive tract, the place where nutrients pass into the
blood.

Note: In some people who switch to a high-fiber diet, the

change may cause the need for an adjustment in insulin dosage or oral agents. Never change your diet radically without consulting your doctor and diet counselor.

WHAT OTHER BENEFITS DOES FIBER HAVE?

Fiber can be helpful in the following additional ways:

IT RELIEVES CONSTIPATION. Fiber absorbs water like a sponge, and water makes stools soft and easier to pass. The best sources of natural laxatives are whole-grain (bran-containing) breads and breakfast cereals. Fruits and vegetables are also good.

IT EASES OR PREVENTS HEMORRHOIDS AND DIVERTICULITIS. Hemorrhoids are swollen blood vessels at or near the anus, and diverticula are small bulges in the large intestines that can become infected. (Infected diverticula are referred to as diverticulitis.) By softening stools, fiber allows them to pass more easily through the intestine and out of the body. As a result, less strain is put on the bowel walls and blood vessels. Once again, bran and bran-containing foods are good choices.

IT MAY LOWER CHOLESTEROL AND FAT LEVELS IN THE BLOOD. When eaten as part of a diet high in complex carbohydrate, pectins (found in most fruits), guar gum (found in beans), rolled oats, oat bran, and chick peas have been found to lower cholesterol and fat levels, at least in some studies of animals and people. Wheat bran has not been effective. More study is needed, however, before anything definitive can be said about fiber's impact on blood fats.

WHAT ARE THE DRAWBACKS?

Fiber can cause gas if you eat too much too suddenly. It can also make you feel bloated or nauseous. Furthermore, people who rely too heavily on fiber-rich foods, particularly if they do not vary their choices, may exclude other important nutrients from their diets. In addition, fiber might bind with certain minerals (such as iron and zinc) and so prevent them from being absorbed into the blood, although this has not been conclusively proven. Eating a well-balanced diet, however, should prevent any vitamin and nutrient deficiencies, and increasing fiber *gradually* should prevent discomfort.

DOES THE FORM OF THE FOOD AFFECT FIBER'S IMPACT?

Increasing evidence shows that the way food is prepared can affect fiber's impact on blood sugar. Early reports indicate that raw, whole, and solid foods cause less of a blood-glucose rise than do forms that are cooked, ground, or liquid. For instance, raw potatoes seem to be absorbed into the blood much more slowly than well-cooked mashed potatoes. Beans that are slightly cooked are absorbed more slowly than well-cooked ones. Whole apples cause less of a blood-glucose rise than pureed ones. Oranges cause a lower rise than orange juice. Or so it seems. More study of individual foods and their action is needed.

ANY OVERALL ADVICE?

High-fiber foods seem to be helpful, although researchers still need more information on how fiber does its work, which fibers are best, and how much fiber is optimal for blood-glucose control and other benefits. For the moment, however, it seems prudent to gradually increase the amount of fiber you eat. The best way to do this is to consult a dietitian and doctor to be sure that your diet includes plenty of nutrients, vitamins, and minerals.

GUIDELINES FOR ADDING FIBER TO YOUR MEAL PLAN

"Everything in moderation." Your grandmother probably had this advice in her repertoire. And wise advice it is. The best way to add fiber to your diet is to continue with your balanced meal plan. Don't rely on any one food. Don't bother with fiber supplements or start compulsively to count grams. Just learn to identify high-fiber foods (complex carbohydrates such as whole-grain cereals, beans, vegetables, and fruits are often excellent sources) and substitute a *variety* of them for low-fiber items. Variety is important because nutrients vary from food to food and a mixture will help ensure that you are getting all you need.

OTHER GUIDELINES:
DISCUSS FIBER WITH YOUR DOCTOR AND DIETITIAN BEFORE CHANGING YOUR EATING HABITS. They will tell you if you need to take special precautions. For instance, high-fiber diets sometimes reduce people's insulin needs, so if you take insulin or oral agents, you have to be on the lookout for unusual blood-glucose changes. Your dietitian can help you find high-fiber foods you'll enjoy eating, and the doctor can help you make any needed reductions in medication.

GO FOR CARBOHYDRATES PACKAGED IN THEIR NATURAL FIBROUS COATINGS. Good choices are beans, peas, fruits, and vegetables. Other examples are brown rice instead of white and whole-grain flour instead of white. Increase your intake of whole grain, whole-wheat, or rye breads, crackers, and cereals.

SUBSTITUTE HIGH-FIBER FOODS FOR LOW-FIBER ONES GRADUALLY. A common recommendation—though not gospel—is to *slowly* work up to about 30 to 40 grams of fiber a day. This equals about 20 to 25 grams for every 1,000 calories you eat. The "gradual" part is important because it will cause the fewest side effects. Remember, this is only a guideline.

DRINK MORE FLUIDS WHEN YOU EAT MORE FIBER; otherwise, fiber can be constipating.

WATCH THOSE CALORIES! Keep in mind that fiber is not a medicine. If you eat extra calories by *adding* high-fiber foods to your daily diet instead of *substituting* them for some food choices, you will probably gain weight and cause a blood-glucose rise. To save calories, trim your intake of high-fat, high-caloric foods such as cream, gravies, sauces, and salad dressings. Eat bread and vegetables without margarine or butter; use noncaloric products for "greasing" pans, or use nonstick pans.

TIPS FOR USING LEGUMES, WHOLE GRAINS, AND RICE

You may be under the impression that starches and beans are fattening, but that simply isn't true. It's the gobs of margarine or butter on rice or bread that heap on the calories! Grain products in the raw, brown rice, whole-wheat breads, and legumes (dried beans and peas) give you a lot of value for the calories—they're excellent sources of protein, B vitamins, and iron. (An average slice of bread or ½ cup of rice contains about 80 calories.) Try experimenting with the various foods in these categories, such as barley, brown rice, buckwheat groats (kasha), bulgur (cracked wheat), cornmeal or polenta, and whole-grain flours (whole wheat, rye, or buckwheat).

LEGUMES. Beans, peas, and lentils are among the best sources of fiber and are full of protein. However, when eaten by themselves, they are "incomplete proteins." That is, they lack, or are low in, certain amino acids needed by the body. There are eight to ten amino acids that cannot be made by the body and must come from food. Most beans (except soybeans) are deficient in two of these amino acids, but whole wheat, whole grains, nuts, seeds, and dairy products are rich in them. Therefore, these foods should be combined with legumes in order to provide complete protein to your diet if you substitute legumes for meat. (See chart in Chapter 14 pages 398–399.)

Because legumes may be hard to digest and can cause intestinal gas, especially if you aren't used to eating them, it is best to start with the most easily digested legumes, such as lentils, split peas, and lima beans.

Before cooking beans, make sure you rinse and sort them

thoroughly, since they come directly from the fields. To cut cooking time, soak all beans overnight. (Soybeans should be refrigerated during soaking to prevent fermentation.) Another method is to put beans and water in a pot, bring the water to a boil, simmer for two minutes, then remove from heat and allow to stand covered for one hour. Salt should not be added until the beans are tender, otherwise they will not cook properly and might get tough. Also, don't mix different kinds of beans when cooking unless you are using a slow-cooking pot. (See Bean Cookery Conversion Chart.) Keep beans covered with liquid during cooking. If you're cooking beans for a salad or any dish where they should be firm, cook just until tender. For soups, beans may be cooked much longer.

The following procedures can be used to reduce the amount of gas (called "flatulence" in medical jargon) that results from eating beans:

- □ Soak the dried beans for 4 to 5 hours; discard the water.
- □ Add fresh water, cook beans for a half hour, and again discard the water.
- □ In each step above, for best results, use 9 cups of water for each cup of beans.
- □ If the beans still require cooking, add more water and discard after cooking unless otherwise directed by the recipe.

The disadvantage of this procedure is that approximately 50 percent of the water-soluble vitamins and a small amount of the protein is lost.

WHOLE GRAINS. Store whole grains in a cool, dry place to prevent spoilage. Whole-grain flour keeps best in a refrigerator or freezer. Because whole-wheat flour is bulkier than white flour, you'll need to make adjustments when baking with it. For each cup of white flour in a recipe, you can substitute:

BEAN COOKERY CONVERSION CHART

Bean	Regular Cooking Time	Pressure Cooker Cooking Time	Minimum Cooking Water	Dry Beans	◆ Cooked Beans
Black beans	1½ hrs.	20–25 min.	4 cups	1 cup	2 cups
Black-eyed peas	1 hr.	20–25 min.	3 cups	1 cup	2 cups
Pinto beans	2½ hrs.	20–25 min.	3 cups	1 cup	2 cups
Kidney beans	1½ hrs.	20–25 min.	3 cups	1 cup	2 cups
Soybeans	3 hrs. or more	20–25 min.	3 cups	1 cup	2 cups
Garbanzo beans	3 hrs.	40–45 min.	4 cups	1 cup	4 cups
Lentils and split peas	1 hr.	10–15 min.	3 cups	1 cup	2 ¼ cups
Great Northern beans	2 hrs.	20–25 min.	3½ cups	1 cup	2 cups
Navy beans	1½ hrs.	20–25 min.	3 cups	1 cup	2 cups
Lima beans	1½ hrs.	20–25 min.	2 cups	1 cup	1¼ cups

Source: *Nutrition Action*, Jan/Feb 1983. (Pressure cooking times come from *Recipes for a Small Planet*, by E. Ewald, New York: Ballantine, 1973, p. 310. The rest of the data are from *Laurel's Kitchen*, by L. Robertson, et al. New York: Bantam, 1976, p. 288.)

- □ One cup whole-wheat flour minus 2 Tbsp. (Decrease the amount of oil, and increase the liquid, by 1 or 2 Tbsp.); or
- □ Three-quarters cup white flour plus either ¼ cup wheat germ or ¼ cup bran; or
- □ Half cup of white flour and ¼ cup whole-wheat flour.

BROWN RICE. Brown rice takes longer to cook than white rice, but is relatively easy to prepare. Follow package instructions but, in general, put rice in boiling water in a 1:2 ratio, return to boil, cover, reduce heat, and cook for 45 minutes until the water steams off. When rice is thoroughly cooked, remove from heat and let stand several minutes to allow it to steam and dry. If you have fully cooked the rice, and it still seems hard or tough, add a little boiling water, cover, and continue cooking. To enhance the nutty flavor of the rice, stir washed, uncooked rice in a dry sauce pan over medium heat until the grain is dry and lightly toasted. When cooking, don't add salt until after the rice is cooked. (Salt tends to harden the kernels.) Also don't stir rice or grain while cooking; stirring makes rice pasty and grains gummy.

Now you know the basics of high-fiber eating, but how do you plan your meals? The "Fiber Exchange" with this chapter gives you the approximate fiber content of many foods. Based on that listing, you can easily construct high-fiber menus like this one:

SAMPLE MENU—1500 Calories, High Carbohydrate, High Fiber

Meal Plan	Sample Menu	Fiber
Breakfast:		
½ Skimmed milk	½ cup skim milk	0 gms.
1 Fruit	1 small orange	2 gms.
2 Starch/Bread	1 cup All-Bran	18 gms.
1 Starch/Bread	1 slice whole-wheat toast	2 gms.
1 Fat	1 tsp. margarine	0 gms.

SAMPLE MENU—1500 Calories, High Carbohydrate, High Fiber

Meal Plan	Sample Menu	Fiber
Snack:		
1 Fruit	1 small apple	2 gms.
Lunch:		
1 Skimmed milk	1 cup skim milk	0 gms.
1 Vegetable	2 cups lettuce w/diet dressing	2 gms.
1 Vegetable	1 medium tomato	2 gms.
1 Fruit	15 grapes	2 gms.
	Sandwich	
2 Starch	2 slices whole-wheat bread	4 gms.
2 Meat	2 oz. sliced turkey	0 gms.
1 Fat	1 tsp. margarine	0 gms.
Snack:		
1 Starch	4 squares Ry Krisp	3 gms.
Dinner:		
2 Vegetable	1 cup broccoli	4 gms.
1 Vegetable	2 cups lettuce w/diet dressing	2 gms.
1 Fruit	⅓ cup pineapple chunks	2 gms.
1 Starch	⅓ cup brown rice	3 gms.
3 Meat	3 oz. broiled fish	0 gms.
1 Fat	1 tsp. margarine	0 gms.
Evening Snack:		
1 Starch	3 cups popcorn, no butter	2 gms.
½ Skim milk	½ cup skim milk	0 gms.
Total:		
1,500 calories	210 gms. carbohydrate (57%)	49 gms.
	90 gms. protein (23%)	Fiber
	35 gms. fat (20%)	

Fiber seems to have many benefits and may have special benefits for people with diabetes, so trying to substitute some high-fiber foods for some high-fat items is probably worth the effort. And don't despair if you're one of those people who insist they'd rather starve than eat broccoli. Lots of foods have fiber, so chances are good that you can find a selection you like.

THE FIBER EXCHANGE*

The following is an adaptation of the American Diabetes Association/The American Dietetic Association's *Exchange Lists for Meal Planning*. To the six basic food groups listed there (See Appendix I) have been added the approximate fiber content of foods and guidelines for choosing high-fiber foods. Keep in mind, however, that the nutrient and fiber measures are *averages*. The nutrient and fiber contents of one food on any given list may differ from those of another food on the list and may affect your blood glucose differently. In addition, portion size and the form of food (cooked or raw, for example) can also affect a food's impact on your body. The letters CHO stand for "carbohydrate."

LIST 1: STARCH/BREAD

(This category is subdivided because of wide variations in fiber content and nutrients. The nutrients listed may vary from the ones in the *Exchange Lists* because the lists give an average for *all* of the foods in the category.)

LEGUMES (BEANS AND PEAS)
Nutrients: 15 gm. CHO; 6 gm. pro.; 1 gm. fat; 90 calories.
Serving size: Beans, peas, lentils (cooked)—⅓ cup; canned
        baked beans (no pork)—¼ cup.
Fiber: 8 gm.

*All servings here represent one "exchange," or portion as listed in the *Exchange Lists for Meal Planning*. The fiber values are from *HCF: A User's Guide to High-Carbohydrate, High-Fiber Diets,* by James W. Anderson *et al.* University of Kentucky Diabetes Fund, Lexington, 1979.

GUIDELINES FOR HIGH-FIBER CHOICES: Fiber is found in cooked or canned dried beans (lima, kidney, navy, pinto, etc.), in dried peas, and in lentils.

STARCHY VEGETABLES
Nutrients: 15 gm. CHO; 3 gm. pro.; 1 gm. fat; 80 calories.
Serving size (cooked): winter squash and parsnips—¾ cup; corn, barley, peas—½ cup; sweet potatoes or wheat bulgar (cracked wheat)—⅓ cup; baked potato (w/skin)—1 small.
Fiber: 3 gm.
GUIDELINES FOR HIGH-FIBER CHOICES: All above are good.

CEREALS (BRAN AND WHOLE GRAIN TYPES)
Nutrients: 15 gm. CHO; 3 gm. pro.; 0 fat; 80 calories.
Serving size: Varies
Fiber: 3 gm.
GUIDELINES FOR HIGH-FIBER CHOICES: Cereals can be excellent sources of fiber and make good choices for breakfast. Read labels, though—many bran-type cereals contain a moderate amount of sugar. Some of those can be eaten but should be alternated with ones that contain little or no sugar. (See "Cereals" chart below for the best choices and portion sizes.)

CEREALS: Does high in fiber mean low in sugar?

Although many cereals with "healthy" sounding names are indeed high in fiber and low in sugar, others—especially bran cereals and granolas—can have a lot of sugar. The cereals here are listed in order of how much sugar they contain. Those marked with an asterisk are good choices—low in sugar and high in fiber. Cereals that contain more than 10% sugar should not be eaten every day, and ones higher than 30% sugar should be left on supermarket shelves.

Cereal	Serving size	Sugar (gms)[1]	Fiber (gms)[2]
Cereals containing approximately 10% sugar or less			
Oatmeal, Oats*	½ cup, cooked	—	2.9
Puffed Wheat*	¾ cup	—	3.4
Shredded Wheat*	1 biscuit	—	2.8
Ralston*	½ cup, cooked	1	2.1
Cheerios*	1 cup	1	2.5
Chex, Corn*	⅔ cup	1	2.6
Chex, Wheat*	½ cup	1	2
Corn Flakes*	⅔ cup	1	2.6
Grape Nuts*	3 Tbsp.	1	2.7
Nutri-Grains*	½ cup	1	2
Corn Bran*	½ cup	2	4.4
Grape Nut Flakes*	⅔ cup	2	2.5
Oat Bran*	¼ cup	2	5.3
Total*	¾ cup	2	2.5
Wheaties*	¾ cup	2	2.6
Cereals containing approximately 10 to 30% sugar			
40% Bran Flakes*	⅔ cup	4	3
Bran Chex*	½ cup	4	4.1
Most*	⅓ cup	4	3
All-Bran*	⅓ cup	5	9
Honey Bran	⅔ cup	5	2.4
Frosted Mini-Wheats	2½ biscuits	5	1.3
Cracklin' Bran	⅓ cup	5	3
Raisin Bran	¾ cup	8	3.4
Cereals containing approximately 30 to 40% sugar			
Wheat and Raisin Chex	½ cup	6	2
Bran Buds	⅓ cup	8	8

[1]Source: USDA Nutrient Composition Laboratory of the Nutrition Institute, Human Nutrition Center, Beltsville, MD. *Journal of Food Science* 45 (1): 138–141, 1980.
[2]Sources: Anderson, J. W., *et al.*, *Plant Fiber in Foods*, HCF Diabetes Research Foundation, Inc., Lexington, KY; Kellogg's; Ralston Purina.

BREADS AND GRAINS
Nutrients: 15 gm. CHO; 3 gm. pro.; 0 fat; 80 calories.
Serving size: Breads—1 slice; graham crackers—3 squares;
             popcorn—3 cups.
Fiber: 2 gm.

GUIDELINES FOR HIGH-FIBER CHOICES: Choose items made from grains that retain their natural fibrous coatings. (Beware: "wheat flour" on an ingredients list is usually white flour.) Good choices are whole-grain breads or crackers, such as cracked wheat, whole meal (stone ground), whole wheat, or rye bread; rye crackers; and bran muffins.

LIST 2: (MEDIUM-FAT MEAT)

FROM ANIMAL SOURCES (LEAN MEATS)
Nutrients: 0 CHO; 7 gm. pro.; 5 gm. fat; 75 calories.
Serving size: Mostly 1 oz. (cooked).
Fiber: 0 gm.

LIST 3: VEGETABLE

Nutrients: 5 gm. CHO; 2 gm. pro.; 0 fat; 25 calories.
Serving size: ½ cup cooked, or 1 cup raw.
Fiber: 2–3 gm.

GUIDELINES FOR HIGH-FIBER CHOICES: Pick foods with edible skins and seeds. May be fresh, frozen, or canned but should not have added fat, sauces, glazes, cheese, etc. (*Note:* Cooking reduces volume and destroys some nutrients but does not alter fiber content.)

LIST 4: FRUIT

Nutrients: 15 gm. CHO; 0 pro.; 0 fat; 60 calories.
Serving size: Varies (see *Exchange Lists*).
Fiber: 2 gm.

GUIDELINES FOR HIGH-FIBER CHOICES: Fruits should be raw, canned in their own juice, unsweetened, or artificially sweetened with a sugar substitute. Select fruits with edible skins and seeds. Eat more whole fruits instead of fruit juice.

LIST 5: MILK

Nutrients: 12 gm. CHO; 8 gm. pro.; trace fat; 90 calories.
Serving size: 1 cup (skim-milk products).
Fiber: 0 gm.

LIST 6: FAT

Nutrients: 0 CHO, 0 pro.; 5 gm. fat; 45 calories.
Serving size: Varies (see *Exchange Lists*).
Fiber: 0 gm.

NOTE: All varieties of nuts contain fiber, as do pumpkin seeds, sesame seeds, and sunflower seeds. Fiber is usually 3 grams per 1-ounce serving.

11 □ RECIPES

Recipes in this book were selected to complement the collection in the first *Family Cookbook*. They emphasize dishes that combine foods from different groups and include several ethnic and regional dishes.

Prior to recipe development and testing, a list of characteristics that each final recipe should have were established—characteristics based on the nutritional guidelines for diabetes as well as the guidelines for all health-conscious people. As a result, the final recipes are generally:

□ Reduced in total fat and saturated fat;
□ Limited to ½ egg per serving when the recipe includes eggs;
□ Limited in salt and sodium-rich ingredients;
□ Limited to about ½ teaspoon of sugar, honey, or molasses when a recipe includes these ingredients.

Note, too, that the preponderance of recipes use low-fat meats, vegetables, dried beans and peas, pasta, and whole grains, rather than fatty meats or processed foods.

RECIPE DEVELOPMENT AND TESTING

Recipes were analyzed, adjusted, and tested in a test kitchen by a registered dietitian experienced in recipe development. The final products were served to customers in a restaurant and only recipes that met with their approval were accepted.

Most recipes are for six, and sometimes two, servings, except soups and items that require long preparation and cooking times. These usually yield eight or more servings. Extra servings may be packaged and frozen, and reheated for later meals. This type of preparation is particularly useful for those who have microwave ovens.

96

Portion sizes for items that are part of a typical meal pattern are the traditional ⅓ to ½ cup. Portion sizes for combination-type dishes are generally 1 to 1½ cups, as they are intended to be the major item in the meal.

INGREDIENTS

Information about basic ingredients found in the first *Family Cookbook* (Volume I) applies to this book as well. Recipe calculations are based on skim milk, fat-free broth,* large eggs, unsifted all-purpose flour, and unsalted water for cooking rice, pasta, vegetables, and the like, unless otherwise specified. For shortening, vegetable oils and margarines were generally used. In your own cooking, choose among those made from corn, cottonseed, safflower, soybean, and/or sunflower oils.

Sugar, when used in recipes, has been calculated in the recipes' total carbohydrate content, as before. Additionally, in this volume, each recipe with added sugar (exceptions: recipes with trace amounts of sugar per serving) has a note describing the amount of refined sugar, honey, or molasses, and the calories from these sources. Discuss the use of the recipes with your dietitian before trying them. Sugar substitutes have been used in some recipes. (See Chapter 14, "The New Sweetener: Aspartame," about uses and limitations of this new sugar substitute.)

In general, granular sugar substitutes are packaged to provide the sweetness of two teaspoons of sugar. Most products also contain about one gram of carbohydrate. But check each product's label before using.

Specialty canned items, such as water chestnuts, ripe olives, mushrooms, green chilies, and pimientos are used in some recipes. Often a whole can is not required; therefore, freeze the remainder of the can for future use or refrigerate and use within a day or two. These can be nice additions to omelets or other recipes.

*Use of homemade broth will reduce sodium content for those who must limit sodium in the diet.

Items such as miller's bran, tofu, wheat germ, pearl barley, and sprouts are usually available in large supermarkets. Growing your own sprouts, however, can be fun. (See the directions on page 277.)

In some areas of the country where miller's bran is not available, you can use all-bran and sugar-free bran breakfast cereal.

Chicken is used extensively in these recipes. If a whole chicken is not required, you can buy breasts, thighs, or quarters of chickens. If buying a whole chicken, keep in mind that a three-pound chicken with bones will yield about 2 to 2½ cups (about 1½ pounds) of diced cooked chicken. To cook chicken, follow the recipe for cold chicken or use the traditional method of simmering until the meat falls from the bones. Chicken parts bought individually will be larger than those from a 2¾- to 3-pound chicken.

SEASONINGS

Most of the seasonings used here are available in large supermarkets. Find fresh ginger root and fresh basil in the fresh vegetable section. Picante sauce and green chili salsa with no added sugar are available in the Mexican food section. (See recipe section for homemade picante sauce, page 321.) They are excellent for seasoning foods in place of catsup. Garlic powder, fresh garlic, and black pepper are very good flavor enhancers and may be increased in recipes to reduce salt content.

"EXCHANGES" AND "ESTIMATED NUTRIENTS" PER SERVING

As in the first *Family Cookbook*, the exchanges and selected estimated nutrients are given for one serving of each recipe. However, in this volume, grams of dietary fiber are listed in addition to the estimated calories, grams of carbohydrate, protein, and fat, and milligrams of sodium, potassium, and cholesterol. The nutrients per serving are expressed in abbreviations and symbols as follows:

Calories (CAL)	Sodium (Na)
Carbohydrates (CHO)	Potassium (K)
Protein (PRO)	Fiber (Fiber)
Fat (FAT)	Cholesterol (Chol)

Optional ingredients and dashes of ingredients were not included in the nutrient analysis. If a choice of ingredients was offered, the first listed was included in the nutrient analysis.

If a given serving size is too large for your meal plan, you can divide the serving size and the listed calculations in half. Similarly, you can double serving sizes if necessary and multiply all calculations by two to find the exchange and nutrient value of the enlarged serving.

The exchanges and nutrients per serving were derived by computer.

RECIPE ANALYSIS*

The data base for the recipe analysis program contains more than seven hundred foods, including all of the ingredients in this cookbook. For each food, the data base includes twenty-eight different nutrients. Of those, the amount per serving of protein, fat, carbohydrate, sodium, potassium, cholesterol, and total dietary fiber appears for each recipe. Nutrient analysis information for calories and the first six nutrients is from the United States Department of Agriculture, Handbook 8 and Handbooks 8-1 through 8-14. Nutrient information for foods not available in these sources was obtained from provisional information or from the producers of the products. Total dietary fiber analysis is from a published source.

The recipe analysis program, developed by Lawrence A. Wheeler, M.D., Ph.D., was written in Pascal and runs on IBM type

---

*The recipe analysis was performed by Madelyn L. Wheeler, M.S., R.D., C.D.E.

computers. The program not only analyzes recipes for individual nutrients per serving (as described above) but also:

1. Provides "exchanges" for an individual serving based on the 1986 edition of *Exchange Lists for Meal Planning*, so that the exchange value of the serving is close to the actual nutrient content.

2. "Flags" key nutrients. A "key nutrient" is defined as a nutrient in a single serving that will provide more than 75 percent of the Recommended Daily Allowance (USRDA).

For some recipes, there were several possible combinations of exchanges that yielded good nutritional approximations. Combinations that might have been "best" in terms of reflecting the actual nutrient content of the recipe, but which seemed inappropriate (for example, a milk exchange in a recipe that did not contain a milk product) were eliminated.

REFERENCES

1. American Diabetes Association. 1987. Nutritional Recommendations and Principles for Individuals with Diabetes Mellitus: 1986, *Diabetes Care* 10: 126–32

2. Anderson, J. W.: 1986. *Plant Fiber in Foods*. Lexington, KY: HCF Diabetes Research Foundation, Inc.

3. United States Department of Agriculture and Health and Human Services. 1985. *Dietary Guidelines for Americans*. Washington, DC: HHS.

4. United States Department of Agriculture Handbook. 1976–86. *8-1: Dairy and Egg Products; 8-2: Spices & Herbs; 8-4: Fats & Oils; 8-5: Poultry Products; 8-6: Soups, Sauces & Gravies; 8-7: Sausages & Luncheon Meats; 8-8: Breakfast Cereals; 8-9: Fruits and Fruit Juices; 8-10: Pork Products; 8-11: Vegetables and Vegetable Products; 8-12: Nut and Seed Products; 8-13: Beef Products; 8-14: Beverages*. Washington, DC: HHS.

5. Watt, B. K., and A. C. P. Merrill. 1984. *Composition of Foods: Raw, Processed, Prepared. USDA Agriculture Handbook No. 8.* Washington, DC: Government Printing Office.
6. Wheeler, L. A., M. L. Wheeler, and P. Ours. 1985. Computer Selected Exchange Lists Approximations for Recipes. *J. Am. Diet. Assoc.* 85:700–703.

Best-Bet Breakfasts

Orange Juice Milk Drink

Yield: 4 servings
Serving Size: 1 cup
Exchange List Approximation:
    Fruit 1
    Milk, low-fat $\frac{1}{2}$

Nutrient Content Per Serving:
CAL: 135   PRO: 4.8 (gm)
FAT: 2.7 (gm)   CHO: 23.4 (gm)
Na: 49.5 (mg)   K: 469.2 (mg)
Fiber: 0   Chol: 73 (mg)

Ingredients

1 6-OUNCE CAN FROZEN CONCENTRATED ORANGE JUICE
1 CUP WATER
1 CUP 2% MILK
1 EGG
6 PACKETS SUGAR SUBSTITUTE
8 ICE CUBES

Method

1. Place all ingredients in blender or food processor.
2. Blend until smooth.

Note: You can cut this recipe in half, but continue to use a whole egg. The change in nutrients per serving is negligible.

Stick-to-the-Ribs Oatmeal

Yield: 1 serving

Serving Size: 1 recipe

Exchange List Approximation:

    Starch/Bread 2

    Meat, lean 1

    Fruit $\frac{1}{2}$

Nutrient Content Per Serving:

CAL: 255   PRO: 14.5 (gm)

FAT: 3.7 (gm)   CHO: 42.2 (gm)

Na: 360.4 (mg)   K: 279 (mg)

Fiber: 4.7 (gm)   Chol: 5 (mg)

Ingredients

⅔ CUP WATER

½ CUP OATMEAL

¹⁄₁₆ TEASPOON SALT

⅓ CUP UNSWEETENED CRUSHED PINEAPPLE

¼ CUP LOW-FAT COTTAGE CHEESE

¼ TEASPOON COCONUT EXTRACT

Method

1. Bring water to a boil, add oatmeal and salt. Stir and cook 1 minute.
2. Stir in pineapple, cottage cheese, and flavoring. Bring to a boil.
3. Serve with sweetener and milk as meal plan permits.

Everyday Oatmeal-Plus

Yield: 1 serving
Serving Size: 1 cup
Exchange List Approximation:
    Starch/Bread 2
    Meat, lean 1

Nutrient Content Per Serving:
CAL: 205   PRO: 14.2 (gm)
FAT: 3.6 (gm)   CHO: 29.1 (gm)
Na: 359.4 (mg)   K: 196 (mg)
Fiber: 4 (gm)   Chol: 5 (mg)

Ingredients

1 CUP WATER
½ CUP OATMEAL (QUICK)
¹⁄₁₆ TEASPOON SALT
¼ CUP LOW-FAT COTTAGE CHEESE
¼ TEASPOON COCONUT EXTRACT OR 2 TEASPOONS SHERRY

Method

1. Bring water to boil. Add oatmeal and salt. Stir. Bring to a boil. Reduce heat, cover, and cook about 3 minutes.
2. Stir in cottage cheese and bring to a boil.
3. Add flavoring and serve with sweetener and milk, if meal plan permits.

Raisin-Apple Oatmeal-Plus-Egg

Yield: 1 serving
Serving Size: 1 recipe
Exchange List Approximation:
    Starch/Bread 1
    Meat, medium-fat 1
    Fruit 2

Nutrient Content Per Serving:

CAL: 271	PRO: 10.9 (gm)
FAT: 7.7 (gm)	CHO: 41.8 (gm)
Na: 72 (mg)	K: 348.2 (mg)
Fiber: 5.3 (gm)	Chol: 274 (mg)

Ingredients

½ SMALL APPLE DICED OR ¼ CUP UNSWEETENED APPLESAUCE
1 TABLESPOON RAISINS
1 CUP WATER
⅓ CUP OATMEAL (QUICK)
1 EGG, BEATEN
⅛ TEASPOON CINNAMON
   DASH NUTMEG

Method

1. Combine diced apple or applesauce, raisins, and water in small saucepan. Bring to boil, cover, and simmer until apple is tender.
2. Stir in oatmeal, bring to a boil, and cook 1 minute.
3. Gradually add half of oatmeal to beaten egg. Add mixture back to oatmeal and cook about 10 seconds. Egg may be added directly to oatmeal if desired.
4. Stir in cinnamon and nutmeg.
5. Serve with milk and sweetener, as meal plan permits.

Fluffy High-Fiber, Low-Fat Pancakes

Yield: 8 4-inch pancakes
Serving Size: 1 pancake
Exchange List Approximation:
    Starch/Bread 1

Nutrient Content Per Serving:
CAL: 68   PRO: 3.7 (gm)
FAT: 1.6 (gm)   CHO: 11.3 (gm)
Na: 217.5 (mg)   K: 145.4 (mg)
Fiber: 2.3 (gm) Chol: 35 (mg)

Ingredients

1   CUP BUTTERMILK OR SOUR MILK (ADD 1 TBSP.
    LEMON JUICE PER 1 CUP MILK)
½   CUP ROLLED OATS (QUICK)
⅔   CUP MILLER'S BRAN (UNPROCESSED, UNCOOKED
    WHEAT BRAN)
1   EGG
¼   CUP WHOLE-WHEAT FLOUR
½   TEASPOON SUGAR
¼   TEASPOON SALT
¾   TEASPOON SODA

Method

1. Combine buttermilk, oats, and bran in large mixing bowl.
    Let stand 5 minutes. Add egg and beat until blended.
2. Mix whole-wheat flour, sugar, salt, and baking soda until
    blended.
3. Add to bran mixture and blend until all flour is moistened.
4. Pour about ¼-cup batter on lightly greased, preheated 375°
    F griddle or frying pan. Cook about 3 minutes or until
    bubbles form and the edge of pancake is dry. Turn and
    cook 2 minutes longer. This is a "fat" pancake.
5. Serve with sugar-free jam or jelly.

Spicy Whole-Wheat Pancakes

Yield: 6 servings
Serving Size: 3 small or 2 large
Exchange List Approximation:
    Starch/Bread 1
    Fat 1

Nutrient Content Per Serving:

CAL: 124	PRO: 5 (gm)
FAT: 4.6 (gm)	CHO: 16.6 (gm)
Na: 225.3 (mg)	K: 149.7 (mg)
Fiber: 1.9 (gm)	Chol: 49 (mg)

Ingredients

1 CUP WHOLE-WHEAT FLOUR
2 TEASPOONS BAKING POWDER
½ TEASPOON CINNAMON
¼ TEASPOON SALT
1 CUP LOW-FAT MILK
1 EGG
1 TABLESPOON VEGETABLE OIL

Method

1. Mix dry ingredients. Add remaining ingredients. Mix until blended.
2. Drop by 1½ tablespoons for small pancakes and 2 tablespoons for large pancakes on hot, lightly greased griddle or frying pan (375° F). Cook until bubbles form on top and the edge appears dry. Turn and cook until lightly browned.
3. Serve with warm applesauce (recipe in Volume I).

Scrambled Tofu

Yield: 6 or 2 servings
Serving Size: $\frac{1}{2}$ cup
Exchange List Approximation:
    Meat, medium-fat 1

Nutrient Content Per Serving:
CAL: 76   PRO: 8.1 (gm)
FAT: 4.3 (gm)   CHO: 2.9 (gm)
Na: 529.3 (mg)   K: 49.7 (mg)
Fiber: 0   Chol: 0

Ingredients

Six servings	Two servings
1-POUND 4-OUNCE PACKAGE TOFU	6⅔ OUNCES
½ TEASPOON ONION POWDER	⅛ TEASPOON
2 CUBES CHICKEN BOUILLON (OR 2 TEASPOONS INSTANT BOUILLON)	1 CUBE
¼ TEASPOON SEASONED SALT	¹⁄₁₆ TEASPOON
VEGETABLE COOKING SPRAY	

Method

1. Spray skillet with vegetable cooking spray.
2. Dice tofu and place in skillet. Add remaining ingredients to tofu and brown lightly. Turn occasionally while cooking.
3. Serve like scrambled eggs for breakfast.

*To reduce sodium content, substitute herb blend recipe (from Chapter 15) for bouillon and seasoned salt.

Breakfast on the Run

Yield: 2 servings
Serving Size: 1¼ cup
Exchange List Approximation:
    Starch/Bread 1
    Fruit 1
    Milk, skim 1

Nutrient Content Per Serving:

CAL: 239	PRO: 12.7 (gm)
FAT: 3.2 (gm)	CHO: 44 (gm)
Na: 108.6 (mg)	K: 931 (mg)
Fiber: 4.9 (gm)	Chol: 6 (mg)

Ingredients

1⅓ CUPS SLICED RIPE BANANAS, FROZEN (ABOUT 2 WHOLE)
  1 CUP SKIM MILK
  ½ CUP PLAIN LOW-FAT YOGURT
  ¼ CUP WHEAT GERM
  1 EGG (OPTIONAL)*
  2 TEASPOONS VANILLA
  1 PACKET SUGAR SUBSTITUTE (IF DESIRED)

Method

1. Slice bananas and freeze overnight.
2. Place ingredients in blender and blend until smooth.
3. Garnish with nutmeg.

*If egg is added, count as an extra ½ Meat, medium-fat.

Crunchy Granola

Yield: 16 servings (5½ cups)
Serving Size: ⅓ cup
Exchange List Approximation:
  Starch/Bread 1½
  Fat 1½

Nutrient Content Per Serving:
CAL: 188   PRO: 5 (gm)
FAT: 8.9 (gm)   CHO: 24 (gm)
Na: 9.2 (mg)   K: 176.3 (mg)
Fiber: 3.7 (gm)   Chol: 0

Ingredients

3½ CUPS OLD-FASHIONED OATS
 ½ CUP WHEAT GERM
 ½ CUP COCONUT
 ¼ CUP SESAME SEEDS
 ¼ CUP ALMONDS
 ¼ CUP SUNFLOWER SEEDS OR MILLET SEEDS
 ¼ CUP HONEY
 ¼ CUP OIL
 1 TABLESPOON VANILLA
 ½ CUP RAISINS, RESERVE

Method

1. Mix all together with electric mixer, spread evenly on 2 baking sheets with edges, and bake in 250° F oven until golden brown (45 to 60 minutes).
2. Turn and stir after 30 minutes.
3. Remove from oven and add raisins. Cool and store in plastic bag. This is very good with milk for breakfast.

Note: Approximately ¾ teaspoon of honey (12 calories) per serving.

Whole-Wheat Granola

Yield: 28 servings
Serving Size: $\frac{1}{2}$ cup
Exchange List Approximation:
    Starch/Bread 1
    Fruit 1
    Fat 2

Nutrient Content Per Serving:
CAL: 227*   PRO: 4.7 (gm)
FAT: 11.9 (gm)* CHO: 27.9 (gm)
Na: 98.4 (mg) K: 189.1 (mg)
Fiber: 4 (gm) Chol: 0

Ingredients

4 CUPS REGULAR OATS, UNCOOKED
3 CUPS WHOLE-WHEAT FLOUR
2 CUPS WHEAT GERM
1 TABLESPOON CINNAMON
1 TEASPOON SALT (OPTIONAL)
1 CUP VEGETABLE OIL
1 CUP HONEY OR SUBSTITUTE
½ CUP ORANGE JUICE
1 CUP FLAKED COCONUT
½ CUP SLICED ALMONDS
1 CUP RAISINS

Method

1. Mix first 5 ingredients in electric mixer.
2. Combine oil, honey, and juice and pour over mixture. Mix until completely blended.
3. Spread evenly in 4 shallow pans and bake in 250° F oven for 45 minutes.
4. Stir in coconut and almonds and bake 30 minutes more.
5. Cool and stir in raisins.

*To cut calories and fat, reduce the coconut and oil by a third.

Yeast Breads, Quick Breads, Muffins

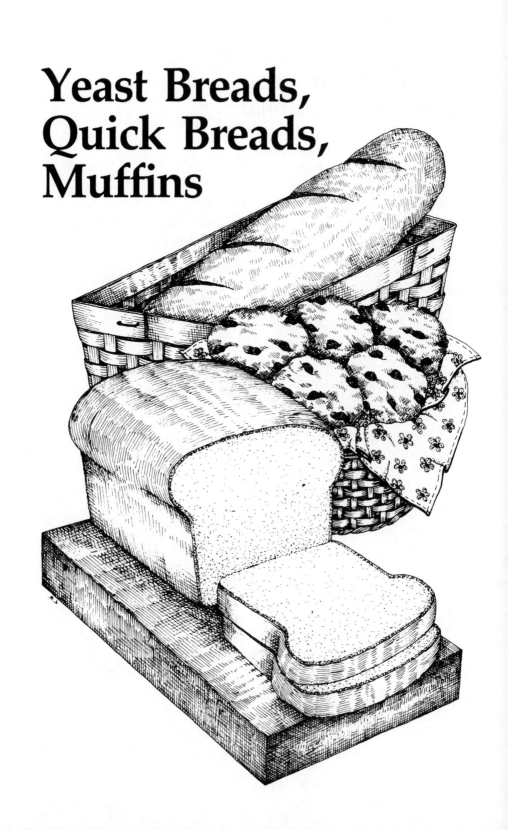

Old World Swedish Limpa or Rye Bread

Yield: 36 servings (2 loaves,
  18 slices per loaf)
Serving Size: 1 slice
Exchange List Approximation:
  Starch/Bread $1\frac{1}{2}$

Nutrient Content Per Serving:
CAL: 125   PRO: 3.4 (gm)
FAT: 1.6 (gm)   CHO: 24.3 (gm)
Na: 181.5 (mg)   K: 117.2 (mg)
Fiber: 1.5 (gm)   Chol: 0

Ingredients

  2 ¼-OUNCE PACKAGES ACTIVE DRY YEAST
  1 CUP WARM WATER
  2 TEASPOONS SUGER
  2 CUPS ALL-PURPOSE FLOUR
1½ CUPS WARM WATER (85° F)
  ½ CUP LIGHT MOLASSES
  3 TABLESPOONS SHORTENING, VEGETABLE, MELTED
  1 TABLESPOON SALT
  1 TABLESPOON CARAWAY SEEDS
1½ CUPS DARK RYE FLOUR
  4 CUPS ALL-PURPOSE FLOUR
  2 TEASPOONS MARGARINE, SOFTENED

Method

1. Sprinkle yeast on 1-cup of warm water (100–110° F). Stir to
    dissolve. Let stand 5 to 10 minutes.
2. In a large mixing bowl, combine dissolved yeast, sugar,
    and 2 cups flour. Beat by hand or mix with mixer at
    number 3 speed until smooth and stretchy.

3. Cover with a cloth. Let rise until double in bulk in a warm place (80° F) free from drafts, approximately 20 minutes.

4. In a separate mixing bowl, thoroughly mix water, molasses, shortening, salt, and caraway seeds. Transfer this mixture to the bowl containing the yeast "sponge." Mix together.

5. To this mixture, add rye and all-purpose flours. Beat by hand or mix on number 2 speed on mixer. Dough will be soft, not stiff.

6. Lightly grease top of dough. Cover with cloth. Let rise until double in bulk in a warm place (80° F) free from drafts.

7. Grease heavily 2 loaf pans, 9¼- by 5¼- by 2¾-inches. Punch down dough. Place soft dough on a floured board. Divide in half. Shape into loaves the size of the pans. Place in greased pans and push down all around the sides so no air is trapped.

8. Cover and let rise until double in size.

9. Preheat oven to 375° F.

10. Place loaves in oven on middle shelf. Bake 45 to 50 minutes. If browning too fast, cover with aluminum foil tent. To check for doneness after 45 minutes, tap top of loaf. It will sound hollow if done. The loaf will shrink from the sides of the pans.

11. Remove from oven. Brush tops with melted margarine. Cool briefly. Carefully remove from pans and cool loaves on wire rack.

Note: Each serving has less than ¾-teaspoon sugar (10 to 11 calories).

Whole-Wheat Batter Bread

Yield: 3 loaves (20 slices per loaf)   Nutrient Content Per Serving:
Serving Size: 1 slice   CAL: 80   PRO: 2.6 (gm)
Exchange List Approximation: FAT: 1.7 (gm)   CHO: 13.9 (gm)
    Starch/Bread 1   Na: 129 (mg)   K: 74.2 (mg)
                                                         Fiber: 1 (gm)   Chol: 9 (mg)

Ingredients

    3 CUPS WHOLE-WHEAT FLOUR
    2 PACKAGES ACTIVE DRY YEAST
2½ CUPS SOUR MILK (2½ CUPS SKIM MILK + 1
        TEASPOON LEMON JUICE OR VINEGAR)
    ¼ CUP MOLASSES
    ¼ CUP HONEY
    1 TABLESPOON SALT
    ⅓ CUP MARGARINE
1½ CUP REGULAR ROLLED OATS
    2 EGGS
3–3½ CUPS UNSIFTED ALL-PURPOSE FLOUR
    1 TABLESPOON MELTED MARGARINE TO BRUSH ON
        DOUGH

Method

1. Combine whole-wheat flour and yeast.
2. Heat margarine, sour milk, molasses, honey, and salt until
    warm. Pour into 3-quart bowl.
3. Add oats, whole-wheat flour-yeast mixture and eggs.
    Blend at low speed with electric mixer until moistened.
    Beat 3 minutes at high speed.
4. Stir in enough white flour to make a stiff dough.

5. Brush with melted margarine.
6. Cover and let rise in a warm place until doubled (about 1 hour).
7. Punch down and shape into 3 loaves. Place in 3 9- by 5-inch loaf pans, greased.
8. Cover loaves and let rise in a warm place until doubled in size (about 45 minutes to 1 hour).
9. Heat oven to 375° F last 10 to 15 minutes of rising time.
10. Bake 25 to 35 minutes or until loaf sounds hollow when tapped.

Note: Each slice of bread has less than ½ teaspoon sugar (6 calories).

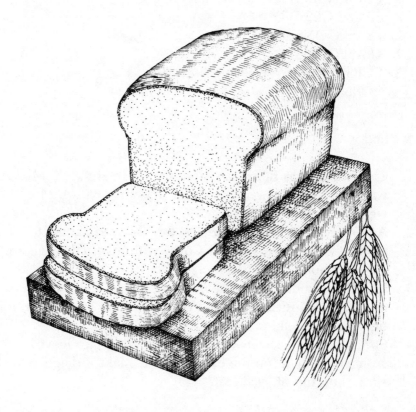

Whole-Wheat French Bread

Yield: 3 loaves (8 slices per loaf)
Serving Size: 1 slice
Exchange List Approximation:
    Starch/Bread 1

Nutrient Content Per Serving:
CAL: 88   PRO: 3.3 (gm)
FAT: 0.4 (gm)   CHO: 18.7 (gm)
Na: 178.8 (mg) K: 87.2 (mg)
Fiber: 2 (gm)   Chol: 0

Ingredients

3½–4 CUPS WHOLE-WHEAT FLOUR
  1 CUP UNBLEACHED WHITE FLOUR
  2 PACKAGES DRY YEAST
  2 TEASPOONS SALT
  2 TEASPOONS HONEY
  2 CUPS WARM WATER
     CORNMEAL

Method

1. Combine 2 cups flour, salt, and dry yeast; stir well. Mix warm water with honey and add to flour mixture. Mix well. Let rest 5 minutes.
2. Add remaining flour, 1 cup at a time. Knead about 10 minutes on floured surface. Cover with inverted bowl, and let rise 1 hour.
3. Punch down dough and divide into thirds. Roll each third into 10- by 14-inch rectangle. With long end facing you, roll tightly into a jelly roll shape.
4. Sprinkle baking sheet with corn meal and place loaves, seam side down, on the baking sheet. Make 4 diagonal slashes on top of each loaf.

5. Place baking sheet in middle of cold oven. Place a pan of hot water on rack below the baking sheet. Let loaves rise about 20 minutes; remove pan of water and brush top of each loaf with cold water.

6. Bake at 425° F oven for 35 to 40 minutes. Do not preheat oven.

Blueberry Banana Bread

Yield: 1 loaf (22 slices)

Serving Size: 2 slices

Exchange List Approximation:

    Starch/Bread 1

    Fruit 1

    Fat $\frac{1}{2}$

Nutrient Content Per Serving:

CAL: 168	PRO: 3.9 (gm)
FAT: 4.3 (gm)	CHO: 30 (gm)
Na: 167.6 (mg)	K: 165 (mg)
Fiber: 2.6 (gm)	Chol: 25 (mg)

Ingredients

  1 CUP WHOLE-WHEAT FLOUR

  ¾ CUP ALL-PURPOSE FLOUR

  1 TEASPOON BAKING SODA

  ½ TEASPOON CINNAMON

  ¼ TEASPOON SALT

  ½ CUP QUICK-COOKING ROLLED OATS

  3 TABLESPOONS MARGARINE

  ⅓ CUP SUGAR

  1 EGG

  1 CUP MASHED BANANAS (ABOUT 2 WHOLE)

  1 TABLESPOON LEMON JUICE

  1 CUP FRESH OR FROZEN BLUEBERRIES, THAWED (ABOUT 4 OUNCES)

Method

1. Preheat oven to 350° F and lightly grease 8½- by 4½-inch loaf pan.
2. Mix flour, soda, salt, and cinnamon. Stir in oats and set aside.
3. Cream margarine and sugar. Whip in egg, add bananas and lemon juice. Stir until blended.
4. Fold in blueberries.
5. Add dry ingredients and mix until just moistened.
6. Pour batter in loaf pan and bake for about 1 hour.
7. Let bread cool in pan for 10 minutes. Turn out on wire rack to cool. Wrap and refrigerate several hours before slicing.

Variation: Double recipe and use canned blueberries; 1 15-ounce can blueberries, drained. Reserve ½ cup juice. Add blueberries and juice in step 4.

Note: Two-slice serving contains less than 1½ teaspoons sugar (approximately 22 calories).

Burgess's Bran Bread

Yield: 2 loaves (20 slices per loaf)
Serving Size: 1 slice
Exchange List Approximation:
 Starch/Bread $\frac{1}{2}$

Nutrient Content Per Serving:
CAL: 40 PRO: 1.2 (gm)
FAT: 1.2 (gm) CHO: 7.4 (gm)
Na: 498.7 (mg) K: 130 (mg)
Fiber: 1.3 (gm) Chol: 0

Ingredients

  1 PACKAGE ACTIVE DRY YEAST
  ¾ CUP WARM WATER
  1 CUP WARM SKIM MILK
  ⅓ CUP MOLASSES
  2 TABLESPOONS SHORTENING
  1 TABLESPOON SALT
  3 CUPS WHOLE-WHEAT FLOUR
  1 CUP UNPROCESSED BRAN

Method

1. Dissolve yeast in warm water. Add warm milk, molasses, shortening, and salt.
2. Mix in bran and enough flour to make a soft dough. Knead until smooth, about 3 minutes.
3. Place in greased bowl, cover, and let rise until double in size; about 2 hours.
4. Punch down and shape into 2 loaves.
5. Place in greased 9- by 5-inch loaf pans.
6. Cover and let rise until doubled in bulk; about 1½ hours.
7. Preheat oven to 375° F last 15 minutes of rising time.
8. Bake for 40 minutes.

Variation: Replace 3 Tablespoons flour with 3 Tablespoons wheat germ.

Basic Rolls

Yield: 8 rolls
Serving Size: 1 roll
Exchange List Approximation:
    Meat, medium-fat $\frac{1}{2}$

Nutrient Content Per Serving:

CAL: 46	PRO: 4 (gm)
FAT: 2.9 (gm)	CHO: 0.5 (gm)
Na: 79.2 (mg)	K: 39.2 (mg)
Fiber: 0	Chol: 138 (mg)

Ingredients

  4 EGGS (SEPARATED)
      PINCH EACH: SALT AND CREAM OF TARTAR
  4 TABLESPOONS LOW-FAT COTTAGE CHEESE, MASHED
  1 PACKET SUGAR SUBSTITUTE

Method

1. Separate egg whites, whip until foamy, add pinch of salt and cream of tartar. Whip until firm peaks are formed.
2. Mix egg yolks, cottage cheese, and sugar substitute.
3. Add slowly to whites while mixing with folding motion.
4. Spray a cookie sheet with vegetable pan spray. Apportion mixture into 8 mounds, bun shaped.
5. Bake in 300° F oven for 1 hour. Lower heat to 250° F if rolls become too brown. This is an unusual item that can be used for sandwiches or hamburger.

Variation: Add 6 packets sugar substitute, 2 teaspoons cinnamon, and ¼ cup chopped nuts for cookie-type rolls. Nutrient information is as follows:

Exchange List Approximation:
    Meat, medium-fat $\frac{1}{2}$
    Fat $\frac{1}{2}$

Nutrient Content Per Serving:

CAL: 71	PRO: 4.6 (gm)
FAT: 5.4 (gm)	CHO: 1.3 (gm)
Na: 79.7 (mg)	K: 59.2 (mg)
Fiber: 0.2 (gm)	Chol: 138 (mg)

Banana Date-Nut Bread

Yield: 2 loaves (16 slices per loaf)
Serving Size: 2 slices
Exchange List Approximation:
Starch/Bread $1\frac{1}{2}$
Fat $1\frac{1}{2}$

Nutrient Content Per Serving:
CAL: 174   PRO: 4 (gm)
FAT: 9.4 (gm)   CHO: 21.1 (gm)
Na: 210.9 (mg)   K: 225.6 (mg)
Fiber: 3 (gm)   Chol: 34 (mg)

Ingredients

1½ CUPS WHOLE WHEAT FLOUR
 1 CUP UNPROCESSED BRAN FLAKES
 ¼ CUP WHEAT GERM (ABOUT 1 OUNCE)
2½ TEASPOONS BAKING POWDER
 ½ TEASPOON BAKING SODA
 ¼ TEASPOON SALT
 ½ CUP MARGARINE (1 STICK)
 2 EGGS
 1 TEASPOON VANILLA
 2 TEASPOONS BROWN SUGAR SUBSTITUTE
1½ CUPS MASHED BANANAS (ABOUT 12 OUNCES)
 ½ CUP CHOPPED WALNUTS OR PECANS (ABOUT 2
    OUNCES)
 ½ CUP CHOPPED DATES (ABOUT 3 OUNCES)

Method

1. In a medium mixing bowl place whole-wheat flour, bran
    flakes, and wheat germ. Sift baking powder, soda, and salt
    over flour and mix all together. Set aside.
2. In a large mixing bowl, cream together margarine and
    brown-sugar substitute. Add eggs and vanilla; mix
    thoroughly.

3. Add flour mixture to creamed mixture alternately with mashed bananas. Blend completely after each addition.
4. Fold in nuts and dates.
5. Pour into 2 lightly greased loaf pans and bake for 50 minutes to 1 hour in 350° F oven.

Southern Cornbread

Yield: 6 servings
Serving Size: 1 wedge
Exchange List Approximation:
    Starch/Bread $1\frac{1}{2}$
    Fat $\frac{1}{2}$

Nutrient Content Per Serving:
CAL: 143   PRO: 4.5 (gm)
FAT: 3.6 (gm)   CHO: 22.7 (gm)
Na: 263.6 (mg)   K: 104 (mg)
Fiber: 2.2 (gm)   Chol: 47 (mg)

Ingredients

- 1 CUP CORNMEAL
- 2 TABLESPOONS FLOUR
- 1 TEASPOON BAKING POWDER
- ½ TEASPOON BAKING SODA
- ¼ TEASPOON SALT
- 1 CUP BUTTERMILK OR SOUR SKIM MILK (ADD 1 TBSP. LEMON JUICE PER 1 CUP MILK)
- 1 EGG
- 1 TABLESPOON VEGETABLE SHORTENING

Method

1. Combine dry ingredients in a bowl.
2. Add milk and egg. Stir until blended and set aside 30 minutes to soften cornmeal.
3. Place shortening in 8-inch ovenproof skillet (preferably iron) or cake pan. Place in oven and heat to 425° F.
4. When shortening is very hot, add to batter, stir, and immediately pour into skillet.
5. Bake in 425° F oven 20 to 25 minutes.

Note: Cornbread is very good with stew, beans, or black-eye peas.

Variation: Add 2 Tablespoons chopped green chilies to batter to make Mexican Cornbread.

Apple-Raisin Muffins

Yield: 12 servings
Serving Size: 1 muffin
Exchange List Approximation:
    Starch/Bread 1
    Fruit $\frac{1}{2}$
    Fat 1

Nutrient Content Per Serving:
CAL: 154   PRO: 3.5 (gm)
FAT: 4.5 (gm)   CHO: 25.2 (gm)
Na: 134.9 (mg)   K: 105.7 (mg)
Fiber: 1.5 (gm)   Chol: 23 (mg)

Ingredients

  2 CUPS ALL-PURPOSE FLOUR
  1 TABLESPOON BAKING POWDER
  ¼ TEASPOON SALT
  1 TEASPOON CINNAMON
  3 PACKETS SUGAR SUBSTITUTE
  1 EGG
  3 TABLESPOONS CORN OIL
  ½ CUP SKIM MILK
  1 CUP UNSWEETENED APPLESAUCE
  ½ CUP RAISINS, WASHED AND DRAINED

Method

1. Preheat oven to 400° F. Prepare 2½-inch muffin tins with vegetable pan spray or grease lightly.
2. Combine dry ingredients in mixing bowl and mix thoroughly.
3. Beat egg and whip in oil, milk, and applesauce.
4. Add to dry ingredients and mix until flour is moistened. Stir in raisins.
5. Fill muffin tins ⅔ full. Bake for 25 minutes. Remove from tin immediately.

Banana Muffins

Yield: 12 servings
Serving Size: 1 muffin
Exchange List Approximation:
    Starch/Bread 1
    Fat $\frac{1}{2}$

Nutrient Content Per Serving:
CAL: 102   PRO: 2.3 (gm)
FAT: 4.6 (gm)   CHO: 14.3 (gm)
Na: 101.4 (mg)   K: 164.9 (mg)
Fiber: 1.5 (gm)   Chol: 23 (mg)

Ingredients

  3 TABLESPOONS VEGETABLE OIL
  1 EGG
  ¼ CUP SKIM MILK
1⅓ CUPS MASHED, VERY RIPE BANANAS (ABOUT 3 MEDIUM)
  1 CUP WHOLE-WHEAT FLOUR
  2 TEASPOONS BAKING POWDER
  ¼ TEASPOON BAKING SODA
  ⅛ TEASPOON SALT

Method

1. Preheat oven to 400° F. Spray 12-cup muffin tin or 3 miniature muffin tins (12 each) with vegetable cooking spray or grease lightly.
2. Beat egg, oil, and milk. Stir in bananas.
3. Mix dry ingredients together and stir into banana mixture until flour is moistened.
4. Fill tins ½ to ⅔ full.
5. Bake about 23 minutes (15 to 18 minutes for small muffins).
6. Let cool about 15 minutes before removing from pans to let texture firm up.

Fresh Peach Muffins

Yield: 12 muffins
Serving Size: 1 muffin
Exchange List Approximation:
    Starch/Bread 1
    Fruit $\frac{1}{2}$
    Fat 1

Nutrient Content Per Serving:
CAL: 151   PRO: 3.9 (gm)
FAT: 5.8 (gm)   CHO: 21.6 (gm)
Na: 139.3 (mg)   K: 132.3 (mg)
Fiber: 1.7 (gm)   Chol: 23 (mg)

Ingredients

- 1 CUP UNPEELED, CHOPPED FRESH PEACHES
- 1 TEASPOON LEMON JUICE
- 1 CUP ALL-PURPOSE FLOUR
- 1 CUP WHOLE-WHEAT FLOUR
- 1 TABLESPOON BAKING POWDER
- 2 TABLESPOONS SUGAR
- 3 PACKETS SUGAR SUBSTITUTE
- ½ TEASPOON MACE
- ¼ TEASPOON SALT
- 1 EGG
- ¼ CUP VEGETABLE OIL
- 1 CUP SKIM MILK

Method

1. Heat oven to 400° F. Lightly grease 12-cup muffin pan.
2. Add lemon juice to peaches. Set aside.
3. Combine sugar, sugar substitute, and remaining dry ingredients and mix thoroughly.
4. Beat egg, oil, and milk together.
5. Add to dry ingredients. Stir until flour is just moistened.

6. Fold in peaches. Fill muffin cups ⅔ full. (Paper baking cups may be used.)
7. Bake about 25 minutes or until brown. Remove from pan immediately.

Note: Each muffin has ½ teaspoon sugar (8 calories).

Bran-Fruit Muffins

Yield: 12 muffins

Serving Size: 2 muffins

Exchange List Approximation:

    Starch/Bread 2

    Fat $1\frac{1}{2}$

Nutrient Content Per Serving:

CAL: 228   PRO: 7.6 (gm)

FAT: 9 (gm)   CHO: 34.9 (gm)

Na: 356.5 (mg)   K: 410.7 (mg)

Fiber: 7.2 (gm)   Chol: 46 (mg)

Ingredients

  1 CUP ALL-BRAN CEREAL

⅓ CUP CHOPPED DATES (OR RAISINS)

1¼ CUPS SKIM MILK

  3 TABLESPOONS VEGETABLE OIL

  1 EGG

  1 CUP WHOLE-WHEAT FLOUR

  1 TABLESPOON BAKING POWDER

Method

1. Preheat oven to 400° F and prepare 12-cup muffin pan; lightly grease or spray with vegetable pan spray or line with paper baking cups.
2. Mix bran cereal and fruit in mixing bowl. Add milk, stir, and let stand several minutes.
3. Add oil and egg. Beat well.
4. Mix flour and baking powder. Add to bran mixture. Stir until flour is just blended or moistened.
5. Spoon mixture into 12 muffin cups.
6. Immediately place in oven. Bake 15 minutes.
7. Remove from pan immediately.

Orange-Bran Muffins

Yield: 12 servings
Serving Size: 1 muffin
Exchange List Approximation:
    Starch/Bread 1

Nutrient Content Per Serving:
CAL: 80   PRO: 3.3 (gm)
FAT: 2.1 (gm)   CHO: 14.1 (gm)
Na: 161.9 (mg)   K: 175.1 (mg)
Fiber: 2.6 (gm)   Chol: 24 (mg)

Ingredients

- 1   CUP WHOLE-WHEAT FLOUR
- ¾   CUP MILLER'S BRAN (UNPROCESSED, UNCOOKED WHEAT BRAN)
- ¾   TEASPOON SODA
- ⅛   TEASPOON SALT
- 1   TABLESPOON GRATED ORANGE RIND
- 1   EGG
- 1   TABLESPOON VEGETABLE OIL
- 2   TABLESPOON DARK MOLASSES
- 1   CUP BUTTERMILK
- ½   CUP RAISINS (OPTIONAL)

Method

1. Preheat oven to 350° F. Spray muffin pan with vegetable pan spray.
2. Combine whole-wheat flour, bran, soda, salt, and orange rind.
3. Beat egg and whip in oil, molasses, and buttermilk.
4. Add dry ingredients and stir until just blended. Fold in raisins.
5. Spoon mixture into 12 muffin cups.
6. Bake for 25 minutes.

Note: Muffin contains ½ teaspoon sugar (8 calories).

Meat

Beef Burgundy

Yield: 4 servings
Serving Size: 1 cup
Exchange List Approximation:
  Meat, lean $2\frac{1}{2}$
  Vegetable 2

Nutrient Content Per Serving:
CAL: 185   PRO: 22 (gm)
FAT: 5.9 (gm)   CHO: 10.1 (gm)
Na: 610.9 (mg)   K: 552.5 (mg)
Fiber: 2.3 (gm)   Chol: 55 (mg)
Key Source Nutrients:
  Vitamin A: 7754 (IU)

Ingredients

¾ POUND BEEF ROUND, WELL-TRIMMED, CUT IN
  1-INCH CUBES
½ TEASPOON SALT
⅛ TEASPOON PEPPER
1 BAY LEAF
⅛ TEASPOON THYME LEAVES
1½ CUPS WATER
1½ CUPS DICED POTATOES
1 CUP SLICED CARROTS
½ CUP DICED CELERY
⅓ CUP CHOPPED ONION
1 CUP SLICED FRESH MUSHROOMS
3 TABLESPOONS FLOUR
¼ CUP WATER
⅓ CUP RED BURGUNDY WINE
  PARSLEY (TO GARNISH)

Method

1. Brown beef cubes in hot frypan.
2. Add salt, pepper, bay leaf, thyme, and 1½ cups water.
3. Simmer, covered, until beef is almost tender, about 1¾
    hours.

4. Remove bay leaf.
5. Add potatoes, carrots, celery, onion, and mushrooms. Simmer, covered, until vegetables are tender, about 20 minutes.
6. Mix flour with ¼ cup water until smooth. Add slowly to meat mixture, stirring gently; cook until thickened.
7. Stir in wine.
8. Garnish with parsley.

Stir-Fried Beef and Broccoli

Yield: 4 or 2 servings
Serving Size: 1 cup
Exchange List Approximation:
 Meat, lean 2
 Vegetable 2
 Fat 2

Nutrient Content Per Serving:
CAL: 259 PRO: 19 (gm)
FAT: 17.2 (gm) CHO: 8.3 (gm)
Na: 585.7 (mg)* K: 559.8 (mg)
Fiber: 3.3 (gm) Chol: 44 (mg)
Key Source Nutrients:
 Ascorbic acid: 65 (mg)

Ingredients

Four Servings		Two Servings	
¾	POUND ROUND OR FLANK STEAK	6	OUNCES
2	TEASPOONS CORNSTARCH	1	TEASPOON
2	TABLESPOONS SOY SAUCE	1	TABLESPOON
3	CUPS BROCCOLI, PEELED, CUT IN STRIPS 1 INCH × ¼ INCH	1½	CUPS
3	CUPS WATER	2	CUPS
2	TABLESPOONS VEGETABLE OIL	1	TABLESPOON
1	CUP WEDGE-CUT ONION	½	CUP
1	TABLESPOON MINCED GINGER ROOT	1½	TEASPOONS
1	TABLESPOON SHERRY (OPTIONAL)	½	TEASPOON
2	TABLESPOONS WATER	1	TABLESPOON

Method

1. Trim fat from steak, slice across the grain in thin slices 1 inch by ¼ inch.

2. Sprinkle with cornstarch and soy sauce. Mix and set aside.
3. Bring water to a boil, add broccoli, stir; bring to a boil and cook 2 minutes. Drain immediately. Set aside.
4. Heat oil in wok or large skillet until very hot. Add onion and ginger root. Stir-fry about 30 seconds.
5. Add steak and stir-fry about 2 minutes.
6. Add broccoli, sherry, and water. Stir contantly until steaming, about 1 minute.
7. Serving suggestion: Serve with rice (½ cup cooked rice = 1 Bread Exchange).

Note: Broccoli may be cooked in hot oil in wok (or skillet) before onions. Stir-fry 3 minutes and remove. This recipe tastes very good. Broccoli is firmer in wok, but color is more attractive when boiled.

*To reduce sodium content, use mild soy sauce or cut back on the quantity of soy sauce used.

Beef Ragout

Yield: 8 or 2 servings
Serving Size: $\frac{2}{3}$ cup
Exchange List Approximation:
    Meat, lean $3\frac{1}{2}$
    Vegetable 1

Nutrient Content Per Serving:
CAL: 211   PRO: 26.9 (gm)
FAT: 9 (gm)   CHO: 4.8 (gm)
Na: 342.6 (mg)   K: 534.2 (mg)
Fiber: 1.9 (gm)   Chol: 74 (mg)

Ingredients

Eight Servings		*Two Servings*	
2	POUNDS BEEF, LEAN, CUBED	½	POUND
1	TABLESPOON MARGARINE	1	TEASPOON
2	CUPS CHOPPED ONION	½	CUP
1	TABLESPOON MINCED GARLIC	¾	TEASPOON
2	BAY LEAVES	1	
2	TABLESPOONS CHOPPED PARSLEY	1½	TEASPOONS
1	TABLESPOON CHOPPED FRESH ORANGE PEEL	¾	TEASPOON
1	TEASPOON CRUSHED ROSEMARY	¼	TEASPOON
1	TEASPOON CINNAMON	¼	TEASPOON
½	TEASPOON SALT	⅛	TEASPOON
½	CUP WATER	¼	CUP
2	CUPS SLICED FRESH MUSHROOMS	½	CUP
1	CUP SLICED GREEN PEPPER	¼	CUP

Method

1. Heat margarine in large skillet. Add one layer of beef cubes, brown over high heat, and remove to stew pot. Continue until all beef is brown.

2. Lower heat and add onions and garlic, stir and cook about 2 minutes. Remove to stew pot.
3. Add bay leaves, parsley, orange peel, rosemary, cinnamon, salt, and water to stew pot.
4. Cover and simmer 1½ hours or until tender. Add a little water if beef becomes dry. Remove bay leaves.
5. Add mushrooms and green pepper, stir, cover, and cook about 5 minutes.
6. Serving suggestion: Serve over noodles (½ cup cooked noodles = 1 Bread Exchange).

Zesty Sauerbraten

Yield: 8 servings

Serving Size: 2 slices meat and
$\frac{1}{2}$ cup sauce

Exchange List Approximation:
Starch/Bread 1$\frac{1}{2}$
Meat, lean 4
Vegtable 2

Nutrient Content Per Serving:
CAL: 381   PRO: 40.5 (gm)
FAT: 11.9 (gm)   CHO: 32.3 (gm)
Na: 256.6 (mg)   K: 856.6 (mg)
Fiber: 6.5 (gm) Chol: 113 (mg)

Ingredients

3 POUNDS BONELESS BEEF ROAST (CHUCK, RUMP, OR ROUND)
2 CUPS WATER
2 CUPS CIDER VINEGAR
1 CUP SLICED ONION
½ CUP SLICED CARROTS
¼ CUP SLICED CELERY
10 PEPPERCORNS
6 WHOLE ALLSPICE
4 WHOLE CLOVES
2 BAY LEAVES
1½ TEASPOONS CHOPPED FRESH GINGER ROOT
1½ CUPS BRAN CEREAL, SUCH AS ALL-BRAN, BRAN-CHEX, OR CRACKLIN' BRAN)
1 TEASPOON GROUND GINGER
½ TEASPOON GROUND CINNAMON
¼ TEASPOON GROUND ALLSPICE
2 TABLESPOONS UNSULPHURED MOLASSES
1 6-OUNCE CAN FROZEN CONCENTRATED APPLE JUICE
2 TEASPOONS CORNSTARCH

Method

1. Trim fat from roast and place in stainless steel bowl or large plastic bag with secure closure.
2. Heat water to boiling and add vinegar, vegetables, and spices. Cool slightly and add to beef. Cover or close bag securely. Refrigerate 24 to 36 hours. Turn meat after 12 hours.
3. Remove meat and bay leaves. Reserve marinade.
4. Drain meat and pat dry. Brown well on all sides in fat-free pan or 425° F oven or under broiler.
5. Place meat on rack in Dutch oven. Add marinade. Cover tightly and braise 2 to 2½ hours. May be covered and cooked in 325° F oven. Cool.
6. Drain cooking liquid and reserve for sauce. Refrigerate meat until firm enough to slice.
7. Prepare sauce. Remove excess fat from cooking liquid, strain, and bring to a boil. Add bran cereal and remaining ingredients. Cook until blended and thickened, stirring constantly.
8. Slice chilled meat. Arrange in baking pan. Cover with sauce. Cover and heat in 300° F oven for 1 hour.

Pepper Steak

Yield: 4 or 2 servings
Serving Size: 1 cup
Exchange List Approximation:
    Meat, lean 3
    Vegetable 1
    Fat 2

Nutrient Content Per Serving:
CAL: 281   PRO: 22.4 (gm)
FAT: 17.8 (gm)   CHO: 8.2 (gm)
Na: 297.8 (mg)   K: 664.2 (mg)
Fiber: 2.9 (gm)   Chol: 58 (mg)
Key Source Nutrients:
    Ascorbic acid: 77 (mg)

Ingredients

Four Servings		*Two Servings*	
1	POUND ROUND OR FLANK STEAK	½	POUND
2	TEASPOONS SOY SAUCE	1	TEASPOON
1	TEASPOON MINCED GARLIC	½	TEASPOON
2	CUPS GREEN PEPPERS, SLICED IN STRIPS	1	CUP
2	CUPS CELERY, CUT DIAGONALLY	1	CUP
⅔	CUP CHOPPED GREEN ONIONS	⅓	CUP
4	TEASPOONS VEGETABLE OIL	2	TEASPOONS
¼	CUP WATER	2	TABLESPOONS
1	TABLESPOON CORNSTARCH	1½	TEASPOONS

Method

1. Trim all fat from steak, cut across grain in slices about 1 inch by ¼ inch.
2. Add soy sauce and garlic, stir, and set aside.
3. Prepare vegetables.
4. Heat half of oil until very hot in large skillet.
5. Add vegetables and stir-fry 2 minutes; remove from skillet to warm pan.

6. Add remaining oil to skillet, heat, add steak and stir-fry 2 minutes.
7. Mix cornstarch with water, add to steak. Cook, stirring constantly until thickened.
8. Add vegetables, mix thoroughly.
9. Serving suggestion: Serve over brown rice (⅓ cup cooked rice = 1 Starch/Bread Exchange).

Italian Ground Beef and Macaroni

Yield: 4 servings
Serving Size: 1⅓ cup
Exchange List Approximation:
    Starch/Bread 2
    Meat, medium-fat 2
    Vegetable 1

Nutrient Content Per Serving:
CAL: 330   PRO: 22.3 (gm)
FAT: 11.3 (gm)   CHO: 35.7 (gm)
Na: 679.5 (mg)*   K: 855.7 (mg)
Fiber: 2.6 (gm)   Chol: 53 (mg)
Key Source Nutrients:
    Ascorbic acid: 54 (mg)

Ingredients

¾ POUND GROUND BEEF, EXTRA LEAN
½ CUP CHOPPED ONION
¼ CUP CHOPPED GREEN PEPPER
¼ CUP CHOPPED CELERY
1 16-OUNCE CAN TOMATOES
1 10¾-OUNCE CAN TOMATO PUREE
1 TEASPOON OREGANO LEAVES
1 TEASPOON BASIL LEAVES
¼ TEASPOON SALT
⅛ TEASPOON PEPPER
3 CUPS COOKED ELBOW MACARONI, UNSALTED
   (ABOUT 1 CUP UNCOOKED)

Method

1. Cook beef, onion, green pepper, and celery in large frypan until beef is lightly browned and onion is clear. Drain.
2. Break up large pieces of tomatoes.
3. Add tomatoes, tomato puree, and seasonings to beef mixture. Simmer 15 minutes to blend flavors.
4. Stir in macaroni. Heat to serving temperature.

*To reduce sodium content, use unsalted tomato products and eliminate the ¼ teaspoon of salt. Try herb blend (from Chapter 15) for extra seasoning.

Verhalen Trainwreck (Burrito Filling)

Yield: 8 servings

Serving Size: $\frac{1}{3}$ cup

Exchange List Approximation:

    Starch/Bread 1

    Meat, medium-fat $1\frac{1}{2}$

Nutrient Content Per Serving:

CAL: 194   PRO: 15 (gm)

FAT: 7.7 (gm)   CHO: 16.3 (gm)

Na: 90.2 (mg)   K: 415.6 (mg)

Fiber: 4.7 (gm)   Chol: 34 (mg)

Ingredients

  1 POUND LEAN GROUND BEEF

  ½ CUP CHOPPED ONION

  1 10-OUNCE CAN TOMATOES AND GREEN CHILIES

  1 3- OR 4-OUNCE CAN GREEN CHILIES (OPTIONAL)

  1 15-OUNCE CAN WESTERN-STYLE PINTO BEANS

      DASH TABASCO SAUCE

Method

1. Cook ground beef in large skillet until it starts to brown. Add onions and cook until limp. Drain excess fat.
2. Add can of tomatoes and green chilies, beans, and Tabasco. Add can of green chilies, if desired. Stir to mix and simmer uncovered 30 minutes, stirring occasionally.
3. Serve on either flour tortillas or corn tortillas.
4. Garnish with shredded cheese, chopped onion, and shredded lettuce.

Mexican Bake with Yogurt

Yield: 6 servings

Serving Size: 1 cup

Exchange List Approximation:

    Starch/Bread $2\frac{1}{2}$

    Meat, medium-fat 3

Nutrient Content Per Serving:

CAL: 409	PRO: 27.9 (gm)
FAT: 16 (gm)	CHO: 39.2 (gm)
Na: 687.2 (mg)	K: 673 (mg)
Fiber: 6.7 (gm)	Chol: 53 (mg)

Ingredients

  6 OUNCES LEAN GROUND BEEF

  ½ CUP CHOPPED ONION

  ½ TEASPOON CUMIN

  ¼ TEASPOON GARLIC POWDER

  ½ TEASPOON CHILI POWDER

  ⅛ TEASPOON CRUSHED RED PEPPER

  1 8-OUNCE CAN TOMATO SAUCE

  1 15-OUNCE CAN RANCH-STYLE PINTO BEANS IN TOMATO AND CHILI SAUCE

  1 CUP LOW-FAT COTTAGE CHEESE

  1 8-OUNCE CONTAINER LOW-FAT PLAIN YOGURT

  ¼ CUP CHOPPED GREEN CHILIES (ABOUT ½ 4-OUNCE CAN)

  4 FLOUR TORTILLAS

1½ CUPS SHREDDED CHEDDAR CHEESE (ABOUT 6 OUNCES)

Method

1. Cook ground beef and onions until crumbly. Drain off any excess fat.
2. Add spices and mix thoroughly with meat.
3. Add tomato sauce and beans. Mix well.

4. In separate bowl, mix yogurt, cottage cheese, and chilies.
5. Bake tortillas on cookie sheet in 400° F oven until crisp and beginning to brown, about 5 minutes. Break tortillas into large pieces.
6. Put half the tortillas in bottom of a 2½-quart casserole. Spoon half the meat mixture evenly over tortillas. Add half of the yogurt mixture and sprinkle with half the cheese. Repeat, ending with the cheese.
7. Bake, covered, in 350° F oven for 30 to 35 minutes.

Variation: Use ¾ cup of sour cream in place of 8-ounce container low-fat plain yogurt. If sour cream is used, nutritional information is as follows:

Serving Size: 1 cup
Exchange List Approximation:
    Starch/Bread 2½
    Meat, medium-fat 3
    Fat ½

Nutrient Content Per Serving:

CAL: 437	PRO: 26.8 (gm)
FAT: 20.4 (gm)	CHO: 37.5 (gm)
Na: 672.7 (mg)*	K: 618.5 (mg)
Fiber: 6.7 (gm)	Chol: 61 (mg)

*To reduce sodium content, use unsalted ingredients.

Breaded Veal Cutlets

Yield: 4 or 2 servings
Serving Size: 1 serving
Exchange List Approximation:
    Starch/Bread 1
    Meat, medium-fat 3
    Fat $\frac{1}{2}$

Nutrient Content Per Serving:
CAL: 319   PRO: 30.7 (gm)
FAT: 19.1 (gm)   CHO: 10.4 (gm)
Na: 272.4 (mg)   K: 620.4 (mg)
Fiber: 0.3 (gm)   Chol: 62 (mg)

Ingredients

Four Servings		*Two Servings*	
1	POUND CHOPPED AND FORMED VEAL CUTLETS (4)	8	OUNCES (2)
4	TABLESPOONS TOMATO JUICE SPRINKLE EACH OF SALT, PEPPER, AND GARLIC POWDER	2	TABLESPOONS SPRINKLE
½	TEASPOON OREGANO	¼	TEASPOON
½	CUP SEASONED BREAD CRUMBS	¼	CUP
2	TEASPOONS VEGETABLE OIL	1	TEASPOON
4	SLICES LEMON	2	SLICES

Method

1. Place cutlets on pan. Spoon tomato juice over cutlets. Sprinkle each side lightly with salt, pepper, garlic powder, and oregano.
2. Spread crumbs on wax paper and press cutlets in crumbs to coat.
3. Heat iron skillet or grill. Grease lightly with vegetable oil. Reduce heat and cook cutlets about 5 minutes per side over medium heat.
4. Serve with lemon slice.

Curried Ham and Vegetable Pie

Yield: 4 servings
Serving Size: $\frac{1}{4}$ pie
Exchange List Approximation:
    Starch/Bread 1$\frac{1}{2}$
    Meat, lean 2
    Fat $\frac{1}{2}$

Nutrient Content Per Serving:
CAL: 253   PRO: 18.5 (gm)
FAT: 9.2 (gm)   CHO: 25.9 (gm)
Na: 1222.7 (mg) K: 556.7 (mg)
Fiber: 4.6 (gm)   Chol: 47 (mg)

Ingredients

½ CUP BEEF BROTH OR WATER
2 TEASPOONS CORNSTARCH
½ TEASPOON CURRY POWDER
2 CUPS DICED COOKED HAM
1 10-OUNCE PACKAGE FROZEN MIXED VEGETABLES, THAWED
2 CUPS MASHED POTATOES
   DASH PAPRIKA

Method

1. In medium bowl blend broth, cornstarch, and curry powder. Stir in ham and vegetables. Pour into a greased 10-inch pie plate.
2. Spread potatoes evenly to cover filling; sprinkle with paprika. Bake in preheated oven at 425° F for 25 minutes or until potatoes are lightly browned.

*This recipe is high in sodium and may not be suitable for some people.

Herbed Pork Kabobs

Yield: 4 servings
Serving Size: 1 serving
Exchange List Approximation:
    Meat, lean 4
    Fat 1

Nutrient Content Per Serving:
CAL: 263   PRO: 32.4 (gm)
FAT: 14.1 (gm) CHO: 0.3 (gm)
Na: 174.3 (mg) K: 607.5 (mg)
Fiber: 0   Chol: 103 (mg)

Ingredients

1¼ POUNDS PORK TENDERLOIN
¼ CUP DRY WHITE WINE
¼ TEASPOON DRY MARJORAM LEAVES
¼ TEASPOON DRY ROSEMARY LEAVES
1 MINCED GARLIC CLOVE
3 TABLESPOONS MARGARINE, SOFTENED
½ TEASPOON DRY MARJORAM LEAVES
½ TEASPOON DRY ROSEMARY LEAVES
¼ TEASPOON SALT (OPTIONAL)
PINCH PEPPER

Method

1. Combine trimmed pork, wine, ¼ teaspoon marjoram, ¼ teaspoon rosemary, and garlic in medium-size bowl; toss to coat. Let stand at room temperature 20 minutes.
2. Cream margarine, ½ teaspoon marjoram, ½ teaspoon rosemary, salt, and pepper.
3. Drain pork; reserve marinade. Beat marinade into margarine mix.
4. Cut pork into 1½-inch cubes and thread on 4 skewers.
5. Place on wire rack over shallow baking dish. Broil 4 inches from heat. Turn frequently; baste occasionally with herb-butter mix until brown on all sides. Serve with lemon wedges.

Cantonese Pork

Yield: 6 servings

Serving Size: 7 meat balls and $\frac{2}{3}$ cup sauce

Exchange List Approximation:
    Starch/Bread 1
    Meat, medium-fat $1\frac{1}{2}$
    Vegetable $\frac{1}{2}$

Nutrient Content Per Serving:

CAL: 235   PRO: 19.5 (gm)
FAT: 7.6 (gm)   CHO: 23.3 (gm)
Na: 355.1 (mg)   K: 664.3 (mg)
Fiber: 2.5 (gm)   Chol: 48 (mg)

Ingredients

  1 POUND LEAN GROUND PORK
  ¼ TEASPOON SALT
  ⅛ TEASPOON PEPPER'
  ¼ CUP FINELY CHOPPED ONIONS
  ¼ CUP EVAPORATED SKIM MILK

Sweet and Sour Sauce

  1 15½-OUNCE CAN PINEAPPLE TIDBITS, UNSWEETENED JUICE
  ¼ CUP VINEGAR
  1 TABLESPOON SUGAR
  1 TABLESPOON SOY SAUCE
  ½ CUP WATER
  2 TABLESPOONS CORNSTARCH
  1 TEASPOON MARGARINE
  ¼ CUP SLIVERED TOASTED ALMONDS
  1 CUP SLICED CELERY
  ½ CUP SLICED GREEN ONIONS
  ½ CUP GREEN PEPPER STRIPS
  2 MEDIUM TOMATOES, CUT IN 6 WEDGES

Method

1. Mix pork, salt, pepper, onions, and milk together thoroughly. Place on board and roll out in rectangle. Cut into 42 pieces. Roll each piece into a ball.
2. Place in shallow pan and bake in 350° F oven 30 to 40 minutes. Turn after 15 minutes.
3. Drain juice from pineapple and combine with vinegar, sugar, soy sauce, water, and cornstarch in 2-quart saucepan. Bring to a boil, stirring constantly, and cook until clear and thickened. Add margarine.
4. Ten minutes before serving, add almonds and vegetables. Heat until vegetables are just heated through.
5. Serve meat balls over rice and cover with ⅔ cup sauce (⅓ cup cooked rice = 1 Starch/Bread Exchange).

Note: Approximately ½ teaspoon sugar (8 calories) per serving.

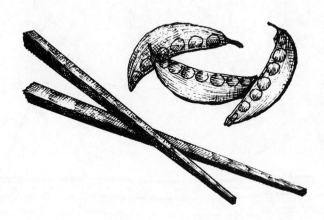

Poultry

Cold Chicken

Yield: 4 servings
Serving Size: breast half or
  leg quarter
Exchange List Approximation:
  Meat, lean 3

Nutrient Content Per Serving:
CAL: 154   PRO: 25 (gm)
FAT: 5.1 (gm)   CHO: 0
Na: 98.1 (mg)   K: 194.5 (mg)
Fiber: 0   Chol: 75 (mg)

Ingredients

3 POUNDS FRYING CHICKEN, CUT UP
1 TEASPOON MINCED GARLIC
1 TEASPOON SALT
3 QUARTS WATER
8 WHOLE PEPPERCORNS
1 TEASPOON CHOPPED FRESH GINGER ROOT
1 SLICED GREEN ONION
2 TEASPOONS DRY SHERRY (OPTIONAL)

Method

1. Remove excess fat from chicken, wash, rub with garlic and salt, set aside.
2. Bring water to a boil in heavy pot.
3. Rinse chicken and add with peppercorns to water.
4. Heat until water is summering, turn off heat, and let stand 30 minutes.
5. Repeat process and let stand 1 hour.
6. Remove chicken; cool enough to handle. Remove skin and discard.
7. Remove breast meat and leg quarters. Bone remaining chicken pieces for later use.
8. Place meat of breast, and leg quarters in refrigerator container.

9. Add ginger, onion, sherry, and enough hot broth to cover. Chill.
10. Serving suggestion: Serve cold breast or leg quarter with green salad or hot vegetables. (See Appendix I for exchange values of salad ingredients or vegetables.) Sprinkle chicken with picante sauce.

*To reduce sodium, eliminate the salt.

Greek Chicken Salad

Yield: 6 or 2 servings
Serving Size: 1 cup
Exchange List Approximation:
    Starch/Bread 1
    Meat, lean 1
    Vegetable 1
    Fat 1

Nutrient Content Per Serving:
CAL: 200   PRO: 13 (gm)
FAT: 6.9 (gm)   CHO: 21.6 (gm)
Na: 148.3 (mg) K: 414.2 (mg)
Fiber: 2.8 (gm)   Chol: 32 (mg)

Ingredients

Six Servings		Two Servings	
2	CUPS COOKED BROWN RICE	⅔	CUP
1½	CUPS COOKED, DICED CHICKEN	½	CUP
⅛	TEASPOON SALT		DASH
½	CUP PLAIN LOW-FAT YOGURT	3	TABLESPOONS
2	TABLESPOONS MAYONNAISE	2	TEASPOONS
1	MINCED GARLIC CLOVE	⅓	
1	CUP SLICED CELERY	⅓	CUP
2	CUPS SHREDDED RAW SPINACH	⅔	CUP
¼	CUP CHOPPED GREEN ONIONS	1	TABLESPOON
1	CUP DICED TOMATO	⅓	CUP
2	TABLESPOONS LEMON JUICE	2	TEASPOONS

Method

1. Combine rice and chicken. Sprinkle with salt and chill.
2. Combine yogurt, mayonnaise, and garlic. Mix with rice and chicken.
3. Add remaining ingredients and toss lightly.
4. Serve on lettuce with Greek- or ripe-olive garnish.

Note: Very good salad. Serving is slightly more than a cup.

Chicken Paprika

Yield: 4 or 2 servings
Serving Size: $\frac{1}{2}$ breast plus
   $\frac{1}{2}$ cup sauce
Exchange List Approximation:
    Starch/Bread $\frac{1}{2}$
    Meat, lean $3\frac{1}{2}$
    Vegetable 1

Nutrient Content Per Serving:
CAL: 262   PRO: 32.5 (gm)
FAT: 9 (gm)   CHO: 11.5 (gm)
Na: 266.4 (mg) K: 528.9 (mg)
Fiber: 3 (gm)   Chol: 85 (mg)

Ingredients

Four Servings		*Two Servings*
4	CHICKEN BREAST HALVES, SKINNED AND BONED	2
1	CLOVE GARLIC, MINCED	½ CLOVE
2	CUPS CHOPPED ONIONS	1 CUP
1	TABLESPOON MARGARINE	1½ TEASPOON
2	TABLESPOONS LEMON JUICE	1 TABLESPOON
1	TEASPOON PAPRIKA	½ TEASPOON
¼	TEASPOON SALT	⅛ TEASPOON
⅛	TEASPOON PEPPER	SPRINKLE
1	TABLESPOON FLOUR	1½ TEASPOON
⅔	CUP SKIM MILK	⅓ CUP
¼	CUP SOUR CREAM	2 TABLESPOONS
1	CUP SLICED FRESH MUSHROOMS (ABOUT 2 OUNCES)	½ CUP

Method

1. Mix chicken with garlic and set aside.
2. Cook onions in margarine in a large skillet for 2 or 3 minutes.

3. Push onions to one side and cook chicken breasts about 3 minutes.
4. Sprinkle chicken with lemon juice, paprika, salt, and pepper.
5. Cover tightly and cook over low heat until tender, about 30 minutes.
6. Remove chicken to another pan.
7. Make sauce by sprinkling flour over onions, stir, and cook about 1 minute. Add milk, stir, and cook until thickened.
8. Stir in sour cream and mushrooms. Add chicken and heat to serving temperature. Do not boil.
9. Serve over noodles (½ cup cooked noodles = 1 Starch/Bread Exchange).

Lemon Barbecued Chicken

Yield: 6 or 2 servings
Serving Size: 1 breast half
Exchange List Approximation:
    Meat, medium-fat 3

Nutrient Content Per Serving:
CAL: 237   PRO: 29.2 (gm)
FAT: 12.6 (gm)   CHO: 0
Na: 157.6 (mg)   K: 240.7 (mg)
Fiber: 0   Chol: 83 (mg)

Serving Size: 1 leg
Exchange List Approximation:
    Meat, medium-fat 4
    Fat $\frac{1}{2}$

Nutrient Content Per Serving:
CAL: 320   PRO: 30.2 (gm)
FAT: 21.2 (gm)   CHO: 0
Na: 180.9 (mg)   K: 219.2 (mg)
Fiber: 0   Chol: 105 (mg)

Ingredients

Six Servings		*Two Servings*	
6	CHICKEN BREASTS, HALVES OR LEGS AND THIGHS	2	
1	TEASPOON GRATED LEMON RIND	½	TEASPOON
1½	TEASPOONS SALT	¾	TEASPOON
½	TEASPOON DRY MUSTARD	¼	TEASPOON
½	TEASPOON DRIED OREGANO LEAVES	¼	TEASPOON
½	CUP LEMON JUICE	¼	CUP
½	CUP SALAD OIL	¼	CUP
2	TABLESPOONS CHOPPED SCALLIONS	1	TABLESPOON
1	TEASPOON WORCESTERSHIRE SAUCE	½	TEASPOON

Method

1. Mix lemon rind, salt, dry mustard, oregano, and Worcestershire sauce in small bowl.
2. Gradually stir in lemon juice, then oil, and scallions.
3. Pour over chicken in large bowl; marinate in refrigerator for 2 hours.
4. Remove chicken from marinade and place skin-side down on grill.
5. Set 3 to 6 inches from charcoal that has reached light gray stage.
6. Cook for 45 minutes to 1 hour, turning once.

Note: Marinade imparts a very good flavor and drains from the chicken, so probably no more than 5 grams of oil remain on each piece. For the two-serving quantity, the marinade ingredients are only cut in half to provide enough to cover chicken.

*To reduce sodium, eliminate the 1½ teaspoon of salt.

Chicken Curry

Yield: 4 servings
Serving Size: $\frac{1}{4}$ recipe
Exchange List Approximation:
    Meat, lean 3
    Vegetable 1

Nutrient Content Per Serving:

CAL: 198	PRO: 25.7 (gm)
FAT: 6.6 (gm)	CHO: 7.9 (gm)
Na: 190.3 (mg)	K: 463.2 (mg)
Fiber: 1.8 (gm)	Chol: 72 (mg)

Ingredients

2½ CUPS DICED COOKED CHICKEN
1 CUP CHOPPED ONION
½ TEASPOON SALT (OPTIONAL)
2 TEASPOONS CURRY POWDER
1 TEASPOON CHILI POWDER
1 TEASPOON MINCED DEHYDRATED GARLIC
½ TEASPOON PEPPER
½ CUP LOW-FAT YOGURT
1 CUP CANNED TOMATOES

Method

1. Cook onion in water (sufficient to cover) until transparent.
2. Add chicken and remaining ingredients. Mix thoroughly and simmer 15 minutes.
3. Serve on rice or toast points.

*Sodium content of salt is not included in the nutrient estimate.

Oven-Fried Chicken

Yield: 6 or 2 servings
Serving Size: $\frac{1}{2}$ breast
Exchange List Approximation:
    Starch/Bread $\frac{1}{2}$
    Meat, lean 3

Nutrient Content Per Serving:
CAL: 230   PRO: 31.3 (gm)
FAT: 7.3 (gm)   CHO: 7.4 (gm)
Na: 341.1 (mg)   K: 287.8 (mg)
Fiber: 0.3 (gm)   Chol: 81 (mg)

Ingredients

Six Servings		Two Servings
6	CHICKEN BREAST HALVES, SKINNED	2
18	SALTINE CRACKER SQUARES, CRUSHED	6
2	TABLESPOONS GRATED PARMESAN CHEESE	2 TEASPOONS
¾	TEASPOON PEPPER	¼ TEASPOON
½	TEASPOON EACH: BASIL, CELERY SEED, ONION POWDER, OREGANO, PAPRIKA	⅛ TEASPOON
⅜	TEASPOON SALT	⅛ TEASPOON
¼	CUPS EVAPORATED SKIM MILK	1½ TABLESPOONS
1	TABLESPOON VEGETABLE OIL	1 TEASPOON

Method

1. Combine cracker crumbs, cheese, pepper, basil, celery seed, onion powder, oregano, paprika, and salt in bowl.
2. Dip chicken in evaporated milk and then coat with crumb mixture. Place in lightly greased shallow roasting pan.
3. Bake in 400° F oven for 30 minutes. Brush with oil and bake 10 minutes longer.

Mock Chicken Kiev

Yield: 4 or 2 servings
Serving Size: $\frac{1}{2}$ breast
Exchange List Approximation:
　Starch/Bread $\frac{1}{2}$
　Meat, lean 3

Nutrient Content Per Serving:

CAL: 218	PRO: 30.6 (gm)
FAT: 6.2 (gm)	CHO: 7.5 (gm)
Na: 177.3 (mg)	K: 273.1 (mg)
Fiber: 0.3 (gm)	Chol: 84 (mg)

Ingredients

Four Servings		*Two Servings*	
4	CHICKEN BREAST HALVES, SKINNED, BONED	2	
4	TABLESPOONS SOUR CREAM	2	TABLESPOONS
2	TABLESPOONS CHOPPED PARSLEY	1	TABLESPOON
¼	TEASPOON OREGANO	⅛	TEASPOON
¼	TEASPOON MARJORAM	⅛	TEASPOON
	SPRINKLE SALT		SPRINKLE
	SPRINKLE PEPPER		SPRINKLE
6	TABLESPOONS DRY BREAD CRUMBS	3	TABLESPOONS

Method

1. Place chicken breast halves between sheets of waxed paper and pound to flatten.
2. Mix sour cream, parsley, oregano, and marjoram.
3. Salt and pepper chicken breasts and brush with sour cream mixture.
4. Roll up, beginning at long side, and secure with toothpicks. Brush remaining sour cream mixture on outside of the rolls and roll in dry bread crumbs.

5. Place rolls in shallow pan or casserole which has been sprayed with vegetable pan spray.
6. Cover and bake in 350° F oven for 45 minutes; uncover and bake 15 minutes longer.

Chicken Peanut Pasta

Yield: 6 or 3 servings
Serving Size: 1 cup
Exchange List Approximation:
    Starch/Bread $1\frac{1}{2}$
    Meat, lean 3
    Fat $\frac{1}{2}$

Nutrient Content Per Serving:
CAL: 304   PRO: 25.9 (gm)
FAT: 11.1 (gm)   CHO: 24.4 (gm)
Na: 399.8 (mg)   K: 302.1 (mg)
Fiber: 1.6 (gm)   Chol: 53 (mg)

Ingredients

Six Servings		*Three Servings*	
3	CUPS SPAGHETTI, BROKEN IN 2-INCH LENGTHS (ABOUT 6 OUNCES)	1½	CUPS (ABOUT 3 OUNCES)
2	QUARTS WATER	1	QUART
4	CHICKEN BREAST HALVES, SKINNED AND BONED	2	
1	EGG WHITE, BEATEN UNTIL FOAMY	1	
¼	TEASPOON WATER	¼	TEASPOON
2	TEASPOONS CORNSTARCH	1	TEASPOON
2	TEASPOONS MINCED GARLIC CLOVE	1	TEASPOON
2	TEASPOONS CHOPPED FRESH GINGER ROOT	1	TEASPOON
4	TEASPOONS VEGETABLE OIL	2	TEASPOONS

Six Servings		*Three Servings*	
	SPRINKLE CRUSHED RED PEPPER		SPRINKLE
2	TABLESPOONS SOY SAUCE	1	TABLESPOON
⅓	CUP VIRGINIA PEANUTS, COCKTAIL TYPE (ABOUT 1½ OUNCES)	¾	OUNCE
¼	CUP WHITE WINE OR WATER	2	TABLESPOONS
2	TEASPOONS SESAME SEED OIL	1	TEASPOON

Method

1. Cook spaghetti in boiling water about 12 minutes while preparing chicken.
2. Cut chicken into bite-size pieces.
3. Combine egg white, water, and cornstarch. Mix with chicken pieces.
4. Heat oil in wok or large skillet over medium heat. Add garlic and ginger root. Stir, then add half of chicken. Stir constantly until chicken meat turns white, about 2 minutes. Place in serving bowl. Stir-fry remaining chicken.
5. Return cooked chicken to skillet. Sprinkle lightly with crushed red pepper.
6. Add soy sauce, peanuts, and wine or water. Stir.
7. Drain spaghetti, add to chicken. Sprinkle with sesame seed oil, toss, and serve.
8. Garnish with chopped parsley.

Chicken Breasts in Sour Cream

Yield: 6 or 2 servings
Serving Size: 1 breast half plus
$\frac{1}{3}$ cup sauce
Exchange List Approximation:
  Starch/Bread $\frac{1}{2}$
  Meat, lean 4

Nutrient Content Per Serving:

CAL: 252	PRO: 31.4 (gm)
FAT: 10.3 (gm)	CHO: 6 (gm)
Na: 561.4 (mg)	K: 377.1 (mg)
Fiber: 0.4 (gm)	Chol: 87 (mg)

Ingredients

Six Servings		*Two Servings*
6	CHICKEN BREAST HALVES, SKINNED	2
¼	TEASPOON GARLIC POWDER	DASH
1	10½-OUNCE CAN CREAM OF MUSHROOM SOUP	⅓ OF CAN
½	CUP SKIM MILK	3 TABLESPOONS
½	CUP SOUR CREAM	3 TABLESPOONS
¼	CUP SHERRY	1 TABLESPOON
1	4-OUNCE CAN MUSHROOM STEMS AND PIECES, DRAINED PAPRIKA	⅓ OF CAN

Method

1. Place chicken breasts in baking pan so they do not overlap. Sprinkle with garlic powder.
2. Mix soup, milk, sour cream, sherry, and drained mushrooms to make a sauce.
3. Spread over chicken. Sprinkle paprika lightly over top.
4. Bake in 375° F oven 45 minutes or until tender.
5. Serve with noodles or over whole-wheat toast (½ cup cooked noodles or 1 slice toast = 1 Starch/Bread Exchange).

Deviled Chicken Thighs

Yield: 6 or 2 servings
Serving Size: 1 thigh
Exchange List Approximation:
    Meat, lean 2

Nutrient Content Per Serving:
CAL: 113   PRO: 14.2 (gm)
FAT: 4.8 (gm)   CHO: 2.5 (gm)
Na: 179.8 (mg) K: 178.6 (mg)
Fiber: 0.3 (gm) Chol: 57 (mg)

Ingredients

Six Servings		*Two Servings*	
6	CHICKEN THIGHS, SKINNED	2	
1	TABLESPOON MARGARINE	1	TEASPOON
1	TABLESPOON PREPARED MUSTARD	1	TEASPOON
1	TABLESPOON VINEGAR	1	TEASPOON
½	TEASPOON PAPRIKA	⅛	TEASPOON
¼	TEASPOON BLACK PEPPER	¹⁄₁₆	TEASPOON
⅛	TEASPOON SALT		DASH
½	CUP FRESH BREAD CRUMBS (1 SLICE WHOLE-WHEAT BREAD)	3	TABLESPOONS

Method

1. Wash and dry chicken thighs.
2. Mix softened margarine with mustard, vinegar, and spices.
3. Place thighs meaty side up on shallow baking pan.
4. Spread mixture evenly over chicken.
5. Sprinkle with crumbs.
6. Bake in 425° F oven for 25 minutes. Do not overbake.

Key Lime Chicken Thighs

Yield: 4 or 2 servings
Serving Size: 2 thighs
Exchange List Approximation:
    Meat, lean 3

Nutrient Content Per Serving:
CAL: 175   PRO: 27.3 (gm)
FAT: 6.4 (gm)   CHO: 0.8 (gm)
Na: 219 (mg)   K: 328.5 (mg)
Fiber: 0   Chol: 114 (mg)

Ingredients

Four Servings		*Two Servings*	
8	CHICKEN THIGHS, SKINNED (ABOUT 2 POUNDS)	4	
1	TEASPOON MARGARINE	½	TEASPOON
2	TABLESPOONS LIME JUICE (1 LIME)	1	TABLESPOON
¼	TEASPOON ROSEMARY, CRUSHED	⅛	TEASPOON
¼	TEASPOON POULTRY SEASONING	⅛	TEASPOON
¼	TEASPOON CHICKEN BOUILLON GRANULES	⅛	TEASPOON
¼	TEASPOON PEPPER	⅛	TEASPOON
¼	TEASPOON PAPRIKA	⅛	TEASPOON

Method

1. Lightly grease baking pan. Space chicken thighs, meat side up, on pan. Do not overlap.
2. Squeeze lime juice over chicken.
3. Sprinkle seasonings evenly over chicken.
4. Bake in 425° F oven for 25 minutes. Do not overbake.
5. Remove chicken. Deglaze baking pan with about ⅓ cup water. Serve as sauce over chicken.

Oriental Chicken with Vegetables

Yield: 6 or 2 servings
Serving Size: 1 cup
Exchange List Approximation:
    Meat, lean 2
    Vegetable 2
    Fat 1

Nutrient Content Per Serving:
CAL: 209   PRO: 19.4 (gm)
FAT: 9.5 (gm)   CHO: 11.3 (gm)
Na: 574.1 (mg) K: 476.5 (mg)
Fiber: 3.8 (gm) Chol: 50 (mg)

Ingredients

Six Servings	*Two Servings*
¾ CUP THINLY SLICED ONION	¼ CUP
2 TABLESPOONS VEGETABLE OIL	2 TEASPOONS
3 CUPS DIAGONALLY SLICED CELERY	1 CUP
1½ TEASPOONS MINCED FRESH GINGER	½ TEASPOON
1 CUP UNCOOKED PEAS OR HALF 10-OUNCE PACKAGE FROZEN PEAS	⅓ CUP
1½ CUPS CHICKEN BROTH OR BOUILLON	½ CUP
3 TABLESPOONS CORNSTARCH	1 TABLESPOON
1 TABLESPOON SOY SAUCE	1 TEASPOON
2 3-OUNCE CANS MUSHROOM CROWNS WITH BROTH	1 CAN
¾ POUND DICED, COOKED CHICKEN	¼ POUND

Method

1. In large, deep skillet, cook onion in oil until transparent. Stir in celery and ginger and cook for 1 minute. Stir in

peas, cover, and cook for about 4 minutes. Vegetables should be bright and tender-crisp. Remove vegetables and set aside.

2. Combine broth from one can of mushrooms, chicken broth, soy sauce, and cornstarch; pour into skillet. Cook, stirring constantly, until sauce thickens.

3. Stir in mushrooms, vegetables, and chicken; toss gently until all ingredients are covered with sauce. Cover and cook over moderate heat until meat is hot, about 5 minutes.

4. Serving suggestion: Serve over hot rice (1/3 cup cooked rice = 1 Starch/Bread Exchange).

*To reduce the sodium content, use salt-free broth and cut back on the amount of soy sauce used.

Smoked Fruity Roast Chicken

Yield: 4 servings
Serving Size: $\frac{1}{4}$ chicken and
$\frac{1}{2}$ cup stuffing
Exchange List Approximation:
  Starch/Bread $1\frac{1}{2}$
  Meat, medium-fat 6
  Fruit 1

Nutrient Content Per Serving:
CAL: 640   PRO: 57 (gm)
FAT: 28.6 (gm)   CHO: 39.9 (gm)
Na: 406.8 (mg)* K: 754.3 (mg)
Fiber: 4.2 (gm)   Chol: 234 (mg)
Key Source Nutrients:
  Protein: 57 (gm)
  Niacin: 17.2 (mg)

Ingredients

    4 SLICES WHOLE-WHEAT BREAD
 1½ CUPS UNPEELED, DICED APPLES (WINESAP OR
       ROME)
   ½ CUP RAISINS
   ¼ CUP CHICKEN BROTH
    2 TABLESPOONS UNSWEETENED APPLE CIDER
    1 TEASPOON CINNAMON
    1 EGG, BEATEN
    1 BROILER-FRYER CHICKEN, 3 TO 3½ POUNDS
   ⅓ CUP LIQUID HICKORY SMOKE
   ¼ TEASPOON MONOSODIUM GLUTAMATE*
       SPRINKLE PAPRIKA

Method

1. Prepare stuffing for chicken. Tear bread into pieces and mix
    with apples, raisins, broth, cider, and cinnamon. Lightly
    stir in egg.
2. Spoon stuffing mix into cavity of cleaned whole chicken.
    Hook wing tips back and tie legs together.
3. Place in a shallow baking pan on rack. Brush liquid smoke

over chicken and sprinkle with paprika and monosodium glutamate.

4. Bake uncovered in 350° F oven about 1½ hours or until legs move freely when lifted or turned.
5. When chicken is done, brush again with liquid smoke.

*If you eliminate monosodium glutamate, sodium content will be reduced.

NOTE: If chicken is skinned, nutrient information is as follows:

Exchange List Approximation:
    Starch/Bread 1½
    Meat, lean 5
    Fruit 1

Nutrient Content Per Serving:
CAL: 457   PRO: 45.8 (gm)
FAT: 13.1 (gm) CHO: 39.9 (gm)
Na: 377.9 (mg)* K: 671.1 (mg)
Fiber: 4.2 (gm) Chol: 192 (mg)

Chicken with Tortilla Dressing

Yield: 6 servings
Serving Size: 1 cup
Exchange List Approximation:
   Starch/Bread 1
   Meat, lean 2
   Vegetable 2
   Fat $\frac{1}{2}$

Nutrient Content Per Serving:
CAL: 255   PRO: 18.2 (gm)
FAT: 8.9 (gm)   CHO: 25.6 (gm)
Na: 556.9 (mg) K: 331.9 (mg)
Fiber: 2.8 (gm) Chol: 42 (mg)

Ingredients

2½ POUNDS FRYING CHICKEN, FAT REMOVED
  3 CUPS WATER
  1 10½-OUNCE CAN CREAM OF MUSHROOM SOUP
  1 CUP DICED CELERY
  1 CUP CHOPPED ONION
  1 TEASPOON POULTRY SEASONING
½ TEASPOON PEPPER
  9 CORN TORTILLAS

Method

1. Place chicken and water in large saucepan. Bring to a boil. Cover and simmer about 1 hour until tender.
2. Remove chicken and boil stock gently about 5 minutes to concentrate. There should be 2½ to 3 cups.
3. Stir in soup, celery, onions, and seasonings.
4. Skin and bone chicken. Cut into large pieces (about 2 cups).
5. Pour ½ cup of stock into 2½-quart casserole.
6. Dip tortillas (one at a time) in stock. Break into pieces and place layer of 3 in casserole.

7. Add layer of chicken, cup of stock, layer of tortillas, layer of chicken, and stock; top with layer of tortillas.
8. Pour remaining stock over top. Cover and bake in 350° F oven for 30 minutes. Remove cover. Bake another 10 minutes.

Two-Way Chicken Enchiladas

Yield: 6 servings
Serving Size: 2 enchiladas or
  1 piece, $4\frac{1}{2}$ by 4 inches
Exchange List Approximation:
    Starch/Bread $2\frac{1}{2}$
    Meat, lean 4
    Fat 1

Nutrient Content Per Serving:
CAL: 466   PRO: 35.6 (gm)
FAT: 20.2 (gm)* CHO: 36.3 (gm)
Na: 999.2 (mg)* K: 546.4 (mg)
Fiber: 3.7 (gm)   Chol: 97 (mg)

Ingredients

  4 CHICKEN BREAST HALVES
     WATER TO COVER
¼ TEASPOON SALT
  1 16-OUNCE CAN TOMATOES, CHOPPED
  1 10½-OUNCE CAN CREAM OF CHICKEN SOUP
  1 4-OUNCE CAN CHOPPED GREEN CHILIES
  1 TEASPOON GROUND CUMIN
     SCANT ½ TEASPOON GARLIC POWDER
  1 CUP CHOPPED ONION
  2 CUPS SHREDDED CHEDDAR CHEESE
12 CORN TORTILLAS

Method

1. Cover chicken with water and simmer 30 minutes. Remove chicken and reserve broth.
2. Skin and bone chicken. Cut each half into 3 strips. Sprinkle with salt and set aside.
3. Mix tomatoes, soup, chilies, cumin, and garlic powder.
4. Assemble each enchilada individually: dip tortilla in warm broth to soften and place in a flat plan. Place strip of chicken on tortilla, add 2 Tablespoons cheese, 1 teaspoon chopped onion, and 1 teaspoon sauce. Roll up and place seam side down in baking pan.
5. Sprinkle with onion, pour remaining sauce evenly over enchiladas and sprinkle with remaining cheese.
6. Bake in 350° F oven for 35 minutes or until bubbly.

Variation in Method

1. For Casserole: follow directions 1 to 3 above, then dip half of tortillas in warm broth to soften, break into pieces and place in a layer in 9-inch × 13-inch baking pan.
2. Spread chicken evenly over tortillas. Sprinkle with half the onions. Spread with layer of sauce and half the cheese.
3. Dip remaining tortillas in broth, break apart, and layer over sauce. Sprinkle with onion.
4. Pour sauce over casserole. Sprinkle with remaining cheese.
5. Bake in 350° F oven for 40 minutes or until bubbly.
6. Let cool 5 minutes. Cut casserole 2 by 3 into pieces 4½ inches × 4 inches each.

*This recipe is high in fat and sodium. You may want to reserve it for occasional use only.

Chicken Tacos

Yield: 12 tacos
Serving Size: 1 taco
Exchange List Approximation:
    Starch/Bread 1
    Meat, medium-fat 2
    Vegetable 1

Nutrient Content Per Serving:
CAL: 256   PRO: 20.5 (gm)
FAT: 10.5 (gm)   CHO: 19.2 (gm)
Na: 152.8 (mg)   K: 199.8 (mg)
Fiber: 1.3 (gm)   Chol: 56 (mg)

Ingredients

  1 PACKAGE FLOUR TORTILLAS (12 6-INCH)
  1 CHICKEN (3 TO 3½ POUNDS)
  1 PACKAGE TACO SEASONING MIX
  6 OUNCES CHEDDAR CHEESE, SHREDDED
12 TABLESPOONS SOUR CREAM (OPTIONAL)*
    SHREDDED LETTUCE
    CHOPPED TOMATO
    CHOPPED ONION

Method

1. Remove skin from chicken and simmer until meat falls off the bone. Cut meat into small pieces.
2. In a skillet combine cooked chicken, taco seasoning, and 1½ cups water. Bring to a boil then simmer to desired consistency (10 to 15 minutes).
3. Shred cheese. Heat tortillas in microwave or iron skillet. Place 2 ounces chicken mix in the center of each tortilla. Top with ½ ounce cheddar cheese, 1 Tablespoon sour cream,* shredded lettuce, chopped tomato, and chopped onion. Roll up.

*If sour cream is used, add ½ Fat to exchanges, and 2 grams fat and 20 calories to estimated nutrients.

Chicken Green-Bean Casserole

Yield: 6 or 2 servings
Serving Size: 1 cup
Exchange List Approximation:
    Starch/Bread 1
    Meat, lean 1
    Vegetable 1
    Fat 1

Nutrient Content Per Serving:
CAL: 210   PRO: 13.2 (gm)
FAT: 9.4 (gm) CHO: 19.8 (gm)
Na: 377.8 (mg) K: 256.4 (mg)
Fiber: 3.2 (gm) Chol: 36 (mg)

Ingredients

Six Servings		*Two Servings*	
½	CUP LONG-GRAIN AND WILD RICE	3	TABLESPOONS
2	CUPS WATER	1	CUP
½	10½-OUNCE CAN CREAM OF CELERY SOUP	3	TABLESPOONS
½	CUP SKIM MILK	3	TABLESPOONS
3	TABLESPOONS MAYONNAISE	1	TABLESPOON
1½	CUPS COOKED, DICED CHICKEN	½	CUP
1	16-OUNCE CAN FRENCH-STYLE GREEN BEANS, DRAINED	⅓	CUP
½	CUP DICED ONION	3	TABLESPOONS
¾	CUP SLICED WATER CHESTNUTS (ABOUT 4 OUNCES)	¼	CUP
4	TABLESPOONS CHOPPED PIMENTO	4	TEASPOONS

Method

1. Add rice to boiling water; bring to a boil, cover, reduce heat, and simmer until tender, 30 minutes to 1 hour. Water will be absorbed. Do not use seasoning packet.

2. Add remaining ingredients to rice. Mix well.
3. Pour in lightly greased 2½ quart casserole.
4. Cover and bake in 350° F oven 30 minutes.

Note: This casserole is so good, make 6 servings, package extra servings, and freeze for later use.

Fanny's Chicken and Rice

Yield: 6 or 2 servings
Serving Size: 1 breast half
    or 1 leg
Exchange List Approximation:
    Starch/Bread 1
    Meat, lean $3\frac{1}{2}$
    Vegetable 2

Nutrient Content Per Serving:
CAL: 322   PRO: 32.8 (gm)
FAT: 9 (gm)   CHO: 26.4 (gm)
Na: 373.3 (mg) K: 574.5 (mg)
Fiber: 4.4 (gm) Chol: 79 (mg)

Ingredients

Six Servings	*Two Servings*
¾ CUP BROWN RICE	¼ CUP
3 CUPS WATER	1 CUP
3 CHICKEN BREASTS, SPLIT AND SKINNED	1 BREAST
or	
6 CHICKEN LEG QUARTERS, SKINNED	2
1 TABLESPOON VEGETABLE OIL	1 TEASPOON
1 CUP CHOPPED ONIONS	⅓ CUP
¾ CUP CHOPPED GREEN PEPPER	¼ CUP
¾ TEASPOON MINCED GARLIC	¼ TEASPOON

Six Servings		*Two Servings*	
2	TEASPOONS CURRY POWDER	¾	TEASPOON
½	TEASPOON SALT	⅛	TEASPOON
½	TEASPOON THYME	⅛	TEASPOON
1	16-OUNCE CAN TOMATOES	⅓	CAN (ABOUT ⅔ CUP)
1	TABLESPOON CHOPPED PARSLEY	1	TEASPOON
2	TABLESPOONS CURRANTS	2	TEASPOONS
¼	CUP TOASTED ALMONDS (ABOUT 1 OUNCE)	1	TABLESPOON

Method

1. Cook rice while preparing chicken and sauce. Add to boiling water, cover, and simmer 1 hour.
2. Place chicken in 2-inch-deep baking pan. Bake chicken in 425° F oven, 25 minutes. Do not overbake.
3. Make sauce. Saute onion, peppers, and garlic in oil, add spices and blend thoroughly. Add tomatoes and parsley. Heat.
4. Pour sauce over chicken, sprinkle with currants. Cover and bake at 350° F for 30 minutes.
5. Arrange chicken serving with ½ cup rice on plate. Pour ½ cup sauce over rice. Sprinkle 2 teaspoons almonds over chicken.

Chicken Livers Oregano

Yield: 6 or 2 servings
Serving Size: ½ cup
Exchange List Approximation:
    Meat, medium-fat 1
    Vegetable ½

Nutrient Content Per Serving:
CAL: 84   PRO: 12.2 (gm)
FAT: 2.8 (gm)   CHO: 2.3 (gm)
Na: 302.4 (mg)   K: 111.4 (mg)
Fiber: 1.3 (gm)   Chol: 307 (mg)
Key Source Nutrients:
    Vitamin A: 8103 (IU)
    Folacin: 387 (mcg)
    Vitamin B$_{12}$: 9 (mcg)

Ingredients

Six Servings		*Two Servings*
1	POUND CHICKEN LIVERS	5 OUNCES
SCANT ½	TEASPOON SALT	⅛ TEASPOON
SCANT ½	TEASPOON OREGANO	⅛ TEASPOON
	SPRINKLE PEPPER	SPRINKLE
1	CUP WATER	⅓ CUP
1¾	CUPS CUT GREEN BEANS, DRAINED (ABOUT 1 16-OUNCE CAN)	½ CUP

Method

1. Wash and trim chicken livers.
2. Place in skillet. Sprinkle with seasonings. Add water. Bring to a simmer, cover tightly, and simmer 10 minutes, turning occasionally.
3. Remove liver. Bring broth to a boil. Add green beans and heat to a simmer. Add livers and stir to mix.
4. Serving suggestion: Serve ½ cup over cooked rice or toasted bread points (⅓ cup cooked rice or 1 full slice of bread = 1 Starch/Bread Exchange).

Duke of Kent Chicken

Yield: 6 or 2 servings
Serving Size: 1 cup
Exchange List Approximation:
    Starch/Bread 2
    Meat, lean 2
    Fat 1

Nutrient Content Per Serving:
CAL: 312   PRO: 19.7 (gm)
FAT: 13.6 (gm)   CHO: 28.7 (gm)
Na: 319.9 (mg)   K: 321.1 (mg)
Fiber: 3.5 (gm)   Chol: 48 (mg)

Ingredients

Six Servings	Two Servings
¾ CUP BROWN RICE	¼ CUP
2¼ CUPS WATER OR CHICKEN STOCK	1 CUP
½ 10½-OUNCE CAN CREAM OF MUSHROOM SOUP	3 TABLESPOONS
½ CUP SKIM MILK	3 TABLESPOONS
3 TABLESPOONS LEMON JUICE	1 TABLESPOON
2 CUPS COOKED, DICED CHICKEN	⅔ CUP
4 TABLESPOONS PIMENTO, CHOPPED	4 TEASPOONS
½ CUP SLIVERED ALMONDS	2½ TABLESPOONS
¾ CUP WATER CHESTNUTS, SLICED (ABOUT ½ 8-OUNCE CAN)	¼ CUP
½ CUP SHREDDED CHEDDAR CHEESE	3 TABLESPOONS

Method

1. Place brown rice in boiling chicken stock; bring back to a boil, reduce heat, cover, and cook 50 minutes.

2. Combine soup and milk and stir in lemon juice.
3. Add chicken, pimento, almonds, chestnuts, and rice. Toss together to mix.
4. Place in a 2½-quart casserole sprayed with vegetable spray.
5. Sprinkle shredded cheese over top, cover, and bake 30 minutes at 350° F.

*May be too high in salt for frequent use, but ideal for entertaining.

Veggie Fried Rice

Yield: 6 or 2 servings
Serving Size: 1½ cup
Exchange List Approximation:
    Starch/Bread 1½
    Meat, lean 2
    Vegetable 1

Nutrient Content Per Serving:
CAL: 260   PRO: 18.8 (gm)
FAT: 7.2 (gm)   CHO: 29.6 (gm)
Na: 749.1 (mg)   K: 366.9 (mg)
Fiber: 2 (gm)   Chol: 87 (mg)
Key Source Nutrients:
    Vitamin A: 3772 (IU)

Ingredients

Six Servings	Two Servings
1 TABLESPOON VEGETABLE OIL	1 TEASPOON
4 TABLESPOONS SOY SAUCE	4 TEASPOONS
2 TEASPOONS CIDER VINEGAR OR LEMON JUICE	½ TEASPOON
1 TEASPOON BROWN SUGAR	¼ TEASPOON
¼ TEASPOON CRUSHED RED PEPPER	SPRINKLE
SCANT ½ TEASPOON CHINESE 5-SPICE	⅛ TEASPOON
½ CUP CHOPPED GREEN ONIONS	3 TABLESPOONS
1 TEASPOON MINCED GARLIC CLOVE	⅓ TEASPOON

Six Servings	*Two Servings*
½ CUP THINLY SLICED CARROTS	3 TABLESPOONS
1½ CUPS BROCCOLI PIECES, CUT INTO ½" CHUNKS	½ CUP
2 CUPS DICED, COOKED CHICKEN (ABOUT 10 OUNCES)	⅔ CUP
1 EGG, LIGHTLY BEATEN	⅓
3 CUPS COOKED RICE	1 CUP

Method

1. In a wok or large skillet, add oil and coat surface. Add soy sauce, vinegar, sugar, and spices. Heat over medium heat.
2. Add vegetables and stir-fry 2 to 3 minutes.
3. Add chicken and egg. Stir-fry until egg is cooked.
4. Add rice, toss, and cook until heated through.

*To reduce sodium content, use mild soy sauce or cut back on the amount of soy sauce used.

Chicken Livers Oregano with Wild Rice

Yield: 6 or 2 servings
Serving Size: $\frac{1}{6}$ recipe
Exchange List Approximation:
    Starch/Bread $\frac{1}{2}$
    Meat, medium-fat 1
    Vegetable 2

Nutrient Content Per Serving:
CAL: 155   PRO: 15.1 (gm)
FAT: 2.9 (gm)   CHO: 17.4 (gm)
Na: 303.9 (mg)   K: 155.4 (mg)
Fiber: 2.8 (gm)   Chol: 307 (mg)
Key Source Nutrients:
    Vitamin A: 8103 (IU)
    Folacin: 390 (mcg)
    Vitamin B_{12}: 9 (mcg)

Ingredients

Six Servings	*Two Servings*
¾ CUP LONG-GRAIN AND WILD RICE	¼ CUP
3 CUPS WATER	1 CUP
1 POUND CHICKEN LIVERS	⅓ POUND
SCANT ½ TEASPOON SALT	⅛ TEASPOON
SCANT ½ TEASPOON OREGANO	⅛ TEASPOON
SPRINKLE PEPPER	SPRINKLE
1 CUP WATER	⅓ CUP
1¾ CUPS CUT GREEN BEANS, DRAINED (ABOUT 1 16-OUNCE CAN)	½ CUP

Method

1. Wash rice. Add water, bring to a boil, reduce heat, cover, and cook until water is absorbed, about 1 hour.
2. Wash and trim livers.
3. Place in skillet. Sprinkle with seasonings, toss. Add water. Bring to a boil, cover tightly, and simmer 10 minutes, turning once.

4. Remove liver. Bring broth to a boil, add beans, and heat to a simmer.
5. Add rice and livers. Toss and heat.

Turkey and Wild-Rice Casserole

Yield: 6 servings
Serving Size: $\frac{1}{6}$ recipe
Exchange List Approximation:
    Starch/Bread $1\frac{1}{2}$
    Meat, lean 2

Nutrient Content Per Serving:
CAL: 233   PRO: 22.2 (gm)
FAT: 7.7 (gm)   CHO: 20 (gm)
Na: 415.2 (mg)   K: 412.8 (mg)
Fiber: 2.6 (gm)   Chol: 45 (mg)

Ingredients

½ CUP NATURAL LONG-GRAIN AND WILD RICE (ABOUT 3 OUNCES)
2 CUPS WATER
¼ TEASPOON SALT
8 OUNCES FRESH MUSHROOMS, SLICED
1 TABLESPOON MARGARINE
2 TABLESPOONS FLOUR
1 CUP SKIM MILK
1 TEASPOON CHICKEN BOUILLON GRANULES
1/16 TEASPOON PEPPER
2 CUPS CUBED, COOKED TURKEY (ABOUT 12 OUNCES)
4 TABLESPOONS SLICED PIMENTO
½ CUP SLICED WATER CHESTNUTS (ABOUT 2 OUNCES)
¼ CUP SLICED ALMONDS (ABOUT 1 OUNCE)

Method

1. Wash rice. Add water and salt, bring to boil, cover, and simmer about 1 hour until water is absorbed.
2. In large skillet, saute mushrooms in margarine about 3 minutes. Stir in flour. Add milk, bouillon and pepper. Cook until thickened, stirring constantly.
3. Add turkey, pimento, water chestnuts, and rice. Mix and pour into 7- by 11-inch baking dish. Sprinkle with sliced almonds.
4. Cover and bake in 350° F oven for 30 minutes. Uncover and bake about 3 minutes. Cut into 6 servings, 2 inches by 3 inches.

Ground Turkey Loaf

Yield: 1 loaf (12 slices)
Serving Size: 1 slice
Exchange List Approximation:
    Meat, medium-fat 2
    Fat $\frac{1}{2}$

Nutrient Content Per Serving:

CAL: 167	PRO: 14.4 (gm)
FAT: 11.4 (gm)	CHO: 2.2 (gm)
Na: 595.1 (mg)	K: 240.3 (mg)
Fiber: 0.2 (gm)	Chol: 88 (mg)

Ingredients

  2 POUNDS GROUND TURKEY, UNCOOKED
⅓ CUP OATMEAL
¼ CUP CATSUP
  2 TABLESPOONS CHOPPED ONION
½ TEASPOON SALT
½ TEASPOON OREGANO
½ TEASPOON PEPPER
  2 EGGS

Method

1. Place ingredients, except turkey, in mixing bowl. Mix thoroughly and let stand a few minutes.
2. Mix in turkey until well blended.
3. Shape into loaf. Place in 5- by 9-inch loaf pan or in shallow pan with a little water.
4. Bake in 325° F oven for 1 hour or until meat thermometer registers 160° to 165° F.
5. Cool to set loaf. Slice into ½-inch slices. Extra slices may be used for sandwiches.

Fish

Twenty-Minute Bouillabaise

Yield: 4 servings (4½ cups)
Serving Size: 1 cup
Exchange List Approximation:
    Meat, lean 2
    Vegetable 2

Nutrient Content Per Serving:
CAL: 160   PRO: 24.1 (gm)
FAT: 3.9 (gm)   CHO: 7 (gm)
Na: 468.8 (mg)   K: 569.9 (mg)
Fiber: 1.5 (gm)   Chol: 77 (mg)

Ingredients

- 2 TEASPOONS VEGETABLE OIL
- ½ CUP CHOPPED ONION
- ½ TEASPOON MINCED GARLIC CLOVE (ABOUT ½)
  PINCH THYME
- 1 TEASPOON CHOPPED FRESH BASIL (OPTIONAL)
- 1 15-OUNCE CAN TOMATOES
- ½ CUP WATER
- ½ CUP WHITE WINE OR WATER
- ½ POUND ROCK COD, BUTTERFISH, OR TURBOT
- ¼ POUND COOKED SHRIMP
- 1 6¼-OUNCE CAN CHOPPED CLAMS

Method

1. Saute onion, garlic, and herbs in oil until tender, about 5 minutes.
2. Add can of tomatoes, water, and wine. Simmer 5 minutes, stirring to break up tomatoes.
3. Cut fish into 1-inch pieces and add to tomatoes. Bring to a boil and simmer 5 to 7 minutes until fish is done.
4. Add shrimp and clams with juice. Heat thoroughly.
5. Serve immediately or hold over very low heat. Salt and pepper may be added to taste.

Poached Fish and Peas

Yield: 6 or 2 servings
Serving Size: 1 cup
Exchange List Approximation:
    Starch/Bread $\frac{1}{2}$
    Meat, lean $3\frac{1}{2}$

Nutrient Content Per Serving:
CAL: 232   PRO: 27.8 (gm)
FAT: 9.1 (gm)   CHO: 8.1 (gm)
Na: 285 (mg)   K: 651.9 (mg)
Fiber: 3.1 (gm)   Chol: 60 (mg)

Ingredients

Six Servings		*Two Servings*
1	TABLESPOON MARGARINE	1 TEASPOON
½	CUP CHOPPED ONION	3 TABLESPOONS
1	TEASPOON MINCED GARLIC CLOVE	¼ TEASPOON
½	CUP CARROTS, CUT INTO 1-INCH STRIPS	3 TABLESPOONS
2¼	CUPS FROZEN PEAS (ABOUT 1 10-OUNCE PACKAGE)	¾ CUP
1	BAY LEAF	⅓
¾	TEASPOON TARRAGON OR MINT	¼ TEASPOON
¼	TEASPOON SALT	¹⁄₁₆ TEASPOON
¼	TEASPOON PEPPER	¹⁄₁₆ TEASPOON
½	CUP WHITE WINE	3 TABLESPOONS
½	CUP WATER	3 TABLESPOONS
6	STUFFED SPANISH OLIVES (OPTIONAL)	2
1½	POUNDS FRESH OR FROZEN FISH, CUT INTO 2-INCH PIECES	8 OUNCES

Method

1. Use a large skillet or saucepan. Cook onions and garlic in margarine about 2 minutes.
2. Add remaining ingredients except fish. Bring to a boil, cover, and simmer about 8 minutes.
3. Add fish, bring to a simmer. Cover and poach (just below boiling) for about 5 minutes.
4. Serve over rice or in soup bowls. (⅓ cup cooked rice = 1 Starch/Bread Exchange).

Tomato-Glazed Fish Fillets

Yield: 4 servings
Serving Size: 1 fillet and
$\frac{1}{2}$ cup sauce
Exchange List Approximation:
   Meat, lean 3
    Vegetable 1

Nutrient Content Per Serving:
CAL: 175   PRO: 30.1 (gm)
FAT: 2.2 (gm)   CHO: 8.7 (gm)
Na: 658.7 (mg) K: 714.6 (mg)
Fiber: 1.6 (gm) Chol: 42 (mg)

Ingredients

  1 MEDIUM ONION, THINLY SLICED
  1 TEASPOON VEGETABLE OIL
  1 4-OUNCE CAN MUSHROOMS, STEMS AND PIECES, DRAINED
  1 POUND COD OR HADDOCK FILLETS
 ½ TEASPOON GARLIC SALT*
 ½ TEASPOON GRATED LEMON RIND
 ¼ TEASPOON DILL WEED
1½ CUPS TOMATO JUICE
  4 TEASPOONS LEMON JUICE

1 TABLESPOON FLOUR
1 PACKET SUGAR SUBSTITUTE (OPTIONAL)
1 TABLESPOON CHOPPED PARSLEY

Method

1. Heat oil in large skillet. Add onions and saute about 5
    minutes. Add mushrooms.
2. Arrange fish over onions. Sprinkle with garlic salt, lemon
    rind, and dill weed. Add tomato juice.
3. Bring to a simmer, cover, and cook over moderate heat 10
    minutes or until fish is easily flaked with a fork. Remove
    fish to a heated platter.
4. Blend lemon juice and flour together. Gradually add ½ cup
    of tomato sauce. Stir back into sauce.
5. Add sweetener, stir, and cook over moderate heat until
    thickened, about 2 minutes.
6. Serve ½ cup sauce over each fillet and sprinkle with
    parsley.

*To reduce sodium content, substitute fresh garlic or garlic powder
for garlic salt.

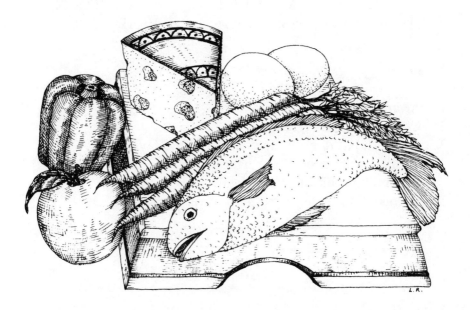

Broiled Fillet of Sole with Parmesan Sauce

Yield: 6 or 2 servings
Serving Size: $\frac{1}{6}$ recipe
Exchange List Approximation:
    Meat, lean $2\frac{1}{2}$

Nutrient Content Per Serving:
CAL: 148   PRO: 29.5 (gm)
FAT: 1.8 (gm)   CHO: 1.6 (gm)
Na: 297.8 (mg)   K: 594.5 (mg)
Fiber: 0.1 (gm)   Chol: 45 (mg)

Ingredients

Six Servings	Two Servings
1½ POUNDS SOLE OR FLOUNDER (FRESH OR FROZEN)	½ POUND
6 TABLESPOONS PLAIN LOW-FAT YOGURT	2 TABLESPOONS
2 TABLESPOONS GRATED PARMESAN CHEESE	2 TEASPOONS
1 TABLESPOON DIJON-STYLE MUSTARD	1 TEASPOON
1 TABLESPOON LEMON JUICE	1 TEASPOON
1½ TEASPOONS HORSERADISH	½ TEASPOON

Method

1. Arrange fish on broiler pan.
2. Combine sauce ingredients.
3. Spread mixture over the fillets in a thin layer.
4. Broil about 8 inches from heat for about 6 minutes (time depends on thickness of fillets).
5. Garnish with lemon wedges and dill sprigs.

Fish-Tomato Sauce for Rice

Yield: 6 or 2 servings
Serving Size: $\frac{2}{3}$ cup sauce plus
$\frac{1}{2}$ cup rice
Exchange List Approximation:
    Starch/Bread 2
    Meat, lean $1\frac{1}{2}$
    Vegetable 1

Nutrient Content Per Serving:
CAL: 273   PRO: 24.2 (gm)
FAT: 3.5 (gm)   CHO: 36.1 (gm)
Na: 613.5 (mg)   K: 930.3 (mg)
Fiber: 2.3 (gm)   Chol: 31 (mg)

Ingredients

Six Servings		Two Servings
1½	CUPS SLICED ONION	½ CUP
1	TEASPOON MINCED GARLIC CLOVE	⅓ TEASPOON
1	TABLESPOON OLIVE OIL	1 TEASPOON
1	8-OUNCE CAN TOMATO SAUCE	⅓ CAN
1	6-OUNCE CAN TOMATO PASTE	⅓ CAN
¾	CUP WATER	¼ CUP
1	POUND FILLET OF SOLE OR FLOUNDER (6 PIECES)	5 OUNCES (2)
3	CUPS COOKED RICE	1 CUP

Method

1. Saute sliced onion and garlic in olive oil in deep pan about 10 minutes. Do not burn garlic.
2. Add tomato sauce, paste, and water. Stir. Bring to a simmer and cook 10 minutes, stirring occasionally.
3. Add fish and cook until tender, about 5 minutes. Stir occasionally. Fish breaks apart. Do not overcook fish as it will become tough.
4. Serve ⅔ cup sauce over ½ cup cooked rice.

Variation: Fish-tomato sauce is also good served over spaghetti.

Oven-Fried Catfish

Yield: 4 servings
Serving Size: $\frac{1}{4}$ recipe
Exchange List Approximation:
    Starch/Bread $\frac{1}{2}$
    Meat, lean 2

Nutrient Content Per Serving:
CAL: 155   PRO: 19 (gm)
FAT: 5.8 (gm)   CHO: 5.3 (gm)
Na: 379.5 (mg)   K: 363.8 (mg)
Fiber: 0.2 (gm)   Chol: 75 (mg)

Ingredients

1¼ POUNDS WHOLE, HEADLESS CATFISH (4)
  2 TABLESPOONS LOW-FAT YOGURT
  2 TEASPOONS VEGETABLE OIL
1½ TEASPOONS LEMON JUICE
  ¼ TEASPOON PAPRIKA
  ½ TEASPOON SALT
  ⅛ TEASPOON PEPPER
  4 TABLESPOONS DRY WHOLE-WHEAT BREAD CRUMBS

Method

1. Wash and drain fish.
2. Combine yogurt, oil, lemon juice, and seasonings in shallow dish.
3. Sprinkle bread crumbs on wax paper.
4. Dip fish in yogurt mixture, then press in crumbs, lightly coating both sides.
5. Place fish on lightly greased cookie sheet or shallow baking pan.
6. Bake in 475° F oven for 10 minutes or until done.

Note: One pound flounder or sole fillets may be used. Reduce baking time to 8 minutes.

Fish-Spinach Birds

Yield: 6 servings
Serving Size: 1 fillet
Exchange List Approximation:
    Meat, lean 2
    Vegetable 2

Nutrient Content Per Serving:
CAL: 169   PRO: 26.1 (gm)
FAT: 1.8 (gm)   CHO: 11.5 (gm)
Na: 551.7 (mg) K: 720.5 (mg)
Fiber: 1.8 (gm) Chol: 36 (mg)

Ingredients

1	10-OUNCE PACKAGE FROZEN CHOPPED SPINACH
½	CUP DRY BREAD CRUMBS
1	4-OUNCE CAN MUSHROOMS, STEMS AND PIECES
6	TABLESPOONS LIGHT ITALIAN SALAD DRESSING (DIVIDED)
1¼	POUNDS FLOUNDER FILLETS (ABOUT 6 PIECES)
10	OUNCES FRESH TOMATOES (ABOUT 3 SMALL)

Method

1. Thaw spinach and drain thoroughly. Chop mushrooms and combine with spinach, bread crumbs, and 4 tablespoons salad dressing.
2. Spread mixture equally over fillets. Roll and secure with toothpicks.
3. Place in lightly greased baking dish. Drizzle with remaining 2 tablespoons salad dressing.
4. Bake in 350° F oven for 10 minutes. Add tomatoes, cut into wedges. Bake 10 minutes, or until fish flakes.

Swordfish or Salmon Kabobs

Yield: 4 servings
Serving Size: $\frac{1}{4}$ recipe
Exchange List Approximation:
    Meat, lean $2\frac{1}{2}$
    Vegetable 2

Nutrient Content Per Serving:
CAL: 191   PRO: 22 (gm)
FAT: 5.9 (gm)   CHO: 12.9 (gm)
Na: 93.5 (mg)   K: 711.6 (mg)
Fiber: 5 (gm)   Chol: 33 (mg)
Key Source Nutrients:
    Ascorbic acid: 46 (mg)

Ingredients

  ¾ POUND SWORDFISH, CUBED, OR SALMON
  1 SMALL ONION, CHOPPED
  ⅛ TEASPOON GROUND BLACK PEPPER
  3 TABLESPOONS LEMON JUICE
10 BAY LEAVES
  4 SMALL ONIONS OR WEDGES
  4 GREEN-PEPPER SQUARES
  1 TOMATO, CUT INTO 4 WEDGES
  4 ZUCCHINI WEDGES
  4 MUSHROOM CAPS

Method

1. Combine onion, pepper, salt,* lemon juice, and fish cubes. Marinate for 4 to 6 hours in refrigerator.
2. One hour before cooking time, pour a cup of boiling water over bay leaves. Let stand.
3. On skewers, alternate: fish, bay leaves, vegetable cubes. Pour marinade over skewered food.
4. Barbecue or broil 8 to 10 minutes, turning once, until fish is golden brown and flakes easily. Discard bay leaves.
5. Serving suggestion: Serve on rice (⅓ cup cooked rice = 1 Starch/Bread Exchange).

*Note: Salt only if desired.

Tasty Cod

Yield: 6 servings
Serving Size: $\frac{1}{6}$ recipe
Exchange List Approximation:
    Meat, lean 2
    Vegetable 1

Nutrient Content Per Serving:
CAL: 140   PRO: 29.1 (gm)
FAT: 0.8 (gm)   CHO: 2.9 (gm)
Na: 214.4 (mg) K: 540.3 (mg)
Fiber: 1.1 (gm)   Chol: 42 (mg)
Key Source Nutrients:
    Vitamin A: 5351 (IU)

Ingredients

1½ POUNDS FROZEN COD FILLET
¼ TEASPOON SALT
¼ TEASPOON PEPPER
1 TEASPOON TARRAGON
1 TABLESPOON LEMON JUICE
1 CUP CHOPPED MUSHROOMS
1 CUP THINLY SLICED CARROTS
½ CUP CHOPPED CELERY
2 TABLESPOONS FRESH CHOPPED PARSLEY

Method

1. Place the frozen fish on a sheet of aluminum foil; lightly salt and pepper.
2. Sprinkle with tarragon and lemon juice. Add all the chopped vegetables and the fresh parsley. Dot with butter and wrap well.
3. Bake at 350° F for 35 to 45 minutes.

Note: Fillet may be cut into 6 pieces and individual servings wrapped in foil before baking.

Tuna- or Salmon-Rice Pie

Yield: 6 servings
Serving Size: $\frac{1}{6}$ pie
Exchange List Approximation:
    Starch/Bread 1
    Meat, lean 2
    Fat $\frac{1}{2}$

Nutrient Content Per Serving:
CAL: 222   PRO: 16.5 (gm)
FAT: 9.4 (gm)   CHO: 17.2 (gm)
Na: 273.1 (mg)   K: 268.6 (mg)
Fiber: 2.8 (gm)   Chol: 118 (mg)

Ingredients

- ⅓ CUP RICE
- 1 CUP WATER
- ⅛ TEASPOON SALT
- 1 TEASPOON MARGARINE
- 2 EGGS (DIVIDED)
- 1 6½-OUNCE CAN WATER-PACKED TUNA OR SALMON, DRAINED
- ¾ CUP SKIM MILK
- 2 CUPS FROZEN PEAS
- ½ TEASPOON PARSLEY FLAKES
- ¼ TEASPOON PEPPER
- ⅛ TEASPOON NUTMEG
- 4 SLICES LOW-FAT SWISS CHEESE

Method

1. Bring rice to boil in salted water, cover, and simmer 14 minutes. Mix with fork and stir in margarine and 1 beaten egg.
2. Place in 9-inch pie pan sprayed with vegetable pan spray. Press against sides and bottom of pan to make crust.
3. Spread tuna or salmon evenly over rice.
4. Heat milk and peas to a simmer. Add seasonings.

5. Beat remaining egg. Gradually stir in milk mixture. Pour over tuna.
6. Layer slices of cheese over top. Bake in 350° F oven for 25 minutes.

Mock Lobster Salad

Yield: 6 or 2 servings
Serving Size: $\frac{1}{2}$ cup
Exchange List Approximation:
    Meat, lean 2
    Vegetable 1

Nutrient Content Per Serving:

CAL: 131	PRO: 19.4 (gm)
FAT: 4.3 (gm)	CHO: 3.1 (gm)
Na: 177.1 (mg)	K: 332 (mg)
Fiber: 0.3 (gm)	Chol: 31 (mg)

Ingredients

Six Servings	Two Servings
1 POUND SCROD OR COD FILLETS	⅓ POUND
WATER TO COVER	
1 TABLESPOON VINEGAR	1 TEASPOON
½ CUP FINELY CHOPPED CELERY	3 TABLESPOONS
2 TABLESPOONS MAYONNAISE	2 TEASPOONS
2 TABLESPOONS CATSUP	2 TEASPOONS
1 TABLESPOON LEMON JUICE	1 TEASPOON
1 TABLESPOON LOW-FAT YOGURT	1 TEASPOON
1 TABLESPOON PICKLE RELISH	1 TEASPOON
1 TEASPOON HORSERADISH	½ TEASPOON
¼ TEASPOON ONION POWDER	⅟₁₆ TEASPOON
⅛ TEASPOON PEPPER	⅟₁₆ TEASPOON

Method

1. Wash fish, place in shallow pan. Cover with water. Bring to a simmer. Do not boil. Cook about 4 minutes or until fish changes to white and flakes.
2. Drain fish, rinse with cold water. Drain and flake into large pieces.
3. Add remaining ingredients. Mix lightly and chill.
4. Serving suggestion: Serve on slit rolls or lettuce (½ hamburger-type roll = 1 Starch/Bread Exchange; lettuce is free).

Dad's Shrimp Over Pasta

Yield: 6 or 2 servings
Serving Size: 1 cup pasta and
$\frac{2}{3}$ cup sauce
Exchange List Approximation:
    Starch/Bread 3
    Meat, lean 2

Nutrient Content Per Serving:

CAL: 308	PRO: 20.6 (gm)
FAT: 4.8 (gm)	CHO: 44.1 (gm)
Na: 566.1 (mg)	K: 189.2 (mg)
Fiber: 1.4 (gm)	Chol: 90 (mg)

Ingredients

Six Servings		Two Servings	
12	OUNCES PASTA (VERMICELLI OR LINGUINE)	4	OUNCES
2	QUARTS WATER	3	CUPS
1	TABLESPOON MARGARINE	1	TEASPOON
1½	TEASPOONS CHICKEN BOUILLON GRANULES	½	TEASPOON
1	TABLESPOON MINCED GARLIC CLOVE (ABOUT 3)	1	TEASPOON

SCANT ½ TEASPOON EACH:	⅛	TEASPOON
PAPRIKA AND OREGANO		
⅓ CUP CHOPPED ITALIAN	2	TABLESPOONS
PARSLEY (OR AMERICAN)		
1 BAY LEAF	⅓	
3 CUPS WATER	1	CUP
12 OUNCES COOKED SHRIMP*	4	OUNCES
6 TABLESPOONS GRATED	2	TABLESPOONS
PARMESAN CHEESE		

Method

1. Cook pasta in unsalted water about 12 minutes while preparing sauce. Drain.
2. In a saucepan, combine all ingredients except shrimp and cheese. Bring to a simmer and cook about 5 minutes.
3. Wash shrimp to remove excess salt. Add to simmering sauce, cover, remove from heat, and let stand 5 minutes. Remove bay leaf.
4. Serve ⅔ cup shrimp sauce over 1 cup pasta. Sprinkle with 1 Tablespoon cheese.

*One pound shelled, deviled, raw shrimp may be used; add to sauce and cook 7 minutes.

Pasta with Clam Sauce

Yield: 2 servings
Serving Size: 1¼ cup
Exchange List Approximation:
    Starch/Bread 3
    Meat, lean 1
    Fat 1

Nutrient Content Per Serving:
CAL: 338   PRO: 15.2 (gm)
FAT: 10.2 (gm)   CHO: 45.5 (gm)
Na: 459.3 (mg) K: 167.1 (mg)
Fiber: 2 (gm)   Chol: 27 (mg)

Ingredients

  2 CUPS SPAGHETTI, BROKEN INTO 2-INCH LENGTHS (ABOUT 4 OUNCES)
1½ QUARTS WATER
  1 TABLESPOON VEGETABLE OIL
 ¼ CUP CHOPPED ONION
  2 TEASPOONS MINCED GARLIC CLOVE
 ½ CUP CHOPPED PARSLEY
 ½ TEASPOON OREGANO
1/16 TEASPOON PEPPER
  1 6½-OUNCE CAN MINCED CLAMS
  2 TABLESPOONS WHITE WINE OR WATER
  1 TABLESPOON GRATED PARMESAN CHEESE

Method

1. Cook spaghetti in boiling water about 15 minutes while preparing sauce.
2. Saute onions and garlic in oil about 2 minutes.
3. Add parsley, oregano, pepper, and juice drained from clams. Add wine and simmer about 5 minutes.
4. Add clams and heat about 1 minute.
5. Drain spaghetti. Add to sauce and toss until mixed.
6. Sprinkle each serving with Parmesan cheese before serving.

Note: Recipe may be doubled.

Noodle Supreme Salad

Yield: 6 or 2 servings
Serving Size: 1 cup
Exchange List Approximation:
    Starch/Bread 1½
    Meat, lean 1
    Vegetable 1

Nutrient Content Per Serving:
CAL: 196   PRO: 14.3 (gm)
FAT: 3.4 (gm)   CHO: 26.4 (gm)
Na: 547.3 (mg) K: 279.2 (mg)
Fiber: 2.2 (gm) Chol: 47 (mg)

Ingredients

Six Servings		Two Servings
6	OUNCES NOODLES	2 OUNCES
¾	CUP FROZEN PEAS	¼ CUP
2	QUARTS WATER	3 CUPS
⅔	CUP CREAM OF MUSHROOM SOUP (ABOUT HALF 10½-OUNCE CAN)	3 TABLESPOONS
1	6½-OUNCE CAN TUNA FISH PACKED IN WATER	2 OUNCES
½	CUP SHREDDED RED CABBAGE	2 TABLESPOONS
1	CUP DICED TOMATOES (ABOUT 1 LARGE)	¼ CUP
⅛	TEASPOON SALT	SPRINKLE
	SPRINKLE PEPPER	SPRINKLE

Method

1. Bring water to a boil. Add noodles and peas. Cook uncovered 5 minutes. Drain.
2. Combine noodles, peas, soup, and drained tuna. Mix lightly. Cool.
3. Add red cabbage and tomatoes. Sprinkle with salt and pepper.
4. Serve on lettuce leaf and garnish with chopped green onion.

Note: Some noodles require longer cooking. Check package.

Tuna Cakes

Yield: 3 servings
Serving Size: 2 cakes
Exchange List Approximation:
    Starch/Bread 1
    Meat, lean 2
    Vegetable 1

Nutrient Content Per Serving:
CAL: 205   PRO: 22.7 (gm)
FAT: 5.9 (gm)   CHO: 15.4 (gm)
Na: 916.6 (mg)   K: 388.9 (mg)
Fiber: 3 (gm)   Chol: 130 (mg)

Ingredients

1 CUP SHREDDED ZUCCHINI (ABOUT 4 OUNCES)
2 TABLESPOONS CHOPPED ONION
½ TEASPOON MINCED GARLIC CLOVE
2 TEASPOONS MARGARINE
1 6½-OUNCE CAN TUNA PACKED IN WATER
1 EGG
1½ CUPS WHOLE-WHEAT BREAD CUBES (ABOUT 3 SLICES)
¼ TEASPOON SALT
¼ TEASPOON PEPPER

Method

1. Saute zucchini, onion, and garlic in 1 teaspoon margarine about 5 minutes.
2. Mix with remaining ingredients until blended.
3. Form into 6 patties and brown in margarine in large skillet over medium heat, about 3 minutes per side.
4. Serve with lemon or horseradish dip (see recipe, page 308).

Salmon-Noodle Bake

Yield: 6 or 2 servings
Serving Size: 1 cup
Exchange List Approximation:
    Starch/Bread 2
    Meat, medium-fat 2
    Fat $\frac{1}{2}$

Nutrient Content Per Serving:
CAL: 326   PRO: 22.3 (gm)
FAT: 13.2 (gm)   CHO: 28 (gm)
Na: 403.7 (mg)   K: 484.1 (mg)
Fiber: 1.2 (gm)   Chol: 58 (mg)

Ingredients

Six Servings	*Two Servings*
6 OUNCES NOODLES	2 OUNCES
2 QUARTS WATER	3 CUPS
2 TABLESPOONS MARGARINE	2 TEASPOONS
3 TABLESPOONS FLOUR	1 TABLESPOON
2 CUPS SKIM MILK	⅔ CUP
3 TABLESPOONS CHOPPED ONION	1 TABLESPOON
¼ TEASPOON PEPPER	¹⁄₁₆ TEASPOON
1 15½-OUNCE CAN SALMON	4 OUNCES
2 TABLESPOONS MAYONNAISE	2 TEASPOONS

Method

1. Cook noodles according to package directions and drain.
2. Prepare sauce in small saucepan. Melt margarine, stir in flour, and cook 1 minute. Add milk, stir until blended, bring to a boil, and cook 2 minutes, stirring constantly.
3. Add onion and pepper to sauce.
4. Drain salmon and reserve juice. Remove bones and flake salmon.
5. Add 6 tablespoons juice, mayonnaise, and sauce. Stir. Add noodles and mix.

6. Pour into a lightly greased 2-quart casserole. Bake in 350° F oven for 30 minutes.

Variation: Twelve ounces of chicken or tuna may be used instead of salmon.

Vegetarian Main-Meal Dishes

Vegetable Medley

Yield: 6 or 2 servings

Serving Size: 1 cup

Exchange List Approximation:

    Starch/Bread 2

    Vegetable 1

    Fat 1

Nutrient Content Per Serving:

CAL: 229	PRO: 10
FAT: 7.1 (gm)	CHO: 35.2 (gm)
Na: 164.1 (mg)	K: 414.2 (mg)
Fiber: 6.7 (gm)	Chol: 10 (mg)

Ingredients

Six Servings	*Two Servings*
3 OUNCES SPAGHETTI, BROKEN INTO 1-INCH LENGTHS	1 OUNCE
2 QUARTS WATER	1 QUART
1 TABLESPOON VEGETABLE OIL	1 TEASPOON
3 TABLESPOONS CHOPPED ONION	1 TABLESPOON
1 6-OUNCE PACKAGE FROZEN CHINESE PEA PODS	⅓ PACKAGE
1 CUP FROZEN CORN OR DRAINED WHOLE-KERNEL CANNED CORN	⅓ CUP
2 CUPS GARBANZO BEANS, DRAINED (ABOUT 1 15-OUNCE CAN)	⅔ CUP
2 TABLESPOONS WHITE-WINE VINEGAR	2 TEASPOONS
½ TEASPOON SUGAR	⅛ TEASPOON
½ TEASPOON BASIL	⅛ TEASPOON
½ TEASPOON OREGANO	⅛ TEASPOON
¼ TEASPOON GARLIC POWDER	⅛ TEASPOON
⅛ TEASPOON PEPPER	DASH

1 TABLESPOON CHOPPED
  PIMENTO (OPTIONAL)

1 TEASPOON

2 OUNCES CHEDDAR CHEESE,
  CUT INTO ¼-INCH CUBES
  (ABOUT ½ CUP)

⅔ OUNCE (ABOUT 3
  TABLESPOONS)

Method

1. Add spaghetti to boiling water, stir, and cook about 12 minutes until just tender. Drain and rinse with cold water.
2. In a large skillet, heat oil. Add onions and stir-fry about 1 minute. Add pea pods and stir-fry about 1 minute. Add corn and stir-fry until steaming, about 2 minutes.
3. Place in large mixing bowl. Add remaining ingredients and spaghetti.
4. Toss to mix well. Cover and chill several hours.
5. Place serving on large lettuce leaf.

Variation: If you prefer raw vegetables, combine oil, onions, corn, and pea pods with remaining ingredients. This recipe is delicious both ways.

Ratatouille II*

Yield: 6 servings
Serving Size: $\frac{3}{4}$ cup
Exchange List Approximation:
    Vegetable 2
    Fat 1

Nutrient Content Per Serving:
CAL: 82   PRO: 1.9 (gm)
FAT: 4.9 (gm)   CHO: 9.3 (gm)
Na: 97.6 (mg)   K: 413.9 (mg)
Fiber: 3.9 (gm) Chol: 0

Ingredients

    2 TABLESPOONS OLIVE OIL
    1 CUP SLICED ONION (ABOUT 1 LARGE ONION)
    1 TEASPOON MINCED GARLIC
    3 CUPS DICED EGGPLANT (ABOUT 1 SMALL)
 2½ CUPS SLICED ZUCCHINI (ABOUT 2 SMALL)
    ¾ CUP GREEN PEPPER, CUT INTO STRIPS (ABOUT 1
       MEDIUM)
    2 CUPS TOMATOES, PEELED AND CUBED (ABOUT 2
       MEDIUM)
    1 TEASPOON SWEET BASIL
    ¼ TEASPOON SALT
    ⅛ TEASPOON PEPPER

Method

1. Heat oil in large frying pan. Add onions and garlic; stir-fry
    about 2 minutes.
2. Add eggplant, stir-fry about 2 minutes. Add layer of
    zucchini, green pepper, and tomato.
3. Sprinkle basil, salt, and pepper over tomatoes. Cover and
    simmer 30 minutes over low heat.
4. Uncover, stir gently, and simmer 10 minutes.
5. Serve over brown rice or chill and serve with crackers or as
    a vegetable or relish.

Note 1: 1 16-ounce can of tomato wedges, drained, may be used for fresh tomatoes. Use juice if needed. Ratatouille is delicious cold. Make the whole recipe.

Note 2: This is a complete meal when served with tofu.

*Ratatouille I can be found in Volume I.

Garden Stir-Fry

Yield: 3 servings (2 cups)
Serving Size: $\frac{2}{3}$ cup
Exchange List Approximation:
    Meat, medium-fat 1
    Vegetable 1
    Fat 2

Nutrient Content Per Serving:

CAL: 181	PRO: 6.4 (gm)
FAT: 14.9 (gm)*	CHO: 7.1 (gm)
Na: 81.1 (mg)	K: 356.4 (mg)
Fiber: 2.9 (gm)	Chol: 183 (mg)

Key Source Nutrients:
    Vitamin A: 6270 (IU)
    Ascorbic acid: 64 (mg)

Ingredients

- 2 TABLESPOONS SALAD OIL
- 1 LARGE CLOVE GARLIC, MINCED OR PRESSED
- 1 CUP BROCCOLI FLOWERETS, CUT INTO ½" CHUNKS
- 1 CUP CAULIFLOWER FLOWERETS, CUT INTO ½" CHUNKS
- 3 TABLESPOONS WATER
- ½ CUP CARROTS, CUT INTO ½-INCH SLANTING SLICES
- ¼ CUP RED BELL PEPPER, CUT INTO ¼-INCH STRIPS
  SALT (OPTIONAL)
- ⅛ TEASPOON PEPPER
- 2 TEASPOONS WHOLE CASHEWS
- 2 EGGS
- 1 TABLESPOON SKIM MILK
- 1 TABLESPOON SOY SAUCE (OPTIONAL)

Method

1. Place wok over high heat. When wok is hot, add 1 tablespoon of the oil. When oil is hot, add garlic and stir-fry for 30 seconds. Reduce heat to medium.
2. Add broccoli and cauliflower and stir-fry for 1 minute. Add 2 tablespoons water; cover and cook, stirring frequently for about 3 minutes. Remove from wok and set aside.
3. Add remaining 1 tablespoon oil to wok. When oil is hot, add carrots and red pepper. Stir-fry for 1 minute. Add remaining 1 tablespoon water; cover and cook, stirring frequently, for about 2 minutes or until vegetables are tender-crisp.
4. Return broccoli and cauliflower to wok and stir-fry to heat through (about 1 minute).
5. Combine eggs, milk, salt, and pepper. Beat until foamy and well-blended.
6. Pour egg mixture over vegetables. Cook, stirring from bottom until eggs are done.
7. Serve with garnish of cashews and sprinkle with soy sauce.

Note: This is a complete meal when served with tofu.

*To reduce fat content, cut back on the oil and add some broth for stir-frying.

Vegetable Platter with Peanut Sauce

Yield: 16 party or 8 main-meal
  servings (party = ¾ vegetables
  with ¼ cup sauce; main
  meal = 1½ cups vegetables
  with ½ cup sauce)
Serving Size: 1/16 recipe
Exchange List Approximation:
    Vegetable 2
    Fat 2

Nutrient Content Per Serving:
CAL: 135   PRO: 6.7 (gm)
FAT: 9.2 (gm)   CHO: 9.8 (gm)
Na: 93 (mg)   K: 458.9 (mg)
Fiber: 4.4 (gm)   Chol: 0
Key Source Nutrients:
    Vitamin A: 4692 (IU)
    Ascorbic acid: 49 (mg)

Ingredients

    4 CUPS FRESH BROCCOLI, PEELED AND CUT INTO 3-
       INCH LENGTHS
    2 CUPS FRESH GREEN BEANS, CUT INTO 2-INCH
       LENGTHS
    2 CUPS CARROTS, CUT INTO 2-INCH STRIPS
    4 CUPS CAULIFLOWER, CUT INTO FLOWERETS
    3 CUPS YELLOW SUMMER SQUASH, CUT INTO 2½-
       INCH PIECES
    2 CUPS CUCUMBER, CUT INTO 2½-INCH STICKS
    8 RADISHES, SLICED
    2 TEASPOONS VEGETABLE OIL
   ½ CUP CHOPPED ONION
    2 TEASPOONS MINCED GARLIC CLOVES
 3½ CUPS HOT WATER OR VEGETABLE STOCK
    1 CUP PEANUT BUTTER
    2 TEASPOONS CHOPPED FRESH HOT PEPPER OR 1
       TEASPOON HOT SAUCE

2 TEASPOONS LEMON JUICE
1 TEASPOON GRATED LEMON RIND
1 TEASPOON CHOPPED FRESH GINGER ROOT
1 BAY LEAF

Method

1. Steam the first five vegetables until crisp-tender; drain stock for use in sauce.
2. Arrange vegetables on 2 platters while making sauce.
3. Garnish with cucumber sticks and radishes.
4. Prepare sauce in large skillet. Heat oil, add onions and garlic. Stir-fry about 2 minutes.
5. Add remaining ingredients; stir until blended; simmer for 15 minutes, stirring occasionally. Taste for seasoning; ½ teaspoon salt may be added if diet permits.
6. Pour in 2 bowls and place in center of vegetable platters.
7. For main meal, arrange vegetables in portions on 8 plates with mound of hot rice (⅓ cup cooked rice = 1 Starch/Bread Exchange). Serve ½ cup sauce over vegetables. Extra vegetable servings may be combined with sauce, packaged, and frozen.

Impossible Garden Pie

Yield: 6 servings
Serving Size: $\frac{1}{6}$ recipe
Exchange List Approximation:
    Starch/Bread 1
    Meat, medium-fat 1
    Vegetable 1

Nutrient Content Per Serving:

CAL: 175	PRO: 10.2 (gm)
FAT: 7 (gm)	CHO: 18 (gm)
Na: 390 (mg)	K: 373.7 (mg)
Fiber: 2.8 (gm)	Chol: 144 (mg)

Ingredients

2	CUPS ZUCCHINI, QUARTERED AND SLICED
1½	CUPS DICED TOMATOES
½	CUP CHOPPED ONION
½	CUP GRATED PARMESAN CHEESE
¼	TEASPOON PEPPER
1½	CUPS SKIM MILK
¾	CUP BISCUIT MIX (BISQUICK-TYPE)
3	EGGS

Method

1. Heat oven to 400° F. Lightly grease 7- by 11-inch ovenproof glass or ceramic dish.
2. Place layer of zucchini, tomatoes, and onion in dish.
3. Sprinkle Parmesan cheese and pepper evenly over vegetables.
4. Combine milk, biscuit mix, and eggs. Beat until smooth, about 1 minute, and pour over vegetables.
5. Bake about 30 minutes.
6. Let set 5 minutes before cutting.

Quiche I (Broccoli)

Yield: 6 or 3 servings
Serving Size: $\frac{1}{6}$ recipe
Exchange List Approximation:
  Starch/Bread 1
  Meat, medium-fat 2
  Vegetable 1
  Fat 1

Nutrient Content Per Serving:
CAL: 291   PRO: 18.2 (gm)
FAT: 15.3 (gm) CHO: 20 (gm)
Na: 555.9 (mg) K: 249.4 (mg)
Fiber: 2 (gm)   Chol: 190 (mg)

Ingredients

Six Servings		Three Servings	
1	16-OUNCE CONTAINER LOW-FAT COTTAGE CHEESE	1	8-OUNCE
½	CUP SKIM MILK	¼	CUP
4	EGGS	2	
¼	CUP CHOPPED ONION	2	TABLESPOONS
1	10-OUNCE PACKAGE BROCCOLI, THAWED	5	OUNCES
	SPRINKLE APPLE-PIE SPICE		SPRINKLE
1	9-INCH PIE SHELL OR 6 TART SHELLS	1	SMALL PIE SHELL OR 3 TART SHELLS

Method

1. Place cottage cheese, milk, and eggs in blender. Blend about 30 seconds until mixture is smooth. Stir in onion.
2. Distribute broccoli evenly in pie shell. Pour cottage cheese mixture over it. Sprinkle with apple-pie spice.
3. Bake in 400° F oven for 50 minutes.

Variation: If recipe is made without the crust, nutrient information is as follows:

Exchange List Approximation:
    Meat, lean 2
    Vegetable 1

Nutrient Content Per Serving:
CAL: 141   PRO: 16.4 (gm)
FAT: 5.3 (gm)   CHO: 6.8 (gm)
Na: 373.3 (mg)   K: 234.8 (mg)
Fiber: 1.3 (gm)   Chol: 190

Quiche II (Vegetable)

Yield: 6 servings
Serving Size: $\frac{1}{6}$ recipe
Exchange List Approximation:
    Starch/Bread 1
    Meat, medium-fat 1
    Vegetable 1
    Fat $1\frac{1}{2}$

Nutrient Content Per Serving:
CAL: 243   PRO: 13.5 (gm)
FAT: 13 (gm)   CHO: 18.3 (gm)
Na: 291.6 (mg)   K: 225.1 (mg)
Fiber: 1.4 (gm)   Chol: 158 (mg)

Ingredients

  1 CUP SHREDDED CHEDDAR CHEESE
  ½ CUP CHOPPED ONION
  ½ CUP DICED TOMATOES
  1 CUP TOFU, DICED
  ½ CUP ZUCCHINI, DICED
  3 EGGS
  ¼ TEASPOON SALT
  ½ TEASPOON PEPPER
  1 CUP SKIM MILK
  1 TABLESPOON VEGETABLE OIL
  ¾ CUP ALL-PURPOSE FLOUR
  ½ TEASPOON BAKING POWDER

Method

1. Sprinkle cheese, onion, tomatoes, tofu, and zucchini in 9-inch pie plate that has been sprayed with nonstick vegetable spray.
2. Combine eggs, salt, pepper, milk, and oil in small bowl and mix well.
3. Combine flour and baking powder; add to milk and egg mixture. Beat with an egg beater or small hand mixer until smooth.
4. Pour above mixture evenly over ingredients in pie plates.
5. Bake at 400° F for 30 minutes. Let stand 5 minutes before serving.

Spinach Cheese Bake

Yield: 6 or 3 servings
Serving Size: $\frac{3}{4}$ cup
Exchange List Approximation:
    Meat, medium-fat 1
    Vegetable 2
    Fat $\frac{1}{2}$

Nutrient Content Per Serving:

CAL: 152	PRO: 13.9 (gm)
FAT: 6.7 (gm)	CHO: 9.2 (gm)
Na: 407.8 (mg)	K: 209.3 (mg)
Fiber: 1 (gm)	Chol: 150 (mg)

Ingredients

Six Servings		*Three Servings*	
1	10-OUNCE PACKAGE FRESH SPINACH	½	PACKAGE
3	EGGS	1	
¼	CUP ALL-PURPOSE FLOUR	2	TABLESPOONS
1	TEASPOON MINCED GARLIC	½	TEASPOON
1½	CUPS SMALL-CURD LOW-FAT COTTAGE CHEESE (1½% TO 2% MILKFAT)	¾	CUP

½ CUP CRUMBLED FETA CHEESE ¼ CUP
(OR SHREDDED JALAPENO
CHEESE)
1 TEASPOON MARGARINE ½ TEASPOON

Method

1. Cut spinach into small pieces. If garden spinach is used, wash and drain dry.
2. Beat eggs, add cheese, mix well; add flour and mix.
3. Add garlic and spinach; mix well.
4. Pour into lightly greased 2- or 2½-quart casserole. Cover loosely with foil and bake in 350° F oven for 35 to 40 minutes.

Vegetarian Lasagna

Yield: 6 servings
Serving Size: 4½-by-4-inch piece
Exchange List Approximation:
    Starch/Bread 2
    Meat, medium-fat 2½
    Vegetable 1
    Fat ½

Nutrient Content Per Serving:
CAL: 392   PRO: 24.7 (gm)
FAT: 16.8 (gm)   CHO: 36.8 (gm)
Na: 887.9 (mg)   K: 775.9 (mg)
Fiber: 4.1 (gm)   Chol: 129 (mg)
Key Source Nutrients:
    Vitamin A: 11847 (IU)

Ingredients

6 LASAGNA NOODLES (ABOUT 4 OUNCES)
2 QUARTS WATER
2 TABLESPOONS VEGETABLE OIL
1 CUP CHOPPED ONION
1½ CUPS ⅛-INCH BIAS-CUT CARROTS (ABOUT 4 MEDIUM)

2 TEASPOONS MINCED GARLIC (ABOUT 1 CLOVE)
1¾ CUPS SPAGHETTI SAUCE (ABOUT 1 15-OUNCE JAR)
½ CUP WATER
1 TEASPOON BASIL
½ TEASPOON OREGANO
2 EGGS
2 CUPS LOW-FAT (½% MILKFAT) COTTAGE CHEESE
 (ABOUT ONE 16-OUNCE CARTON)
4 TABLESPOONS PARMESAN CHEESE
1 10-OUNCE PACKAGE FROZEN CHOPPED SPINACH,
 THAWED AND DRAINED
1 CUP SLICED MUSHROOMS
1 CUP QUARTERED AND SLICED ZUCCHINI
1 CUP SHREDDED PART-SKIM MOZZARELLA CHEESE
 (ABOUT 4 OUNCES)
¼ CUP SLICED BLACK OLIVES (OPTIONAL)

Method

1. Cook lasagna noodles in boiling water about 12 minutes.
   Drain, rinse, and cover with cold water.
2. Heat vegetable oil in sauce pan. Add onions, carrots, and
   garlic. Saute until carrots are tender, about 10 minutes.
3. Add spaghetti sauce, water, and spices. Bring to a simmer.
4. Beat eggs and blend in cottage cheese, Parmesan cheese,
   and vegetables.
5. Spread a thin layer of sauce over bottom of 9- by 13-inch
   baking pan. Cover with layer of noodles, spoon half of
   cheese mixture over noodles. Cover with half of sauce.
   Repeat.
6. Cover with foil and bake at 350° F oven for 35 minutes.
7. Remove foil. Arrange olive slices over top and sprinkle
   with cheese. Bake uncovered about 15 minutes, or until
   center is bubbly.
8. Let cool about 10 minutes to set layers. Cut 2 by 3 into 4½-
   by 4-inch pieces.

Lasagne with Tofu

Yield: 6 or 2 servings
Serving Size: $\frac{1}{6}$ recipe
Exchange List Approximation:
    Starch/Bread 1$\frac{1}{2}$
    Meat, lean 2
    Vegetable 1
    Fat 1$\frac{1}{2}$

Nutrient Content Per Serving:
CAL: 317   PRO: 19.4 (gm)
FAT: 15.8 (gm)   CHO: 26.6 (gm)
Na: 730.9 (mg)   K: 623.2 (mg)
Fiber: 2.1 (gm)   Chol: 43 (mg)

Ingredients

Six Servings		Two Servings	
6	LASAGNA NOODLES	2	
2	QUARTS WATER	1	QUART
1	TEASPOON VEGETABLE OIL	1	TEASPOON
1	8-OUNCE PACKAGE MUSHROOMS, SLICED	1⅓	CUPS
¾	CUP CHOPPED ONION	¼	CUP
2	TABLESPOONS VEGETABLE OIL	2	TEASPOONS
1	8-OUNCE CAN TOMATO SAUCE	1	8-OUNCE CAN
1	6-OUNCE CAN TOMATO PASTE		OMIT
1	CUP WATER	⅓	CUP
¾	TEASPOON GARLIC POWDER	¼	TEASPOON
¾	TEASPOON BASIL	¼	TEASPOON
¾	TEASPOON OREGANO	¼	TEASPOON
¼	TEASPOON PEPPER	¹⁄₁₆	TEASPOON
1	BAY LEAF	⅓	LEAF
1	TABLESPOON PARSLEY, FRESH, CHOPPED	1	TEASPOON
8	OUNCES TOFU (SOY CHEESE), DRAINED, CRUMBLED	⅔	CUP

Six Servings	*Two Servings*
6 TABLESPOONS PARMESAN CHEESE, GRATED	2 TABLESPOONS
2 CUPS SHREDDED, LOW-MOISTURE, PART-SKIM MOZZARELLA CHEESE	⅔ CUP

Method

1. Cook lasagna noodles in boiling water containing oil about 12 minutes. Drain, rinse, and cover with cold water.
2. Prepare sauce. Saute onions and mushrooms in oil about 2 minutes. Add tomato sauce and paste. Rinse cans with water and add. Add spices and parsley. Simmer over low heat 30 minues.
3. Mash tofu and combine with ¾ ounce of Parmesan cheese (reserve rest for topping).
4. Spread thin layer of sauce over bottom of baking dish. Cover with layer of cooked noodles, spoon half the tofu mixture over noodles, sprinkle with half of cheese. Cover with 1 cup sauce; repeat. Top with layer of noodles and remaining sauce. Omit top layer in small casserole. Sprinkle with Parmesan cheese.
5. Bake in 350° F oven for 30 minutes or until sauce is bubbling.
6. Let cool about 10 minutes to set layers. Cut lasagna 2 by 3 into 3½- by 3¾-inch pieces.
7. Serve with green salad.

Note: Lasagna may be prepared in 9- by 13-inch pan with 2 layers of noodles.

Pasta Primavera

Yield: 6 or 2 servings
Serving Size: 1½ cup
Exchange List Approximation:
    Starch/Bread 2
    Vegetable 1
    Fat 1

Nutrient Content Per Serving:
CAL: 222   PRO: 8 (gm)
FAT: 5.5 (gm)   CHO: 35.8 (gm)
Na: 295 (mg)   K: 337.5 (mg)
Fiber: 4.2 (gm) Chol: 2 (mg)

Ingredients

Six Servings		Two Servings	
8	OUNCES THIN SPAGHETTI, 2-INCH LENGTHS	2⅔	OUNCE (ABOUT 1 CUP)
6	CUPS WATER	2	CUPS
2	TABLESPOONS MARGARINE	2	TEASPOONS
1	CUP ONION, CUT INTO THIN WEDGES	⅓	CUP
2	CUPS BROCCOLI, CUT INTO FLOWERETS AND PEELED STALKS, SLICED	⅔	CUP
1	CUP CARROTS, THINLY SLICED	⅓	CUP
1	CUP ZUCCHINI, THINLY SLICED	⅓	CUP
1	CUP YELLOW SUMMER SQUASH, DICED	⅓	CUP
¾	CUP WATER	¼	CUP
¾	TEASPOON CHICKEN BOUILLON GRANULES	¼	TEASPOON
6	TABLESPOONS PARSLEY, CHOPPED	2	TABLESPOONS
3	TABLESPOONS LEMON JUICE	1	TABLESPOON
1½	TEASPOONS BASIL	½	TEASPOON
¼	TEASPOON PEPPER	¹⁄₁₆	TEASPOON
3	TABLESPOONS GRATED PARMESAN CHEESE	1	TABLESPOON

Method

1. Bring water to a boil, add spaghetti, stir, and boil gently
   until tender, about 10 minutes. Meanwhile prepare
   vegetables.
2. Heat margarine in a large skillet. Add onion.
   Stir-fry about 1 minute.
3. Add vegetables. Stir. Add water and chicken bouillon. Stir.
   Cover and simmer about 6 minutes.
4. Add parsley, lemon juice, basil, and pepper. Stir and cook
   1 minute.
5. Drain spaghetti and add to vegetables.
6. Sprinkle with parmesan cheese, toss to mix well.

Manicotti Crepes

Yield: 6 servings

Serving Size: 2 crepes

Exchange List Approximation:

    Starch/Bread 2

    Meat, medium-fat 3

    Vegetable 1

    Fat 1

Nutrient Content Per Serving:

CAL: 448	PRO: 28.7 (gm)
FAT: 22.6 (gm)	CHO: 32.2 (gm)
Na: 986.9 (mg)	K: 528.1 (mg)
Fiber: 0.6 (gm)	Chol: 278 (mg)

Ingredients

Crepes
- ¾ CUP WATER
- ¾ CUP FLOUR
- ⅛ TEASPOON SALT
- 2 EGGS

Filling
- 2 CUPS LOW-FAT RICOTTA CHEESE
- 1¾ CUPS LOW-FAT MOZZARELLA CHEESE, GRATED
- ¼ TEASPOON SALT
- 3 EGGS*
- 2 CUPS SPAGHETTI SAUCE (CANNED) OR TOMATO SAUCE (CANNED)
- ½ CUP PARMESAN CHEESE

Method

1. Combine first four ingredients and beat or mix in blender until smooth.
2. Heat 5-inch skillet or crepe pan until moderately hot. Film with shortening or margarine. Ladle a few tablespoons of batter into the skillet; tilt quickly to cover pan with thinnest possible layer.

3. Cook until bottom is lightly browned and edges lift easily. Turn and cook for a few minutes on other side. Remove crepe to plate. Film pan with shortening or margarine prior to adding batter. Make 12 crepes.
4. To make filling, beat eggs* and combine with ricotta and mozzarella cheese and salt.
5. Spoon filling down center of each crepe and roll it.
6. Cover bottom of 9- by 13-inch baking dish with about half of the spaghetti sauce. Arrange filled crepes in dish. Cover top with remaining spaghetti sauce. Sprinkle Parmesan cheese on top.
7. Bake at 350° F for 30 minutes.

*To reduce cholesterol, use egg whites as egg replacement.
Nutrient information is as follows:

Exchange List Approximation:
    Starch/Bread 2
    Meat, medium-fat 3
    Vegetable 1
    Fat ½

Nutrient Content Per Serving:

CAL: 425	PRO: 29 (gm)
FAT: 19.8 (gm)	CHO: 32.3 (gm)
Na: 1002.4 (mg)	K: 540.6 (mg)
Fiber: 0.6 (gm)	Chol: 141 (mg)

Pasta with Hot and Cold Sesame-Peanut Sauce

Yield: 6 or 2 servings
Serving Size: $\frac{1}{4}$ cup sauce and
$\frac{3}{4}$ cup spaghetti
Exchange List Approximation:
 Starch/Bread 2$\frac{1}{2}$
 Meat, medium-fat 1$\frac{1}{2}$
 Fat 3

Nutrient Content Per Serving:
CAL: 441   PRO: 18.1 (gm)
FAT: 25.5 (gm) CHO: 39.1 (gm)
Na: 208.2 (mg) K: 346.2 (mg)
Fiber: 4.5 (gm) Chol: 0

Ingredients

Six Servings	Two Servings
1 CUP CRUNCHY PEANUT BUTTER	⅓ CUP
1 TABLESPOON SESAME SEED OIL	1 TEASPOON
1 TABLESPOON SESAME SEEDS	1 TEASPOON
2 TABLESPOONS CIDER VINEGAR	2 TEASPOONS
3 TABLESPOONS CHOPPED GREEN ONION	1 TABLESPOON
⅜ TEASPOON CAYENNE PEPPER	⅛ TEASPOON
½ CUP COLD WATER	3 TABLESPOONS
9 OUNCES SPAGHETTI, BROKEN	3 OUNCES
3 QUARTS WATER	1 QUART

Method

1. Blend peanut butter, oil, seeds, vinegar, onions, and pepper together.
2. Beat in cold water gradually, using fork, until sauce has consistency of thick mayonnaise.
3. Cook spaghetti in boiling water about 15 minutes.

4. Serve ¼ cup sauce on ¾ cup spaghetti.
5. Sauce may be served hot or cold on seafoods and vegetables.

*This is a high-fat dish and should be limited to occasional use.

Tofu Balls

Yield: 6 or 2 servings
Serving Size: 4 balls
Exchange List Approximation:
    Starch/Bread 1
    Meat, medium-fat 1
    Fat 1

Nutrient Content Per Serving:
CAL: 200   PRO: 11 (gm)
FAT: 12.4 (gm)   CHO: 12.5 (gm)
Na: 277.7 (mg)   K: 113.2 (mg)
Fiber: 0.7 (gm)   Chol: 137 (mg)

Ingredients

Six Servings	Two Servings
1 POUND TOFU	5½ OUNCES
BOILING WATER	
1 TEASPOON MARGARINE	½ TEASPOON
3 TABLESPOONS GRATED ONION	1 TABLESPOON
⅓ CUP FINELY SHREDDED CARROTS	1½ TABLESPOONS
3 EGGS, BEATEN	1
¾ CUP DRY, SEASONED BREAD CRUMBS	¼ CUP
⅜ TEASPOON SALT	⅛ TEASPOON
¼ TEASPOON PEPPER	¹⁄₁₆ TEASPOON
1 TABLESPOON CHOPPED PARSLEY	1 TEASPOON

Method

1. Cut tofu in large cubes. Place in sieve and rinse with boiling water. Drain well. Mash fine or process in a food processor.
2. Braise onion and carrot in margarine for about 2 minutes.
3. Mix with tofu and remaining ingredients. Place in refrigerator for at least 2 hours for flavors to blend.
4. Form in walnut-size balls about 1 ounce each. Deep-fat fry in 350° F fat until brown, about 4 minutes.
5. Serve with tartar sauce.

Variation: Five slices of whole-wheat bread can be dried and ground for bread crumbs. Add ⅛ teaspoon each of thyme and garlic powder.

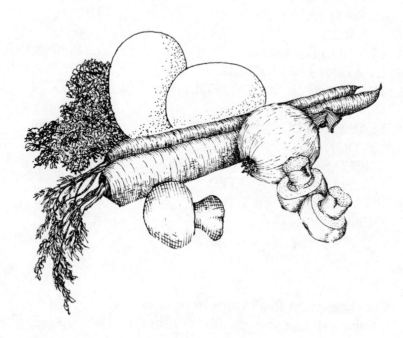

Cheese-and-Sprouts Pita Sandwich

Yield: 6 or 1 serving
Serving Size: 1 sandwich
Exchange List Approximation:
  Starch/Bread 2
  Meat, lean 1
  Vegetable 2
  Fat $1\frac{1}{2}$

Nutrient Content Per Serving:
CAL: 328   PRO: 17 (gm)
FAT: 12.4 (gm)   CHO: 38.2 (gm)
Na: 846 (mg)   K: 500.8 (mg)
Fiber: 6.9 (gm) Chol: 23 (mg)
Key Source Nutrients:
     Vitamin A: 5413 (IU)

Ingredients

Six Servings	One Serving
6 SLICES LOW-FAT CHEESE (ABOUT 6 OUNCES)	1 SLICE
1 CUP SHREDDED CARROTS	3 TABLESPOONS
12 SLICED RADISHES	2
2 CUPS ALFALFA OR BEAN SPROUTS	⅓ CUP
¼ CUP MAYONNAISE	2 TABLESPOONS
¾ CUP LOW-FAT YOGURT	2 TABLESPOONS
1 TEASPOON DIJON OR REGULAR MUSTARD	1/16 TEASPOON
½ TEASPOON CURRY POWDER (OPTIONAL)	⅛ TEASPOON
12 SLICED SALAD ONIONS, THIN-SLICED AND SEPARATED	2 SLICES
6 PITA BREAD (ABOUT 12 OUNCES)	1 (ABOUT 2 OUNCES)

Method

1. Cut cheese into small strips or squares.
2. Combine cheese with carrots, radishes, and sprouts.

3. Mix dressing of mayonnaise, yogurt, mustard, and curry powder.
4. Cut each pita in half to make sandwich pockets. Spread inside with dressing.
5. Fill with cheese-vegetable filling and lay onion slices on top.

Chick Peas and Green Pepper

Yield: 4 servings (3 cups)
Serving Size: $\frac{3}{4}$ cup
Exchange List Approximation:
    Starch/Bread 1
    Vegetable 2
    Fat 1

Nutrient Content Per Serving:
CAL: 179   PRO: 7.9 (gm)
FAT: 5.6 (gm)   CHO: 26 (gm)
Na: 15.2 (mg)   K: 451.2 (mg)
Fiber: 6.6 (gm)   Chol: 0

Ingredients

1 TABLESPOON VEGETABLE OIL
½ CUP CHOPPED ONION (ABOUT 1 SMALL)
½ TEASPOON CHOPPED FRESH GINGER
1 TEASPOON CUMIN SEEDS
1 TEASPOON CORIANDER, GROUND
¼ TEASPOON PEPPER
⅛ TEASPOON SALT (OPTIONAL)
1 CUP CHOPPED GREEN PEPPER
1 15-OUNCE CAN CHICK PEAS (GARBANZO), DRAINED
1 CUP CHOPPED FRESH TOMATOES (ABOUT 2)
2 TABLESPOONS LEMON JUICE

Method

1. Saute onions and ginger in oil.
2. Add seasonings and stir for 1 minute.
3. Add chopped green pepper and chick peas. Cook about 5 minutes.
4. Add tomatoes and lemon juice. Cook about 2 minutes, stirring frequently.
5. Serve hot on flour tortilla (1 Starch/Bread Exchange) or in pita bread (1 Starch/Bread Exchange) with shredded fresh lettuce.

Cheese Enchiladas

Yield: 6 servings
Serving Size: 2 enchiladas
Exchange List Approximation:
    Starch/Bread 2
    Meat, medium-fat 2
    Fat $1\frac{1}{2}$

Nutrient Content Per Serving:
CAL: 371   PRO: 19 (gm)
FAT: 20.8 (gm)   CHO: 29.6 (gm)
Na: 668.2 (mg)   K: 409.4 (mg)
Fiber: 3.8 (gm)   Chol: 60 (mg)

Ingredients

Sauce
- 1 8-OUNCE CAN TOMATO SAUCE, SPANISH STYLE, NO SUGAR ADDED
- 1 4-OUNCE CAN CHOPPED GREEN CHILIES
- 1 CUP CHOPPED, PEELED TOMATO (ONE 7-OUNCE CAN OR ONE CUP FRESH TOMATO)
- 1 TABLESPOON DEHYDRATED MINCED ONION
- 1 TEASPOON MINCED GARLIC CLOVE (ABOUT 1)
- 1 TEASPOON GROUND CUMIN
- ½ TEASPOON OREGANO
- PINCH SUGAR SUBSTITUTE

Enchiladas
- 12 CORN TORTILLAS (ABOUT 10-OUNCE PACKAGE)
- 4 CUPS SHREDDED CHEDDAR CHEESE (ABOUT 12 OUNCES)
- 1½ CUPS CHOPPED ONIONS

Method

1. Combine ingredients for sauce in small saucepan. Bring to boil, cover, and simmer 15 minutes. For smooth sauce, whip in blender.

2. Prepare enchiladas one at a time. Heat tortilla in skillet sprayed with vegetable pan spray.
3. Pour part of sauce in a plate. Place tortilla on sauce and flip to other side.
4. Place 2 Tablespoons cheese and 1 Tablespoon onion on one edge of tortilla and roll up. Place flap-side down in a 9- by 13-inch baking pan spread with a thin layer of sauce.
5. Continue until all tortillas are filled and rolled.
6. Spread remaining sauce over tortillas. Be sure all edges are moistened.
7. Sprinkle remaining cheese evenly over rolls.
8. Bake, uncovered, in 350° F oven until cheese melts and starts to bubble, 15 to 20 minutes.
9. Sprinkle the rest of chopped onions over enchiladas. Serve with garnish of shredded lettuce.

Variation: Sauce used on top of enchiladas may be thinned with ½ cup sour cream, if diet permits. Nutrient information is as follows:

Exchange List Approximation:	Nutrient Content Per Serving:	
Starch/Bread 2	CAL: 406	PRO: 19.5 (gm)
Meat, medium-fat 2	FAT: 24.1 (gm)	CHO: 30.3 (gm)
Fat 2½	Na: 676.2 (mg)	K: 432.1 (mg)
	Fiber: 3.8 (gm)	Chol: 67 (mg)

High-Fiber Main Meals and Side Dishes

To turn many of the lower-calorie dishes into satisfying main meals, simply double the serving size. Just be sure to double the nutrient and exchange information as well.

Soybean Vegetable Casserole

Yield: 6 servings (4 cups)
Serving Size: $\frac{2}{3}$ cup
Exchange List Approximation:
    Starch/Bread 1
    Meat, medium-fat 1
    Vegetable $\frac{1}{2}$

Nutrient Content Per Serving:
CAL: 170   PRO: 12.9 (gm)
FAT: 7.3 (gm)   CHO: 16.5 (gm)
Na: 143.2 (mg)   K: 830 (mg)
Fiber: 6.3 (gm)   Chol: 0

Ingredients

1 CUP DRY SOYBEANS
4 CUPS WATER
1 TEASPOON VEGETABLE OIL
¼ CUP CHOPPED ONION
1 CUP DICED CELERY
¼ CUP CHOPPED GREEN PEPPER
1 16-OUNCE CAN TOMATOES

Method

1. Wash soybeans and soak overnight. Bring to a boil, cover, and simmer until tender, about 2 hours. Add water as needed. Drain and reserve liquid.
2. Saute onion, celery, and peppers in a little oil, about 5 minutes.
3. Add beans, 1 cup bean liquid, and canned tomatoes. Stir to mix and break up tomatoes.
4. Pour into 1½-quart casserole and bake in 350° F oven for 1 hour.

Beans and Sausage Casserole

Yield: 6 or 2 servings
Serving Size: $\frac{1}{6}$ recipe
Exchange List Approximation:
    Starch/Bread $2\frac{1}{2}$
    Meat, lean 1
    Fat 1

Nutrient Content Per Serving:
CAL: 302   PRO: 17.8 (gm)
FAT: 9.4 (gm)   CHO: 38 (gm)
Na: 827.2 (mg)   K: 940.1 (mg)
Fiber: 9.5 (gm)   Chol: 23 (mg)

Ingredients

Six Servings		*Two Servings*	
1½	CUPS DRAINED, COOKED PINTO BEANS	½	CUP
1½	CUPS DRAINED, COOKED LIMA BEANS	½	CUP
1½	CUPS DRAINED, COOKED NAVY OR GREAT NORTHERN BEANS	½	CUP
¾	POUND BULK SAUSAGE (BEEF OR TURKEY MAY BE SUBSTITUTED)	¼	POUND
½	CUP BEEF BROTH (CANNED OR BOUILLON)	¼	CUP
1	8-OUNCE CAN TOMATO SAUCE	⅓	CUP
1	TEASPOON GROUND CUMIN (OPTIONAL)	½	TEASPOON
3	TABLESPOONS RED WINE OR COOKING SHERRY (OPTIONAL)	1	TABLESPOON
½	TEASPOON SALT		DASH
½	TEASPOON PEPPER		DASH
1	TEASPOON MINCED FRESH GARLIC	½	TEASPOON
1	CUP FINELY CHOPPED ONION	⅓	CUP

Method

1. Combine beans in a 2½-quart casserole and set aside.
2. Shape sausage into about 24 small balls and brown in a skillet. Drain fat.
3. While the sausage browns, add beef broth, tomato sauce, cumin, wine, salt, and pepper to the beans.
4. Add browned sausage balls to beans.
5. Saute garlic and onions in sausage drippings. Add to ingredients in the casserole and stir.
6. Cover casserole and bake in 325° F oven for 1 hour.

Red Beans and Brown Rice

Yield: 6 or 2 servings
Serving Size: $\frac{2}{3}$ cup
Exchange List Approximation:
    Starch/Bread $1\frac{1}{2}$

Nutrient Content Per Serving:
CAL: 118   PRO: 5.3 (gm)
FAT: 2.6 (gm)   CHO: 18.7 (gm)
Na: 38.3 (mg)   K: 292.9 (mg)
Fiber: 4.8 (gm)   Chol: 3 (mg)

Ingredients

Six Servings	*Two Servings*
½ CUP BROWN RICE	3 TABLESPOONS
1½ CUPS WATER	⅔ CUP
1 SLICE BACON, DICED	⅓ SLICE
1 CUP CHOPPED ONIONS	⅓ CUP
½ CUP DICED CELERY	3 TABLESPOONS
½ CUP DICED GREEN PEPPER	2 TABLESPOONS
1 15-OUNCE CAN RED KIDNEY BEANS (NEW ORLEANS STYLE), OR PINTO BEANS, OR BLACK-EYE PEAS	⅓ CAN
¼-½ TEASPOON HOT SAUCE	2 DROPS
⅛ TEASPOON PEPPER	DASH

Method

1. Bring rice and water to a boil, cover tightly, reduce heat, and cook until water is absorbed, about 1 hour.
2. In large skillet, cook diced bacon, onion, celery, and green peppers slowly over low heat, about 10 minutes.
3. Add undrained canned beans or peas and seasonings. Bring to a boil, cover, and simmer 5 minutes.

4. Add cooked rice and mix lightly. Add a little water, if mixture is too dry.

Variation: Season pinto beans or black-eye peas and rice with 2 teaspoons Picante sauce. Refer to page 321.

Green-Pea Curry with Rice

Yield: 6 or 2 servings
Serving Size: $\frac{3}{4}$ cup
Exchange List Approximation:
    Starch/Bread $3\frac{1}{2}$

Nutrient Content Per Serving:

CAL: 286	PRO: 12.2 (gm)
FAT: 1.9 (gm)	CHO: 55.8 (gm)
Na: 17.4 (mg)	K: 503 (mg)
Fiber: 8.1 (gm)	Chol: 0

Ingredients

Six Servings		*Two Servings*	
1½	CUPS GREEN SPLIT PEAS (ABOUT 12 OUNCES)	½	CUP
3	CUPS WATER	1	CUP
1½	TEASPOONS VEGETABLE OIL	½	TEASPOON
1	CUP CHOPPED ONION	⅓	CUP
1	TABLESPOON CURRY POWDER	1	TEASPOON
¾	TEASPOON GROUND GINGER	¼	TEASPOON
3	TABLESPOONS RAISINS	1	TABLESPOON
¼	TEASPOON SALT (OPTIONAL)		PINCH
1	CUP WATER	½	CUP
3	CUPS COOKED RICE	1	CUP

Method

1. Wash peas, add water, bring to boil. Cover, remove from heat and let stand 1 hour.
2. Heat oil in sauce pan. Add onions and saute until limp. Add spices and raisins. Stir to blend.
3. Add green peas and water as needed to cover. Stir. Bring to a boil. Cover and simmer 1 hour.
4. Serve over ½ cup cooked rice.
5. Garnish with any of the following as diet permits: chutney (on average, 1 tablespoon = ½ Fruit Exchange), finely diced hard-cooked eggs, shredded fresh coconut, chopped olives, chopped nuts. (For remaining exchanges, see Appendix I.)

Variation: One or combination of the following may be used.

Six Servings	*Two Servings*
¾ TEASPOON CINNAMON	¼ TEASPOON
¾ TEASPOON CUMIN	¼ TEASPOON
1 TABLESPOON TOASTED SESAME SEEDS	1 TEASPOON

Marinated Beans and Corn

Yield: 6 main meal or 12
  salad servings
Serving Size: 1 cup
Exchange List Approximation:
    Starch/Bread 4
    Meat, lean 1
    Vegetable ½

Nutrient Content Per Serving:
CAL: 390   PRO: 19.4 (gm)
FAT: 7.8 (gm)   CHO: 64.8 (gm)
Na: 130.5 (mg)   K: 826 (mg)
Fiber: 14.5 (gm)   Chol: 8 (mg)

Serving Size: ½ cup
Exchange List Approximation:
    Starch/Bread 1½
    Vegetable 1½

Nutrient Content Per Serving:
CAL: 156   PRO: 8.2 (gm)
FAT: 2.3 (gm)   CHO: 27.9 (gm)
Na: 20.1 (mg)   K: 471.9 (mg)
Fiber: 7.3 (gm)   Chol: 0

Ingredients

- 1 15-OUNCE CAN RED KIDNEY BEANS, DRAINED
- 1 15-OUNCE CAN PINK BEANS, DRAINED; RESERVE ¼ CUP SAUCE
- 1 15-OUNCE CAN GARBANZO BEANS, DRAINED
- 1 10-OUNCE PACKAGE FROZEN WHOLE-KERNEL CORN
- 1 CUP SLICED CELERY (ABOUT 2 LARGE STALKS)
- ⅓ CUP WINE VINEGAR
- 1 TABLESPOON VEGETABLE OIL
- 1 TABLESPOON CHOPPED FRESH PARSLEY
- 2 TEASPOONS MINCED GARLIC CLOVES (ABOUT 2)
- ¼ TEASPOON CHILI POWDER

Method

1. Drain beans and save ¼ cup sauce.
2. Cook corn according to packaged directions. Drain.
3. Combine beans and corn in large mixing bowl.
4. Combine all other ingredients and bean sauce. Pour over bean-and-corn mixture. Toss lightly to mix.
5. Cover and refrigerate overnight.
6. For salad, serve ½-cup portions on lettuce. Garnish with onion slice and tomato wedge.
7. For main meal, serve 1-cup portion on heated flour tortilla. Sprinkle with shredded cheese, chopped onion, and shredded lettuce.

New Mexico Green-Chili Zucchini

Yield: 6 servings
Serving Size: ⅙ recipe
Exchange List Approximation:
    Meat, lean 2
    Vegetable 2

Nutrient Content Per Serving:

CAL: 159	PRO: 19.5 (gm)
FAT: 4.9 (gm)	CHO: 10.2 (gm)
Na: 181.7 (mg)	K: 712.4 (mg)
Fiber: 4.6 (gm)	Chol: 45 (mg)

Ingredients

- 1 POUND LEAN BEEF, CUBED
- 1 CUP CHOPPED ONION
- 1 7-OUNCE CAN GREEN CHILIES
- 4 MEDIUM ZUCCHINI, QUARTERED AND SLICED
- 2 TEASPOONS MINCED GARLIC CLOVE (ABOUT 2)
- 1 16-OUNCE CAN TOMATOES
- ½ CUP WATER
- ½ CUP SHREDDED MONTEREY JACK CHEESE (ABOUT 2 OUNCES)

Method

1. Use large electric skillet or other large skillet. Spray with vegetable pan spray.
2. Saute beef until lightly browned; add onions and garlic. Cook about 5 minutes. Add chilies.
3. Add zucchini, toss, and cook until just tender.
4. Chop tomatoes and add. Heat to a simmer. Mixture should be soupy. Add water if needed.
5. Serve in soup bowls with 1½ Tablespoons cheese on top.
6. Serving suggestion: Serve with Southern Cornbread (see recipe on page 125).

Western-Style Beans

Yield: 9 servings (6 cups)
Serving Size: $\frac{2}{3}$ cup
Exchange List Approximation:
    Starch/Bread 2
    Vegetable 1

Nutrient Content Per Serving:
CAL: 190   PRO: 11.8 (gm)
FAT: 1.5 (gm)   CHO: 33.8 (gm)
Na: 160.9 (mg)   K: 682.7 (mg)
Fiber: 9.1 (gm)   Chol: 0

Ingredients

1 POUND DRIED BEANS (PINTO, RED, PINK, OR NAVY)
1 TEASPOON VEGETABLE OIL
1 CUP CHOPPED ONION
2 TEASPOONS CHILI POWDER
½ TEASPOON SALT
5 CUPS WATER
1 CUP GREEN CHILIES SAUCE (SEE RECIPE PAGE 322)

Method

1. Wash and pick over beans. Cover with water and soak overnight. Drain.
2. Heat oil in cooking pot. Add onion and saute until tender, about 5 minutes.
3. Add chili powder, salt, beans, and water.
4. Bring to a boil. Reduce heat, cover, and cook until beans are tender, 1 to 1½ hours.
5. Add Green Chilies Sauce, stir, and simmer uncovered 30 minutes longer. Beans should not be too soupy.

Note: Extra servings can be packaged and frozen.

Simmered Black-Eye Peas

Yield: 10 servings (6⅔ cups)
Serving Size: ⅔ cup
Exchange List Approximation:
    Starch/Bread 1
    Meat, medium-fat ½

Nutrient Content Per Serving:
CAL: 117   PRO: 6.5 (gm)
FAT: 2.7 (gm)   CHO: 17.8 (gm)
Na: 156.8 (mg)   K: 306 (mg)
Fiber: 12.2 (gm)   Chol: 2 (mg)

Ingredients

  1 POUND DRIED BLACK-EYE PEAS
  2 QUARTS COLD WATER
  1 SLICE SALT PORK OR BACON (ABOUT 1 OUNCE)
 ½ TEASPOON SALT
  1 LARGE ONION, SLICED

Method

1. Wash peas and place in large pot. Add water, pork, and salt.
2. Bring to a boil, cover, and cook slowly for 2 hours. Water should cook down so peas are just covered. Add more water if needed.
3. Serve peas with juice and slices of onion. Pepper sauce may be served with peas. Cornbread is a good accompaniment. Peas may be used in salads or to make dip.

Rum-Baked Black Beans

Yield: 6 servings (4 cups)
Serving Size: ⅔ cup
Exchange List Approximation:
    Starch/Bread 2

Nutrient Content Per Serving:
CAL: 172   PRO: 9.2 (gm)
FAT: 2.6 (gm)   CHO: 29.4 (gm)
Na: 142.8 (mg)   K: 564.8 (mg)
Fiber: 11.3 (gm)   Chol: 0

Ingredients

½ POUND DRIED BLACK BEANS
3 CUPS WATER
¾ CUP CHOPPED ONION
1 CUP FINELY CHOPPED CELERY
⅔ CUP CHOPPED CARROTS
1 TEASPOON MINCED GARLIC CLOVE (ABOUT 1)
1 SMALL BAY LEAF
2 TABLESPOONS CHOPPED FRESH PARSLEY
¾ TEASPOON THYME LEAVES
¼ TEASPOON SALT
¼ TEASPOON PEPPER
1 TABLESPOON MARGARINE
2 TABLESPOONS DARK RUM
1 ORANGE, CUT INTO 6 WEDGES

Method

1. Wash beans. Cover with 4 cups water. Soak overnight. Drain.
2. Place beans, 3 cups water, and ingredients except margarine, rum, and orange in cooking pot. Bring to a boil, cover, and simmer until beans are mealy, about 1 hour.
3. Transfer beans and juice to bean pot. Stir in margarine and rum. Cover and bake in 325° F oven 2 hours.

4. Remove cover and bake 30 minutes longer.
5. Serve with wedge of orange and rice.

Cheese-y Lima Beans

Yield: 3 servings
Serving Size: 1 cup
Exchange List Approximation:
    Starch/Bread $1\frac{1}{2}$
    Meat, lean $2\frac{1}{2}$

Nutrient Content Per Serving:
CAL: 255   PRO: 23.2 (gm)
FAT: 7.8 (gm)   CHO: 23 (gm)
Na: 440.1 (mg)   K: 533.8 (mg)
Fiber: 5.6 (gm)   Chol: 112 (mg)

Ingredients

- 1 10-OUNCE PACKAGE FROZEN LIMA BEANS OR 1 16-OUNCE CAN LIMA BEANS, DRAINED
- 1 EGG
- ¾ CUP POT OR FARMER'S CHEESE OR DRAINED LOW-FAT COTTAGE CHEESE
- ¾ CUP SHREDDED SKIMMED MILK MOZZARELLA CHEESE OR MUENSTER OR SWISS (DIVIDED)
- 2 TABLESPOONS CHOPPED ONIONS
- 2 TABLESPOONS CHOPPED PARSLEY
-    SPRINKLE PEPPER

Method

1. Cook frozen lima beans according to package directions. Drain. If canned beans are used, drain.
2. Beat egg, add pot cheese, and ½ cup shredded cheese.
3. Combine with beans. Add onions and parsley. Pour in lightly greased 1-quart casserole. Sprinkle with pepper.
4. Bake in 350° F oven for 20 minutes. Sprinkle with ¼ cup shredded cheese. Place under broiler to brown.

Spanish Beans

Yield: 6 servings
Serving Size: 1 cup
Exchange List Approximation:
  Starch/Bread 3
  Meat, medium-fat $1\frac{1}{2}$
  Vegetable 1

Nutrient Content Per Serving:
CAL: 381   PRO: 21.5 (gm)
FAT: 11.5 (gm) CHO: 49.8 (gm)
Na: 261.1 (mg) K: 1248.1 (mg)
Fiber: 11.4 (gm) Chol: 24 (mg)

Ingredients

1	POUND DRY BABY LIMA BEANS
⅛	TEASPOON CRUSHED RED PEPPER
6	CUPS WATER
1	TEASPOON CHILI POWDER
¼	TEASPOON GARLIC POWDER
1	TEASPOON OLIVE OIL
1	CUP DICED ONIONS
1	CUP DICED CELERY
¾	CUP RED SWEET PEPPER
⅔	CUP SLICED, PITTED RIPE OLIVES
1⅓	CUPS SHREDDED MONTEREY JACK CHEESE

Method

1. Add beans and red pepper to water. Bring to a boil, cover, remove from heat and let stand 1 hour. Bring to boil and simmer 1 hour.
2. Drain beans and save ⅔-cup liquid.
3. Sprinkle beans with chili powder and garlic powder. Add reserved liquid.
4. Saute onions, celery, and red pepper in hot olive oil until onions start to brown, about 3 minutes.

5. Add beans, olives, and one half the cheese to vegetables. Mix well.
6. Pour into a 3-quart casserole. Sprinkle remaining cheese over beans.
7. Bake in 375° F oven until bubbly, about 30 minutes.
8. Serving suggestion: Serve with brown rice (1/3 cup cooked rice = 1 Starch/Bread Exchange) and a tossed salad.

Variation: If red sweet pepper is not available, use green pepper and 2 Tablespoons minced pimento.

Note: Extra beans may be packaged in 1 cup servings and frozen for later use.

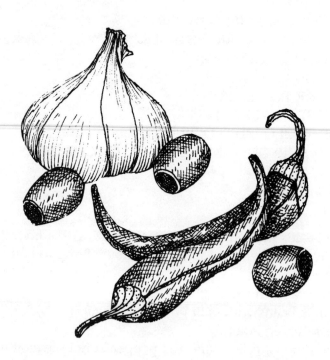

Mexi-Greek Beans

Yield: 6 or 3 servings
Serving Size: 1 cup
Exchange List Approximation:
    Starch/Bread 1
    Meat, medium-fat 2
    Vegetable 2
    Fat 2

Nutrient Content Per Serving:
CAL: 376   PRO: 24.3 (gm)
FAT: 22.3 (gm)   CHO: 24.6 (gm)
Na: 473.5 (mg)   K: 1040.1 (mg)
Fiber: 10.1 (gm)   Chol: 25 (mg)

Ingredients

Six Servings		*Three Servings*
2	CUPS DRY SOYBEANS (ABOUT 12 OUNCES)	1 CUP (ABOUT 6 OUNCES)
8	CUPS WATER	4 CUPS
4	TEASPOONS VEGETABLE OIL	2 TEASPOONS
1	CUP CHOPPED ONION	½ CUP
½	CUP CHOPPED RED OR GREEN PEPPER	¼ CUP
1	TEASPOON MINCED GARLIC CLOVE	½ TEASPOON
1	4-OUNCE CAN CHOPPED GREEN CHILIES	2 OUNCES
½	TEASPOON CUMIN	¼ TEASPOON
¾	CUP CRUMBLED FETA CHEESE (ABOUT 6 OUNCES)	6 TABLESPOONS
1	CUP GREEK OLIVES OR PITTED RIPE OLIVES	½ CUP

Method

1. Wash soybeans and soak overnight. Bring to a boil, cover, and simmer until tender and almost dry, about 2 hours. Add water as needed.

2. Saute onion and peppers in vegetable oil until limp, about 5 minutes.
3. Add garlic, chilies, and cumin. Mix. Add to beans and heat.
4. Serve 1 cup beans in soup bowl. Sprinkle 1 ounce (2 Tablespoons) feta cheese over serving. Garnish with 5 olives.

Dried Beans in Seasoned Tomato Sauce

Yield: 12 servings
Serving Size: 1 cup
Exchange List Approximation:
    Starch/Bread 2
    Vegetable 1

Nutrient Content Per Serving:
CAL: 182   PRO: 10.1 (gm)
FAT: 3.1 (gm)   CHO: 30.3 (gm)
Na: 112.2 (mg)   K: 579.9 (mg)
Fiber: 8.8 (gm)   Chol: 0

Ingredients

1 POUND DRIED MARROW OR PINTO BEANS
6 CUPS WATER
1 TABLESPOON OLIVE OIL
1 TABLESPOON VEGETABLE OIL
1 TABLESPOON MINCED FRESH GARLIC (ABOUT 3 CLOVES)
1½ POUNDS ONIONS, THICKLY SLICED (ABOUT 4 MEDIUM)
¼ TEASPOON MARJORAM OR OREGANO
¼ TEASPOON THYME
1 BAY LEAF, CRUMBLED

2 TABLESPOONS CHOPPED FRESH PARSLEY
1 28-OUNCE CAN TOMATOES OR 4 LARGE FRESH
  TOMATOES
2 TEASPOONS SALT (OPTIONAL)*

Method

1. Wash beans and soak overnight. Bring to a boil, cover, and
   simmer 1 hour. Drain thoroughly and wash with cold
   water.
2. Heat oils in a heavy iron pot. Add garlic, onions, and
   herbs. Saute until onions are soft but not brown, about 5
   minutes.
3. Stir in tomatoes and simmer until well blended.
4. Add drained beans, salt,* and just enough water to cover.
   Bring to a boil, reduce heat, and simmer uncovered 1 hour.

*Optional salt is not accounted for in nutrient analysis.

Refried Beans

Yield: 6 servings (3 cups)
Serving Size: $\frac{1}{2}$ cup
Exchange List Approximation:
    Starch/Bread $1\frac{1}{2}$

Nutrient Content Per Serving:
CAL: 124   PRO: 7.8 (gm)
FAT: 0.5 (gm)   CHO: 23 (gm)
Na: 135.5 (mg) K: 380 (mg)
Fiber: 6.8 (gm) Chol: 0

Ingredients

- 1 CUP DRIED PINTO BEANS (ABOUT 6 OUNCES)
- 4 CUPS WATER
- 1 CUP CHOPPED ONIONS
- 1 TEASPOON MINCED GARLIC CLOVE
- ¼ TEASPOON SALT
- ½ TEASPOON GROUND CUMIN OR CUMINO
- ¼ CUP TACO SAUCE (MILD, MEDIUM, OR HOT TO TASTE)

Method

1. Soak beans overnight in water to cover.
2. Drain beans and place in heavy saucepan with 4 cups water, onions, garlic, salt and cumin. Bring to a boil, then simmer 1½ to 2 hours until beans are soft enough to mash.
3. Mash or blend beans in blender to desired consistency.
4. Mix in taco sauce and reheat in lightly greased skillet.
5. Serve as vegetable or in burrito (1 6-inch flour tortilla = 1 Starch/Bread).

Lentil Bake

Yield: 4 servings
Serving Size: $1\frac{1}{2}$ cup
Exchange List Approximation:
    Starch/Bread 3
    Meat, lean $\frac{1}{2}$
    Vegetable 1

Nutrient Content Per Serving:
CAL: 290   PRO: 16.2 (gm)
FAT: 4.1 (gm)   CHO: 48.8 (gm)
Na: 302.1 (mg)   K: 739.9 (mg)
Fiber: 10.4 (gm)   Chol: 5 (mg)

Ingredients

  1 CUP LENTILS
  3 CUPS WATER
 ⅓ CUP RICE
  1 CUP WATER
  4 SLICES BACON, CHOPPED
  2 TABLESPOONS CHOPPED GREEN PEPPER
  1 CUP CHOPPED ONION (ABOUT 1 MEDIUM)
  1 16-OUNCE CAN TOMATOES

Method

1. Wash and sort lentils. Add water, bring to a boil, and simmer until tender, about 30 minutes.
2. Bring water to a boil, add rice; cover and cook over low heat about 15 minutes.
3. In a Dutch oven, fry chopped bacon until nearly done. Add green pepper and onion. Continue to cook until onions start to brown. Drain fat from mixture.
4. Add tomatoes to onions and stir until tomatoes are broken up. Add rice and lentils. Mix gently.
5. Bake covered in 350° F oven 45 minutes.

Foul Madamis (Beans)

Yield: 4 servings
Serving Size: $\frac{1}{3}$ cup
Exchange List Approximation:
    Starch/Bread 1
    Vegetable $\frac{1}{2}$
    Fat $1\frac{1}{2}$

Nutrient Content Per Serving:
CAL: 162   PRO: 5.5 (gm)
FAT: 8.9 (gm)   CHO: 16.7 (gm)
Na: 68.7 (mg)   K: 346.3 (mg)
Fiber: 4.8 (gm)   Chol: 0

Ingredients

- 1 CUP COOKED FRIZOL, SMALL FAVA BEANS, OR PINTO BEANS
- 1 TABLESPOON TAHINI (SESAME SEED PASTE)
- ¾ CUP DICED TOMATO (ABOUT 1 MEDIUM)
- ¾ CUP CHOPPED ONION (ABOUT 1 MEDIUM)
- 2 TABLESPOONS OLIVE OIL (DIVIDED)
- 1 TABLESPOON TOMATO PASTE
- 1 TEASPOON CUMIN
- PINCH EACH: GINGER, PEPPER, AND SALT

Method

1. Blend beans in a food processor until big chunks disappear (alternately, mash beans). Add tahini and mix well. Set aside.
2. Saute tomato and onion in 1 Tablespoon olive oil about 5 minutes. Stir in tomato paste and spices.
3. Combine with bean mixture.
4. Spread serving on plate and sprinkle with 1 Tablespoon olive oil. Serve with pita bread.

Cowpoke Beans

Yield: 8 cups
Serving Size: 1 cup
Exchange List Approximation:
    Starch/Bread $2\frac{1}{2}$
    Vegetable 1

Nutrient Content Per Serving:

CAL: 226	PRO: 14.4 (gm)
FAT: 0.9 (gm)	CHO: 41.9 (gm)
Na: 365.9 (mg)	K: 742.7 (mg)
Fiber: 12.2 (gm)	Chol: 0

Ingredients

1 POUND DRIED PINTO BEANS
2 QUARTS WATER
1 TEASPOON SALT
½ TEASPOON CRUSHED RED PEPPER
1 CUP CHOPPED ONION
1 TEASPOON MINCED GARLIC
1 16-OUNCE CAN TOMATOES
2 TEASPOONS GROUND CUMIN
1 TABLESPOON CHILI POWDER

Method

1. Presoak beans in water overnight or use quick-cook method on the package.
2. After soaking, add red pepper and salt, and bring beans to a boil; reduce heat, cover, and simmer gently for 2+ hours or until beans are tender.
3. Add remaining ingredients during last hour of cooking and continue to simmer.
4. Serve. Freeze leftover portions and reheat for another meal.

Lentils Italiano

Yield: 8 servings
Serving Size: 1 cup
Exchange List Approximation:
    Starch/Bread 2
    Meat, medium-fat $\frac{1}{2}$

Nutrient Content Per Serving:
CAL: 197   PRO: 10.8 (gm)
FAT: 4.7 (gm)   CHO: 30.3 (gm)
Na: 1258.5 (mg)   K: 652 (mg)
Fiber: 7.1 (gm)   Chol: 1 (mg)

Ingredients

- 1 MEDIUM ONION, CHOPPED
- 1 CLOVE GARLIC, MINCED
- 2 TABLESPOONS OIL
- 1½ CUPS DRIED LENTILS, WASHED
- ½ TEASPOON CRUSHED RED PEPPER
- 1 TEASPOON SALT
- ½ TEASPOON PEPPER
- 4 CUPS WATER
- 2 CUBES BEEF BOUILLON OR 4 TEASPOONS INSTANT BEEF BOUILLON OR 4 CUPS FAT-SKIMMED BEEF BROTH (IF USED, OMIT 4 CUPS WATER)
- ¼ TEASPOON DRIED CRUSHED BASIL
- ¼ TEASPOON DRIED CRUSHED OREGANO
- 1 16-OUNCE CAN TOMATOES
- 1 6-OUNCE CAN TOMATO PASTE
- 1 TABLESPOON VINEGAR
- 1 CUP WATER

Method

1. In heavy 4-quart pot, saute onion and garlic in oil for 5 minutes.
2. Add lentils, red pepper, salt, pepper, bouillon, and water. Cover and simmer for 30 minutes.

3. Add remaining ingredients and simmer uncovered for about 1 hour. Stir occasionally.

4. Serve as a bowl of beans or as a sauce over noodles or rice (½ cup cooked noodles or ⅓ cup rice = 1 Starch/Bread Exchange).

Note: Package extra servings and freeze for later use.

Soups

Russian Cabbage Borscht

Yield: 16 servings
Serving Size: $\frac{1}{4}$ cup meat and
   1 cup vegetable
Exchange List Approximation:
   Starch/Bread $\frac{1}{2}$
   Meat, lean $1\frac{1}{2}$
   Vegetable 1

Nutrient Content Per Serving:
CAL: 151   PRO: 13 (gm)
FAT: 5.7 (gm) CHO: 13.3 (gm)
Na: 458 (mg)   K: 604.6 (mg)
Fiber: 2.4 (gm) Chol: 36 (mg)
Key Source Nutrients:
   Vitamin A: 3958 (IU)
   Ascorbic acid: 46 (mg)

Ingredients

2¾ POUND CHUCK ROAST, BONE IN
1 TEASPOON SALT
¼ TEASPOON PEPPER
2 CUPS CHOPPED ONION
1 2-POUND HEAD OF CABBAGE, SHREDDED
1 28-OUNCE CAN TOMATO PUREE
1 28-OUNCE CAN TOMATOES
1 CUP DICED GREEN PEPPER
1½ CUPS SLICED CARROTS
1 TEASPOON SUGAR
1 CUP PLAIN LOW-FAT YOGURT

Method

1. Trim fat from meat.
2. Place meat in 6-quart pot. Add salt, pepper, and onions.
3. Add water to cover meat; bring to a boil, reduce heat, cover, and simmer 1 hour.
4. Add vegetables in order listed, and sugar.
5. Cover and cook at a simmer for 2½ hours.
6. Cool and refrigerate overnight.
7. To serve, remove meat, slice or cut in 1½-ounce servings (2 slices, about ¼ cup).

8. Heat vegetables and serve 1 cup over meat.
9. Top with 1 tablespoon yogurt.
10. Serve with black bread (1 slice of bread = 1 Starch/Bread Exchange).

Turkey (or Chicken) Gumbo Soup

Yield: 8 servings

Serving Size: 1 cup

Exchange List Approximation:

    Starch/Bread 1

    Meat, lean $\frac{1}{2}$

Nutrient Content Per Serving:

CAL: 107   PRO: 7.7 (gm)

FAT: 2.8 (gm)   CHO: 13.2 (gm)

Na: 406.3 (mg)   K: 318.5 (mg)

Fiber: 2 (gm)   Chol: 14 (mg)

Ingredients

    ROAST TURKEY CARCASS OR MEAT AND BONES FROM CHICKEN

    WATER

1 TEASPOON SALT

1 TABLESPOON MARGARINE

1 CUP SLICED OKRA, FRESH OR FROZEN

1 CUP SLICED CELERY

½ CUP CHOPPED ONION

¼ CUP DICED GREEN PEPPER

1 TEASPOON MINCED GARLIC CLOVE

2 TABLEPOONS FLOUR

1 16-OUNCE CAN TOMATOES

1½ QUARTS TURKEY BROTH

¼ CUP UNCOOKED RICE

2 TABLESPOONS CHOPPED PARSLEY

¼ TEASPOON EACH: CUMIN, PEPPER, TABASCO SAUCE, THYME
1 CUP CHOPPED, COOKED TURKEY

Method

1. Place turkey (or chicken) carcass in large pot, add any uncooked parts (neck, back, wings). Cover with water. Add salt. Simmer about 2 hours.
2. Pour broth into container and chill. Skim off fat. Remove meat from bones and reserve.
3. Saute okra in margarine until it starts to brown, about 5 minutes.
4. Add celery, onion, green pepper, and garlic. Saute for about 2 minutes while stirring.
5. Sprinkle with flour. Stir until blended and starting to brown.
6. Add tomatoes. Stir, break into pieces, and cook until thickened.
7. Add broth, rice, and seasonings.
8. Simmer 30 minutes. Add meat and heat 5 minutes. Serve.

Valley Forge Pepperpot Soup

Yield: 8 servings (2 quarts)
Serving Size: 1 cup
Exchange List Approximation:
    Starch/Bread $\frac{1}{2}$
    Vegetable 1
    Fat 1

Nutrient Content Per Serving:

CAL: 113	PRO: 3.6 (gm)
FAT: 6.7 (gm)	CHO: 10 (gm)
Na: 668.1 (mg)	K: 247.9 (mg)
Fiber: 1.1 (gm)	Chol: 2 (mg)

Ingredients

1¼ CUPS DICED POTATOES
 ¼ CUP FINELY CHOPPED ONION
 ½ CUP JULIENNED GREEN PEPPER
 ½ CUP THINLY SLICED CELERY
 4 TABLESPOONS MARGARINE
1½ QUARTS CHICKEN BROTH, CANNED
    (ABOUT 1 46-FLUID-OUNCE CAN)
 ¼ CUP ALL-PURPOSE FLOUR
 ½ CUP WHOLE MILK
 1 TEASPOON DICED PIMENTO

Method

1. In a soup pot, cook potatoes in 1 quart of the broth until half done. Reserve 2 cups broth for step 3.
2. Add onion, green pepper, and celery. Simmer for 15 minutes.
3. In another pan melt margarine; stir in flour. Add the reserved 2 cups of broth while stirring constantly. Simmer 5 minutes. Stir in milk.
4. Add thickened broth to the cooking vegetables. Add pimento.
5. Simmer 3 to 5 minutes, stirring frequently until smooth and slightly thickened consistency is achieved.

Mulligatawny Soup

Yield: 8 or 2 servings
Serving Size: 1 cup
Exchange List Approximation:
    Meat, lean 1
    Vegetable 2

Nutrient Content Per Serving:
CAL: 109   PRO: 7.4 (gm)
FAT: 4.2 (gm)   CHO: 10.9 (gm)
Na: 424.1 (mg) K: 268.3 (mg)
Fiber: 1.6 (gm)   Chol: 24 (mg)

Ingredients

Eight Servings		*Two Servings*	
4	CHICKEN DRUMSTICKS, FAT REMOVED	1	
1½	QUARTS WATER	2	CUPS
1	TEASPOON SALT	¼	TEASPOON
¼	TEASPOON PEPPER	¹⁄₁₆	TEASPOON
2	TABLESPOONS MARGARINE	1½	TEASPOONS
¼	CUP CHOPPED ONION	1	TABLESPOON
¼	CUP CARROTS, THINLY SLICED	1	TABLESPOON
¼	CUP CELERY, THINLY SLICED	1	TABLESPOON
3	TABLESPOONS FLOUR	2	TEASPOONS
1	TEASPOON CURRY POWDER	¼	TEASPOON
1	16-OUNCE CAN TOMATOES, DICED, WITH JUICE	½	CUP
1	CUP PEELED, DICED APPLE	¼	CUP
1	TABLESPOON PARSLEY, FRESH, CHOPPED	1	TEASPOON

Method

1. Cook chicken legs in seasoned water in large pot about 45 minutes while preparing vegetables.
2. Heat margarine in saucepan. Add vegetables and cook about 5 minutes. Do not burn.

3. Stir flour and curry powder and cook about 2 minutes. Set aside.
4. Remove chicken from broth. Cool slightly, skin, bone, and cut up (yields 1 cup chicken).
5. Add chicken, vegetables, and tomatoes to broth. Bring to a boil while stirring. Cover and simmer 20 minutes.
6. Add apples and parsley, stir, and simmer uncovered for 10 minutes.

Variation: 1 cup of cup-up chicken and 5½ cups of stock may be used. Omit salt.

Fresh Vegetable Chowder

Yield: 8 servings
Serving Size: 1 cup
Exchange List Approximation:
    Starch/Bread 1
    Meat, medium-fat $\frac{1}{2}$
    Vegetable 1
    Fat $\frac{1}{2}$

Nutrient Content Per Serving:
CAL: 160   PRO: 9.1 (gm)
FAT: 6.5 (gm)   CHO: 18.2 (gm)
Na: 798.6 (mg)*   K: 511.3 (mg)
Fiber: 4 (gm)   Chol: 16 (mg)

Ingredients

  1 POUND ZUCCHINI
  1 TABLESPOON MARGARINE
 ½ CUP CHOPPED ONION
  2 TABLESPOONS CHOPPED PARSLEY
 ½ TEASPOON BASIL LEAVES
  3 TABLESPOONS ALL-PURPOSE FLOUR
2½ CUPS WATER
  2 TEASPOONS CHICKEN BOUILLON GRANULES
  1 TEASPOON LEMON JUICE
 ½ TEASPOON PEPPER
  1 CUP FROZEN WHOLE-KERNEL CORN
  1 16-OUNCE CAN TOMATOES
  1 13-OUNCE CAN EVAPORATED SKIM MILK
  1 CUP AMERICAN CHEESE, CUBED (ABOUT 4 OUNCES)

Method

1. Cut zucchini lengthwise in half and slice into ¼-inch pieces.
2. Heat margarine in 3- to 6-quart saucepan. Add zucchini, onion, parsley, and basil. Cook for about 6 minutes, stirring occasionally.

3. Add flour and stir until mixed.
4. Add water, bouillon, lemon juice, and pepper. Stir while heating to a boil.
5. Add corn, bring to a boil, stirring to prevent scorching.
6. Drain tomatoes. Reserve juice for another use. Dice tomatoes and add to chowder.
7. Add milk and heat to just boiling.
8. Add cheese. Stir until melted. Do not boil.

*To reduce sodium content, use salt-free bouillon or substitute an herb blend from Chapter 15 for the bouillon.

Black Bean Soup

Yield: 8 cups (8 servings)
Serving Size: 1 cup
Exchange List Approximation:
    Starch/Bread $2\frac{1}{2}$
    Meat, lean 1

Nutrient Content Per Serving:
CAL: 241   PRO: 13.3 (gm)
FAT: 4.4 (gm)   CHO: 38.8 (gm)
Na: 815.5 (mg)* K: 682.9 (mg)
Fiber: 15.7 (gm) Chol: 0

Ingredients

1 POUND DRIED BLACK BEANS
2 QUARTS WATER
3 TEASPOONS SALT
2 TABLESPOONS OLIVE OIL
2 CUPS CHOPPED ONIONS
1 CUP CHOPPED GREEN PEPPER (OPTIONAL)
2 TEASPOONS MINCED GARLIC
1 TEASPOON GROUND CUMIN
1 TEASPOON OREGANO
¼ TEASPOON DRY MUSTARD
1 TABLESPOON LEMON JUICE

Method

1. Presoak beans in water overnight or use quick-cook method on package.
2. After soaking beans, add 2 teaspoons salt and bring to a boil; cover and simmer on low heat for 2 hours.
3. Heat oil, add onions, and saute about 5 minutes. Add green pepper and sauté until onions are tender.
4. Stir in remaining ingredients. Add about ¾ cup hot bean liquid, cover, and simmer 10 minutes.

5. Add onion seasoning mixture to beans and continue to cook 1 hour, stirring occasionally.
6. Serve over cooked brown rice (½ cup cooked rice = 1 Bread Exchange) and top with chopped green onions. Freeze leftovers and reheat for another meal.

*To reduce sodium content, cut back on, or eliminate, the salt.

Fish Chowder with Black Olives

Yield: 8 servings (8 cups)
Serving Size: 1 cup
Exchange List Approximation:
    Starch/Bread 1
    Meat, lean 1

Nutrient Content Per Serving:
CAL: 137   PRO: 12.6 (gm)
FAT: 2.8 (gm)   CHO: 15.9 (gm)
Na: 335.7 (mg)   K: 504.7 (mg)
Fiber: 2.5 (gm)   Chol: 16 (mg)

Ingredients

3 CUPS DICED POTATOES
½ TEASPOON SALT
¼ TEASPOON PEPPER
3½ CUPS WATER
1 TABLESPOON MARGARINE
1 CUP CHOPPED ONION
2 TEASPOONS MINCED GARLIC CLOVE (ABOUT 2)
1 16-OUNCE CAN TOMATOES
¼ CUP CHOPPED PARSLEY
1 TEASPOON THYME
1 BAY LEAF

¾ POUND COD OR HADDOCK, CUT INTO 1-INCH
   CUBES
¼ CUP QUARTERED, PITTED BLACK OLIVES
½ TEASPOON WORCESTERSHIRE SAUCE (OPTIONAL)

Method

1. Place potatoes in large pot (3-quart). Add salt, pepper, and water. Bring to a boil, cover, and cook about 20 minutes.
2. Saute onions in margarine in saucepan, about 5 minutes. Add garlic and cook 1 minute.
3. Add tomatoes, parsley, thyme, and bay leaf. Mash tomatoes while cooking over moderate heat, about 15 minutes.
4. Add tomato mixture, fish, and olives to potatoes. Cook over low heat 6 to 8 minutes. Add more water, if needed to make 8 cups.
5. Garnish with parsley or capers.

Indiana Senate Bean Soup

Yield: 8 servings

Serving Size: 1 cup

Exchange List Approximation:

    Starch/Bread $2\frac{1}{2}$

    Meat, lean $1\frac{1}{2}$

Nutrient Content Per Serving:

CAL: 278   PRO: 20.1 (gm)

FAT: 6.7 (gm)   CHO: 35.4 (gm)

Na: 478 (mg)   K: 819.3 (mg)

Fiber: 9.6 (gm)   Chol: 20 (mg)

Ingredients

  1 POUND GREAT NORTHERN BEANS, DRIED

  3 QUARTS WATER

  ¼ CUP DICED SALT PORK (ABOUT 1½ OUNCES)

  ½ TEASPOON BLACK PEPPER

  ½ TEASPOON WORCESTERSHIRE SAUCE

1¾ CUPS DICED LEAN HAM (ABOUT 8 OUNCES)

  1 CUP THINLY SLICED CELERY

  ¼ CUP CHOPPED ONION

Method

1. Wash beans thoroughly in cold water. Remove any discolored beans or trash.
2. Place beans in 4- to 6-quart pot. Add water. Let set overnight or bring the beans to a boil, cover, turn off heat, and let stand 1 hour.
3. Add diced salt pork, pepper, and Worcestershire sauce. Bring to a boil and simmer covered for 1 hour.
4. Add ham, celery, and onion. Cover and simmer 1½ to 2 hours longer, until beans are tender and liquid is thickened. Stir occasionally. Add water if needed. Adjust yield to 2 quarts.
5. Garnish with chopped onion.

Cream of Tomato Soup

Yield: 6 servings
Serving Size: $\frac{2}{3}$ cup
Exchange List Approximation:
    Starch/Bread 1
    Fat 1

Nutrient Content Per Serving:
CAL: 122   PRO: 6 (gm)
FAT: 4.3 (gm)   CHO: 15.7 (gm)
Na: 487.8 (mg)   K: 476.5 (mg)
Fiber: 1.1 (gm)   Chol: 2 (mg)

Ingredients

3 CUPS COOKED TOMATOES (ABOUT 1 28-OUNCE CAN)
1 TABLESPOON MINCED ONION
½ TEASPOON SALT
¼ TEASPOON PEPPER
  DASH CAYENNE OR TABASCO SAUCE
2 TEASPOONS SUGAR
2 TABLESPOONS MARGARINE
2 TABLESPOONS FLOUR
1 13-OUNCE CAN EVAPORATED SKIM MILK

Method

1. Cook tomatoes, onions, salt, pepper, cayenne, and sugar together for 15 minutes. Strain into large liquid measuring cup or bowl.
2. Melt margarine in a 2-quart saucepan. Blend in flour. Cook until bubbly. While stirring, gradually add milk and cook until thickened.
3. Add tomato mixture, stirring constantly. Heat just to a simmer. Do not boil.

Variation: 4 cups of chopped fresh tomatoes may be used for canned tomatoes.

Note: Less than ½ teaspoon of sugar per serving (5 calories).

Zucchini Soup

Yield: 8 or 4 servings
Serving Size: 1 cup
Exchange List Approximation:
    Starch/Bread 1
    Vegetable 1

Nutrient Content Per Serving:
CAL: 106   PRO: 4.8 (gm)
FAT: 2.6 (gm)   CHO: 16.9 (gm)
Na: 397.5 (mg)   K: 376.1 (mg)
Fiber: 4.6 (gm)   Chol: 1 (mg)

Ingredients

Eight Servings		*Four Servings*
1	TABLESPOON OLIVE OIL	1½ TEASPOONS
1	CUP CHOPPED ONION	½ CUP
1	TEASPOON MINCED GARLIC CLOVE	½ TEASPOON
½	CUP EACH: DICED CARROTS, CELERY, POTATOES	¼ CUP
2	BOUILLON CUBES	1
1	TEASPOON OREGANO	½ TEASPOON
½	TEASPOON BASIL	¼ TEASPOON
⅛	TEASPOON PEPPER	⅟₁₆ TEASPOON
6	CUPS WATER	3 CUPS
1	CUP RED OR PINTO BEANS, DRAINED (ABOUT ⅔ 15-OUNCE CAN)	½ CUP
4	CUPS ZUCCHINI, QUARTERED AND SLICED, ⅜ INCH (ABOUT 1 POUND)	2 CUPS
½	CUP ELBOW MACARONI (ABOUT 2 OUNCES)	¼ CUP
2	TABLESPOONS GRATED PARMESAN CHEESE	1 TABLESPOON

Method

1. Saute onion and garlic in olive oil in 3- to 4-quart saucepan until lightly browned, about 5 minutes.
2. Add carrots, celery, potatoes, and seasonings. Stir. Add water. Cover and simmer about 15 minutes.
3. Add beans and zucchini. Bring to a boil. Add macaroni. Stir. Cover and simmer 15 minutes.
4. Sprinkle each serving with ¾ teaspoon Parmesan cheese.

Salads and
Side Dishes

Sprouts

Yield: 6 servings
Serving Size: $\frac{1}{3}$ cup
Exchange List Approximation:
    Free food

Nutrient Content Per Serving:
CAL: 3   PRO: 0.4 (gm)
FAT: 0.1 (gm)   CHO: 0.4 (gm)
Na: 0.7 (mg)   K: 8.6 (mg)
Fiber: 0.3 (gm)   Chol: 0

Ingredients

1 TABLESPOON ALFALFA SEEDS
or
2 TABLESPOONS DRIED BEANS (LENTILS, MUNG, SOY, OR BLACK)

Method

1. Use clean wide-mouth, quart, clear-glass jar with mesh or cheese-cloth cover.
2. Place seeds or beans in jar, cover with water, and soak overnight at room temperature.
3. Pour off water, rinse seeds thoroughly, and drain well. Place jar on side away from light at room temperature.
4. Repeat process every morning. Seeds will start sprouting after 2 days, beans after 3 days.
5. Rinsing will remove hulls and prevent souring. In hot, humid climates, the sprouts should be rinsed twice a day.
6. Allow about 6 to 7 days for sprouts' growth. Use in salad or stir-fry recipes.

Note: Sprouts tend to grow best in darkness; however, place alfalfa, mustard, radish, cabbage, and clover in indirect light to develop chlorophyll the last 2 days of growth.

Sprouts Salad

Yield: 6 or 2 servings
Serving Size: 1 cup
Exchange List Approximation:
    Vegetable 1
    Fat 2

Nutrient Content Per Serving:
CAL: 124*   PRO: 3.1 (gm)
FAT: 11.3 (gm)* CHO: 3.8 (gm)
Na: 61 (mg)   K: 180.1 (mg)
Fiber: 1.1 (gm)   Chol: 46 (mg)

Ingredients

Six Servings		*Two Servings*	
4	TABLESPOONS SUNFLOWER SEEDS	4	TEASPOONS
2	CUPS ALFALFA SPROUTS	⅔	CUP
or			
1½	CUPS BEAN SPROUTS	½	CUP
½	CUP SLICED RADISHES	3	TABLESPOONS
¾	CUP CUCUMBER, QUARTERED AND SLICED	¼	CUP
¼	CUP SLICED GREEN ONIONS	2	TABLESPOONS
4	CUPS BITE-SIZED PIECES SALAD GREENS	1¼	CUPS
3	TABLESPOONS SALAD OIL	1	TABLESPOON
2	TABLESPOONS VINEGAR	2	TEASPOONS
⅛	TEASPOON SALT		PINCH
⅛	TEASPOON GARLIC POWDER		PINCH
⅛	TEASPOON BASIL		PINCH
¹⁄₁₆	TEASPOON BLACK PEPPER		SPRINKLE
1	SLICED HARD-COOKED EGG	⅓	

Method

1. Place sunflower seeds in dry skillet. Toast by stirring over medium heat for about 3 minutes (optional).

2. Combine sunflower seeds, sprouts, radishes, cucumbers, and onions in large salad bowl. Add cold, dry salad greens and toss. Cover and chill.
3. Prepare dressing by mixing salad oil, vinegar, salt, garlic powder, basil, and pepper.
4. When ready to serve, pour over salad and toss. Garnish with slices of hard-cooked egg.

*To reduce fat and calories, cut back on the sunflower seeds.

Summer Night Salad

Yield: 6 servings
Serving Size: 1 cup
Exchange List Approximation:
  Meat, medium-fat 1
  Vegetable 2
  Fat 3

Nutrient Content Per Serving:
CAL: 262*   PRO: 10.6 (gm)
FAT: 21.5 (gm)* CHO: 9.3 (gm)
Na: 642.2 (mg)   K: 448 (mg)
Fiber: 3 (gm)   Chol: 165 (mg)

Ingredients

    1 CUP FRESH BROCCOLI CUT INTO FLOWERETS
    1 CUP FRESH CAULIFLOWER CUT INTO FLOWERETS
    1 CUP FRESH YELLOW SQUASH IN STRIPS
    1 CUP ZUCCHINI IN STRIPS
    3 HARD-COOKED EGGS, DICED
    ½ CUP CHOPPED PECANS
    ½ CUP CHOPPED COOKED HAM
    ½ CUP CHOPPED CHEDDAR CHEESE
    ¼ CUP MAYONNAISE
    ¼ CUP CREAM, LIGHT
    1 TABLESPOON VINEGAR
    1 TEASPOON SALT
    1 TEASPOON SUGAR
    2 TOMATOES, CUT INTO WEDGES

Method

1. Steam vegetables together just until broccoli turns bright green, about 5 minutes.
2. Drain and pour into large bowl.
3. Combine mayonnaise, cream, vinegar, salt, and sugar for dressing.
4. Toss vegetables and remaining ingredients with dressing and chill for several hours.

5. Arrange 1-cup serving and garnish with 2 tomato wedges.

*To reduce fat and calories, use low-calorie dressing instead of following step 3 and making your own.

Three-Bean Salad (Mexican Bean Salad)

Yield: 6 servings (3 cups)
Serving Size: $\frac{1}{2}$ cup
Exchange List Approximation:
    Starch/Bread 1
    Meat, medium-fat $\frac{1}{2}$

Nutrient Content Per Serving:
CAL: 118   PRO: 5.2 (gm)
FAT: 3.4 (gm)   CHO: 17.9 (gm)
Na: 62.2 (mg)   K: 254.5 (mg)
Fiber: 4.7 (gm)   Chol: 0

Ingredients

  1 CUP CUT GREEN BEANS (ABOUT ONE HALF 16-OUNCE CAN)
  ¾ CUP RED KIDNEY OR PINTO BEANS (ABOUT ONE HALF 15-OUNCE CAN)
  ⅞ CUP GARBANZOS OR CHICK PEAS (ABOUT ONE HALF 15-OUNCE CAN)
  ¼ CUP FINELY CHOPPED ONION
  ¼ CUP CHOPPED GREEN PEPPER
  3 TABLESPOONS VINEGAR
  ¼ CUP WATER
  1 TABLESPOON VEGETABLE OIL
  2 TEASPOONS SUGAR
  ¼ TEASPOON OREGANO
  1 GARLIC CLOVE

Method

1. Combine drained beans, onion, and green pepper.
2. Mix vinegar, water, oil, sugar, oregano, and garlic clove. Pour over beans. Toss to mix.
3. Cover and chill about 4 hours or overnight before serving. Remove garlic clove.

Variation: For Mexican Bean Salad, omit oregano and add 1 Tablespoon Picante sauce (see recipe page 321). Soy beans, navy beans, black-eye peas, or lima beans may be substituted for garbanzos.

Barley Salad

Yield: 6 servings (3 cups)
Serving Size: $\frac{2}{3}$ cup
Exchange List Approximation:
    Starch/Bread 1
    Fat 1

Nutrient Content Per Serving:
CAL: 111   PRO: 1.9 (gm)
FAT: 5.2 (gm)   CHO: 15.2 (gm)
Na: 93.6 (mg)   K: 123.6 (mg)
Fiber: 2.6 (gm)   Chol: 0

Ingredients

½ CUP QUICK PEARL BARLEY
1½ CUPS WATER
¼ TEASPOON SALT
1 CUP SLICED FRESH MUSHROOMS
⅓ CUP THINLY SLICED CARROTS
⅓ CUP THINLY SLICED ZUCCHINI (OR YELLOW SQUASH)
3 TABLESPOONS SLICED GREEN ONION
3 TABLESPOONS FINELY CHOPPED PARSLEY
3 TABLESPOONS LEMON JUICE
2 TABLESPOONS VEGETABLE OIL
¼ TEASPOON GARLIC POWDER
½ TEASPOON BASIL (OR 1 TEASPOON FRESH BASIL)
⅛ TEASPOON SALT

Method

1. Add barley to boiling salted water; stir. Add drop of oil to prevent boiling over; cover, lower heat, and cook until tender, about 1 hour for regular barley.
2. Drain and chill.
3. Add vegetables.

4. Combine lemon juice, oil, and spices. Add to salad. Toss lightly to coat ingredients. Sprinkle with salt.
5. Chill at least 3 hours or overnight.
6. Serve on lettuce and garnish with tomato wedges, if desired.

Note: This salad will keep well in refrigerator for several days.

Broccoli-Cauliflower Salad with Dressing

Yield: 6 or 2 servings
Serving Size: $\frac{1}{6}$ recipe
Exchange List Approximation:
   Vegetable 1
   Fat $\frac{1}{2}$

Nutrient Content Per Serving:

CAL: 52	PRO: 3.1 (gm)
FAT: 2.5 (gm)	CHO: 5.2 (gm)
Na: 50.4 (mg)	K: 250.4 (mg)
Fiber: 1.7 (gm)	Chol: 4 (mg)

Ingredients

Six Servings		*Two Servings*	
2	CUPS BROCCOLI, PEELED, QUARTERED, CUT INTO BITE-SIZED PIECES	⅔	CUP
1	CUP CAULIFLOWER, SLICED INTO BITE-SIZED PIECES	⅓	CUP
2	TABLESPOONS CHOPPED GREEN ONION	2	TEASPOONS
⅛	TEASPOON PEPPER		SPRINKLE

Horseradish Dressing

1	TABLESPOON PREPARED HORSERADISH	1	TEASPOON
1	TABLESPOON MAYONNAISE	1	TEASPOON
1	8-OUNCE CONTAINER PLAIN LOW-FAT YOGURT	4	TABLESPOONS

Method

1. Mix broccoli, cauliflower, onion, and pepper. Chill.
2. Mix horseradish and mayonnaise until blended. Carefully fold into yogurt.
3. Pour over vegetables and mix lightly.

Banana-Yogurt Mold

Yield: 8 servings
Serving Size: ½ cup
Exchange List Approximation:
    Fruit 1

Nutrient Content Per Serving:

CAL: 59	PRO: 3.4 (gm)
FAT: 0.6 (gm)	CHO: 11.1 (gm)
Na: 32.7 (mg)	K: 250.1 (mg)
Fiber: 0.7 (gm)	Chol: 2 (mg)

Ingredients

  1 ENVELOPE UNFLAVORED GELATIN
  2 TABLESPOONS WATER
⅓ CUP ORANGE JUICE
1⅓ CUPS MASHED BANANAS (ABOUT 3 SMALL)
  1 TEASPOON VANILLA
  1 8-OUNCE CARTON PLAIN LOW-FAT YOGURT
  2 EGG WHITES
  6 PACKETS SUGAR SUBSTITUTE

Method

1. Sprinkle gelatin on water in custard cup; place in pan of hot water; heat until gelatin melts.
2. Place orange juice, bananas, gelatin, and vanilla in mixer bowl. Whip until mixture is smooth. (May be whipped in blender or food processor.)
3. Use wire whip to gently fold in yogurt. Refrigerate while whipping egg whites.
4. Beat egg whites until foamy, add sweetener, and whip until stiff. Fold into yogurt mixture.
5. Spoon into 8 individual serving containers, cover, and freeze.

Variation: Frozen Banana Yogurt. Following step 3, freeze mixture in shallow metal pan. Break into pieces and beat until smooth in electric mixer or food processor. Add whipped egg whites and beat until just blended.

Apple-Cabbage Slaw

Yield: 4 servings
Serving Size: $\frac{1}{2}$ cup
Exchange List Approximation:
    Vegetable $\frac{1}{2}$
    Fruit $\frac{1}{2}$

Nutrient Content Per Serving:
CAL: 42   PRO: 1.3 (gm)
FAT: 0.4 (gm)   CHO: 9.2 (gm)
Na: 154.3 (mg)   K: 170.4 (mg)
Fiber: 1.5 (gm)   Chol: 1 (mg)

Ingredients

¼ CUP PLAIN LOW-FAT YOGURT
¼ TEASPOON SALT
    DASH PEPPER
2 TEASPOONS VINEGAR
¼ TEASPOON PREPARED MUSTARD
1 CUP APPLES, UNPARED, THINLY SLICED
2 CUPS CABBAGE, SHREDDED

Method

1. Mix yogurt, salt, pepper, vinegar, and mustard thoroughly.
2. Lightly mix apples and cabbage.
3. Pour yogurt mixture over apple-cabbage mixture; toss lightly.
4. Serve immediately.

Wine Salad

Yield: 12 servings (6 cups)
Serving Size: $\frac{1}{2}$ cup
Exchange List Approximation:
    Fruit 1
    Fat 1

Nutrient Content Per Serving:
CAL: 101   PRO: 1.8 (gm)
FAT: 3.2 (gm)   CHO: 17.6 (gm)
Na: 34.4 (mg) K: 122.4 (mg)
Fiber: 0.8 (gm) Chol: 0

Ingredients

1 PACKAGE RASPBERRY LOW-CALORIE GELATIN DESSERT POWDER
1 ENVELOPE PLAIN GELATIN
1 CUP JELLIED CRANBERRY SAUCE (ABOUT ONE HALF 16-OUNCE CAN)
1¾ CUPS BOILING WATER
¾ CUP PORT WINE
2¼ CUPS CRUSHED PINEAPPLE IN UNSWEETENED JUICE (ABOUT 1 20-OUNCE CAN)
⅔ CUP CHOPPED CELERY
½ CUP CHOPPED NUTS

Method

1. Mix gelatin and cranberry sauce.
2. Add boiling water and stir until gelatin and sauce are dissolved.
3. Add wine, pineapple and juice, celery, and nuts. Stir and chill until slightly thickened.
4. Mix and pour into 12 individual molds or one large mold. Chill until firm.

Note: This salad may be prepared for 6 servings; use raspberry dessert powder and one half of ingredients.

Garden Green-Salad Mold

Yield: 6 servings
Serving Size: $\frac{1}{2}$ cup
Exchange List Approximation:
    Free food

Nutrient Content Per Serving:

CAL: 15	PRO: 1.2 (gm)
FAT: 0	CHO: 2.3 (gm)
Na: 136.5 (mg)	K: 104.2 (mg)
Fiber: 1 (gm)	Chol: 0

Ingredients

  1 ENVELOPE LOW-CALORIE LIME-FLAVORED GELATIN
  1 CUP BOILING WATER
  1 CUP COLD WATER
  1 TABLESPOON LEMON JUICE
  ¼ TEASPOON SALT
  ½ TEASPOON HORSERADISH
  ½ TEASPOON FINELY CHOPPED JALAPENO PEPPER
      (OPTIONAL)
2½ CUPS FINELY SHREDDED CABBAGE
  ⅓ CUP THINLY SLICED GREEN ONIONS
  ⅓ CUP SLICED RADISHES

Method

1. Add boiling water to gelatin. Stir until dissolved.
2. Add cold water and chill until thickened.
3. Add seasonings and vegetables. Mix thoroughly.
4. Pour into 1 quart mold or individual molds and chill until firm.
5. Serve on lettuce or as relish on salad plate.

Jellied Vegetable Salad

Yield: 4 servings
Serving Size: $\frac{2}{3}$ cup
Exchange List Approximation:
    Vegetable 1

Nutrient Content Per Serving:
CAL: 29   PRO: 2.1 (gm)
FAT: 0.1 (gm)   CHO: 6.2 (gm)
Na: 149.4 (mg)   K: 174.9 (mg)
Fiber: 1.1 (gm)   Chol: 0
Key Source Nutrients:
    Vitamin A: 4262 (IU)

Ingredients

1 ENVELOPE UNFLAVORED GELATIN
¼ CUP WATER
1½ CUPS BOILING WATER
2 TABLESPOONS TARRAGON VINEGAR
¼ TEASPOON SALT
½ TABLESPOON HONEY
¾ CUP FINELY SHREDDED CABBAGE
½ CUP SHREDDED CARROTS
¼ CUP CHOPPED CELERY
½ CUP PARED, DICED CUCUMBER
1 TABLESPOON CHOPPED GREEN ONION
1 TABLESPOON FINELY CHOPPED PIMENTO
   SALAD GREENS (AS DESIRED)

Method

1. Soften gelatin in ¼ cup water for 5 minutes.
2. Add softened gelatin to boiling water. Stir until gelatin is dissolved.
3. Stir in vinegar, salt, and honey.
4. Chill until mixture begins to thicken.
5. Fold in remaining ingredients except salad greens.
6. Pour into 1-quart mold or 8-inch square pan.
7. Chill until set.
8. Unmold and serve on crisp salad greens.

Pineapple Salad

Yield: 8 servings (4 cups)
Serving Size: $\frac{1}{2}$ cup
Exchange List Approximation:
    Fruit $\frac{1}{2}$
    Fat $\frac{1}{2}$

Nutrient Content Per Serving:
CAL: 50   PRO: 1 (gm)
FAT: 1.8 (gm)   CHO: 6.7 (gm)
Na: 43 (mg)   K: 56.6 (mg)
Fiber: 0.2 (gm)   Chol: 0

Ingredients

1 PACKAGE LEMON OR LIME LOW-CALORIE GELATIN DESSERT
1 CUP BOILING WATER
1 8-OUNCE CAN CRUSHED PINEAPPLE IN UNSWEETENED PINEAPPLE JUICE
½ 12-OUNCE CAN CITRUS OR LEMON-LIME SUGAR-FREE CARBONATED BEVERAGE
4 OUNCES WHIPPED TOPPING (ABOUT ONE HALF 8-OUNCE CONTAINER)

Method

1. Add boiling water to gelatin dessert. Stir until dissolved.
2. Add juice from pineapple and beverage.
3. Chill until medium stiff. Whip with mixer until foamy.
4. Gradually whip into whipped topping. Fold in pineapple.
5. Pour into mold and chill until set.

Variation: Orange or raspberry low-calorie gelatin dessert and 1 cup of other unsweetened fruits may be used, such as peaches, apricots, etc.

Vegetable Salad en Gelée

Yield: 8 servings (4 cups)
Serving Size: $\frac{1}{2}$ cup
Exchange List Approximation:
    Vegetable 1
    Fat $\frac{1}{2}$

Nutrient Content Per Serving:
CAL: 46   PRO: 1 (gm)
FAT: 2.8 (gm)   CHO: 4.6 (gm)
Na: 27.8 (mg)   K: 88.5 (mg)
Fiber: 0.5 (gm)   Chol: 2 (mg)

Ingredients

- 1 ENVELOPE UNFLAVORED GELATIN
- 1 12-OUNCE CAN SUGAR-FREE CARBONATED GRAPEFRUIT-LEMON BEVERAGE
- 1 6½-OUNCE CAN UNSWEETENED CRUSHED PINEAPPLE
- 2 TABLESPOONS MAYONNAISE
- 1 CUP SHREDDED OR FINELY CHOPPED CABBAGE
- ⅓ CUP SHREDDED OR FINELY CHOPPED CARROTS

Method

1. Sprinkle gelatin over beverage. Let set 1 minute to soften. Heat over low heat until gelatin is dissolved.
2. Stir in remaining ingredients.
3. Pour into individual molds or into pan. Refrigerate until set.

Cheesy Grits

Yield: 6 or 2 servings
Serving Size: 1 cup
Exchange List Approximation:
    Starch/Bread $1\frac{1}{2}$
    Meat, medium-fat 1
    Fat 2

Nutrient Content Per Serving:
CAL: 286   PRO: 12.3 (gm)
FAT: 15.4 (gm)* CHO: 24.1 (gm)
Na: 253.5 (mg)   K: 124 (mg)
Fiber: 2.2 (gm)   Chol: 122 (mg)

Ingredients

Six Servings		Two Servings	
4	CUPS WATER	2	CUPS
1	CUP QUICK GRITS	½	CUP
1½	CUPS PROCESSED CHEDDAR CHEESE, CHOPPED	¾	CUP
2	TABLESPOONS MARGARINE	1	TABLESPOON
¼	CUP CHOPPED GREEN CHILIES (ABOUT 2 OUNCES) OR PICANTE SAUCE	2	TABLESPOONS
2	EGGS (SEPARATED)	1	
½	CUP SKIM MILK	¼	CUP

Method

1. Bring water to a boil in heavy sauce pan. Stir in grits. Bring to a boil. Reduce heat, partially cover, and cook 5 minutes. Stir occasionally.
2. Add cheese, margarine, and chilies. Stir until cheese is melted.
3. Beat egg yolks with milk and stir into grits.
4. Whip egg whites until stiff and fold into mixture.
5. Pour into lightly greased 7- × 11-inch baking dish (5- × 5-inch casserole for 3 servings) and bake in 350° F oven for 1 hour. Let set 5 minutes before cutting.

*To reduce fat, use half servings. If full servings are used, limit this dish to occasional use.

Cottage Cheese Baked Potatoes

Yield: 4 servings
Serving Size: $\frac{1}{2}$ potato
Exchange List Approximation:
    Starch/Bread $1\frac{1}{2}$

Nutrient Content Per Serving:

CAL: 131	PRO: 6.5 (gm)
FAT: 0.7 (gm)	CHO: 24.9 (gm)
Na: 263.7 (mg)	K: 435.8 (mg)
Fiber: 2.7 (gm)	Chol: 3 (mg)

Ingredients

2 8-OUNCE BAKING POTATOES
½ CUP LOW-FAT COTTAGE CHEESE
¼ CUP SKIM MILK
¼ TEASPOON SALT
⅛ TEASPOON PEPPER
   PAPRIKA (USE AS DESIRED)

Method

1. Wash potatoes well. Prick skins in several places. Bake at 425° F (hot oven) until tender, 50 to 60 minutes.
2. Remove from oven; cut in half. Scoop out insides of potatoes, leaving skins intact; save skins. Mash potatoes thoroughly.
3. Add remaining ingredients except paprika. Beat until fluffy.
4. Put mashed potato mixture into potato skins. Sprinkle paprika over the tops.
5. Bake at 425° F until heated through and tops are lightly browned, about 10 minutes.

Brown Rice Pilaf

Yield: 6 servings
Serving Size: $\frac{3}{4}$ cup
Exchange List Approximation:
   Starch/Bread 2
   Fat $\frac{1}{2}$

Nutrient Content Per Serving:
CAL: 167   PRO: 4.4 (gm)
FAT: 5.1 (gm) CHO: 26.8 (gm)
Na: 264.9 (mg)* K: 94.6 (mg)
Fiber: 2.1 (gm) Chol: 0

Ingredients

1 TABLESPOON MARGARINE
½ CUP VERMICELLI, BROKEN INTO ½-INCH LENGTHS
¾ CUP BROWN RICE
3 CUPS WATER
1 CUBE BOUILLON
3 TABLESPOONS CHOPPED TOASTED NUTS
(ALMONDS, PECANS, PINE NUTS)

Method

1. Heat margarine in large skillet. Add vermicelli. Stir until it starts to brown.
2. Add rice. Stir until rice starts to brown.
3. Add water and bouillon cube. Stir. Bring to a boil, cover, and cook over low heat until rice is tender, about 45 minutes.
4. Add nuts and stir with fork to fluff.

Note: Extra servings can be packaged and frozen for later use.

*Na content minimal if low-sodium bouillon cube used.

Stove-Top Yams and Apples

Yield: 6 or 2 servings
Serving Size: $\frac{2}{3}$ cup
Exchange List Approximation:
    Starch/Bread 1 $\frac{1}{2}$
    Fruit 1
    Fat $\frac{1}{2}$

Nutrient Content Per Serving:
CAL: 202   PRO: 1.6 (gm)
FAT: 4.2 (gm)   CHO: 41.3 (gm)
Na: 96 (mg)   K: 750.2 (mg)
Fiber: 5.3 (gm)   Chol: 0

Ingredients

Six Servings		*Two Servings*	
1½	POUNDS YAMS	½	POUND
1	CUP WATER	½	CUP
2	TABLESPOONS MARGARINE	2	TEASPOONS
1	TABLESPOON SUGAR	1	TEASPOON
⅛	TEASPOON SALT		PINCH
3	TART APPLES	1	
	SPRINKLE CINNAMON		SPRINKLE
1	PACKET SUGAR SUBSTITUTE	1	PACKET

Method

1. Peel and cut yams into ¼-inch slices. Place in large skillet.
2. Pour water over potatoes. Dot with margarine. Sprinkle with salt and sugar. Cover, bring to boil, and cook over moderate heat 20 minutes.
3. Wash, core, and slice apples (peel if desired). Spread over potatoes, sprinkle with cinnamon; cover, and cook 10 minutes longer.
4. Remove cover and cook until sauce is absorbed, about 5 minutes.
5. Sprinkle with sweetener; stir gently.

Vegetables

Broccoli with Mustard-Dill Sauce

Yield: 4 servings
Serving Size: 2 stalks broccoli
   and 2 tablespoons sauce
Exchange List Approximation:
     Vegetable 1
     Fat $\frac{1}{2}$

Nutrient Content Per Serving:
CAL: 50   PRO: 3.2 (gm)
FAT: 1.6 (gm)   CHO: 6.5 (gm)
Na: 273.4 (mg) K: 169 (mg)
Fiber: 1.8 (gm)   Chol: 1 (mg)

Ingredients

- 1 10-OUNCE PACKAGE FROZEN BROCCOLI SPEARS OR FRESH BROCCOLI SPEARS, 4 INCHES LONG
- ½ CUP WATER WITH ¼ TEASPOON SALT
- ¼ TEASPOON SALT
- 1½ TEASPOONS MARGARINE
- 1 TABLESPOON FLOUR
- ½ CUP SKIM MILK
- 1½ TEASPOONS PREPARED MUSTARD
- ¼ TEASPOON DILL WEED

Method

1. Bring broccoli spears and salted water to boil, cover, and cook until just tender, about 6 minutes.
2. Melt margarine in small saucepan, add flour, and cook about 1 minute, stirring constantly. Add milk, mustard, salt, and dill weed. Stir until smooth, bring to a simmer, and cook 2 minutes while stirring.
3. Spoon 2 Tablespoons sauce over each serving of broccoli (2 spears).

Jade-Green Broccoli

Yield: 10 servings
Serving Size: $\frac{1}{2}$ cup
Exchange List Approximation:
    Vegetable 1
    Fat 1

Nutrient Content Per Serving:
CAL: 82   PRO: 2.5 (gm)
FAT: 6.2 (gm)   CHO: 5.2 (gm)
Na: 239.1 (mg)   K: 131.1 (mg)
Fiber: 1.8 (gm)   Chol: 0
Key Source Nutrients:
    Riboflavin: 147.3 (mg)

Ingredients

1 BUNCH BROCCOLI (ABOUT 2 POUNDS)
1 CLOVE GARLIC, MINCED
1 TABLESPOON CORNSTARCH
2 TABLESPOONS SOY SAUCE
½ CUP WATER OR CHICKEN STOCK
¼ CUP VEGETABLE OIL
⅛ TEASPOON SALT
2 TABLESPOONS SHERRY

Method

1. Wash broccoli in cold water. Drain, peel stems, and cut the stems on a slant into ⅛-inch slices.
2. Mix together cornstarch, soy sauce, and chicken stock; put aside.
3. Heat wok or pan hot and dry. Add the oil, then the salt.
4. Turn heat to medium and add the garlic. When garlic is golden brown, add the broccoli. Turn heat up and stir-fry for 3 minutes.
5. Add the sherry and cover wok or pan quickly. Cook, covered, 2 minutes longer.
6. Add cornstarch, soy sauce, and chicken stock. Stir constantly until gravy has thickened.

Green Beans with Sunflower Seeds

Yield: 6 or 2 servings
Serving Size: $\frac{1}{2}$ cup
Exchange List Approximation:
   Vegetable 1
   Fat $\frac{1}{2}$

Nutrient Content Per Serving:

CAL: 51	PRO: 2.2 (gm)
FAT: 2.2 (gm)	CHO: 7.1 (gm)
Na: 45.1 (mg)	K: 244.7 (mg)
Fiber: 2.6 (gm)	Chol: 0

Ingredients

Six Servings	Two Servings
1 POUND FRESH GREEN BEANS	⅓ POUND
½ CUP CHOPPED ONIONS	3 TABLESPOONS
1 TEASPOON MINCED GARLIC	⅓ TEASPOON
⅛ TEASPOON SALT	PINCH
⅛ TEASPOON PEPPER	PINCH
SHAKE CRUSHED RED PEPPER (OPTIONAL)	SHAKE
⅓ CUP WATER	2 TABLESPOONS
3 TABLESPOONS SUNFLOWER SEEDS	1 TABLESPOON
¼ TEASPOON OREGANO	SPRINKLE

Method

1. Snap ends off beans and break into ½" lengths. If very young, leave whole. Wash and place in saucepan.
2. Sprinkle onion, garlic, salt, and pepper over beans. Add water.
3. Cover tightly. Cook on high until steaming, reduce heat, and cook about 20 minutes until beans are crisp-tender.
4. Remove lid. Pour off excess liquid.
5. Sprinkle sunflower seeds and oregano over beans. Mix lightly.

Peas and Celery

Yield: 6 or 2 servings
Serving Size: ½ cup
Exchange List Approximation:
    Starch/Bread ½
    Vegetable ½

Nutrient Content Per Serving:
CAL: 54   PRO: 2.6 (gm)
FAT: 1.5 (gm)   CHO: 8.4 (gm)
Na: 113.3 (mg)   K: 163.3 (mg)
Fiber: 3.4 (gm)   Chol: 0

Ingredients

Six Servings		*Two Servings*
2	TEASPOONS MARGARINE	¾ TEASPOON
1	CUP CELERY, ⅛-INCH BIAS CUT SLICES	⅓ CUP
2	TABLESPOONS FINELY CHOPPED ONION	2 TEASPOONS
½	TEASPOON SAVORY	⅛ TEASPOON
½	CUP WATER	¼ CUP
1	10-OUNCE PACKAGE FROZEN PEAS	¾ CUP
⅓	CUP SLICED CANNED MUSHROOMS, DRAINED	2 TABLESPOONS
2	TABLESPOONS CHOPPED PIMENTO	2 TEASPOONS
	SPRINKLE BLACK PEPPER	SPRINKLE

Method

1. Heat margarine in a saucepan. Add celery, onion, and savory. Stir-fry about 2 minutes.
2. Add water, bring to a boil, cover, and simmer 5 minutes.
3. Add frozen peas, mushrooms, and pimento. Sprinkle with black pepper. Bring to a simmer, cover, and cook over low heat about 5 minutes, until peas are just tender.

Squash Puff

Yield: 6 or 2 servings
Serving Size: $\frac{1}{2}$ cup
Exchange List Approximation:
   Starch/Bread 1$\frac{1}{2}$

Nutrient Content Per Serving:
CAL: 125   PRO: 4.4 (gm)
FAT: 2.9 (gm)   CHO: 22.4 (gm)
Na: 173.5 (mg) K: 372.7 (mg)
Fiber: 3.9 (gm) Chol: 137 (mg)

Ingredients

Six Servings		*Two Servings*	
3	CUPS ACORN SQUASH, COOKED AND MASHED (ABOUT 3 POUNDS)	1	CUP (ABOUT 1 POUND)
3	TABLESPOONS HONEY	1	TABLESPOON
3	TABLESPOONS WHOLE-WHEAT FLOUR	1	TABLESPOON
⅜	TEASPOON SALT	⅛	TEASPOON
¼	TEASPOON EACH: CINNAMON, GINGER, NUTMEG	¹⁄₁₆	TEASPOON
3	EGGS, SEPARATED		

Method

1. Cut acorn squash and scoop out seeds. Steam or bake in 350° F oven until tender. Remove from skin and mash.
2. Combine with honey, flour, salt, spices, and egg yolks. Whip until blended.
3. Beat egg whites until stiff (not dry). Fold into squash mixture.
4. Pour into 1½-quart baking dish, sprayed with nonstick vegetable spray.
5. Bake in 350° F oven until crusty, about 45 minutes.

Note: One serving contains approximately 1½ teaspoons honey (24 calories).

Dilled Zucchini

Yield: 4 servings
Serving Size: $\frac{1}{2}$ cup
Exchange List Approximation:
    Vegetable 1

Nutrient Content Per Serving:
CAL: 19   PRO: 0.8 (gm)
FAT: 0   CHO: 4.6 (gm)
Na: 66.2 (mg)   K: 249.8 (mg)
Fiber: 3.1 (gm)   Chol: 0

Ingredients

1 POUND ZUCCHINI
⅓ CUP CHOPPED ONION
¼ CUP BOILING WATER
⅛ TEASPOON SALT
½ TEASPOON PAPRIKA
½ TEASPOON DILL WEED
1 TABLESPOON VINEGAR

Method

1. Remove ends from zucchini; cut into strips or slices.
2. Add zucchini and onion to boiling salted water. Cover and boil gently until tender, about 10 minutes. Drain.
3. Add paprika, dill weed, and vinegar. Stir gently.

Stir-Fry Zucchini

Yield: 4 or 2 servings
Serving Size: $\frac{3}{4}$ cup
Exchange List Approximation:
    Vegetable 1
    Fat 1

Nutrient Content Per Serving:
CAL: 75   PRO: 1.7 (gm)
FAT: 5 (gm)   CHO: 7.2 (gm)
Na: 239.3 (mg) K: 308.9 (mg)
Fiber: 4.1 (gm)   Chol: 0

Ingredients

Four Servings		Two Servings
1	TABLESPOON VEGETABLE OIL	1½ TEASPOONS
4	CUPS ZUCCHINI, CUT INTO 1½-INCH STRIPS (ABOUT 1 POUND)	2 CUPS
1	CUP ONION, CUT IN WEDGES, SEPARATED	½ CUP
1	TABLESPOON SESAME SEEDS	1 TEASPOON
2	TEASPOONS SOY SAUCE	1 TEASPOON
⅛	TEASPOON SALT	SPRINKLE
½	TEASPOON SESAME SEED OIL (OPTIONAL)	¼ TEASPOON

Method

1. Heat vegetable oil in large skillet over medium heat.
2. Add zucchini and onion. Stir-fry about 5 to 8 minutes.
3. Sprinkle with sesame seeds, soy sauce, salt, and sesame seed oil. Stir until blended.

Summer Squash Pudding

Yield: 6 or 3 servings
Serving Size: $\frac{1}{3}$ cup
Exchange List Approximation:
    Vegetable 1
    Fat 1

Nutrient Content Per Serving:

CAL: 81	PRO: 3.7 (gm)
FAT: 4.4 (gm)	CHO: 7.7 (gm)
Na: 154.5 (mg)	K: 286.2 (mg)
Fiber: 1.1 (gm)	Chol: 92 (mg)

Ingredients

Six Servings		*Three Servings*
4	SUMMER SQUASH, LARGE (ABOUT 2 POUNDS)	1 (ABOUT 1 POUND)
½	CUP WATER	¼ CUP
¼	TEASPOON SALT	⅛ TEASPOON
2	EGGS	1
2	TABLESPOONS LOW-FAT YOGURT	1 TABLESPOON
½	TEASPOON PEPPER	¼ TEASPOON
1	TABLESPOON MARGARINE, DIVIDED	1½ TEASPOONS
2	TABLESPOONS SEASONED BREAD CRUMBS	1 TABLESPOON

Method

1. Slice squash, add to salted water; cover, bring to a boil, and cook until tender, about 20 minutes. Mash.
2. Beat eggs. Stir in yogurt, pepper, and mashed squash.
3. Grease 2-quart casserole with 1 teaspoon margarine. Mix remaining margarine with seasoned crumbs.
4. Pour squash mixture into casserole. Sprinkle crumbs over top.
5. Bake in 350° F oven for 20 minutes.

Dips and Dressings

Delicious Dip

Yield: 8 servings
Serving Size: 3 tablespoons
Exchange List Approximation:
    Milk, skim $\frac{1}{2}$

Nutrient Content Per Serving:
CAL: 36   PRO: 3.6 (gm)
FAT: 0.8 (gm)   CHO: 3.5 (gm)
Na: 105.6 (mg)   K: 105.8 (mg)
Fiber: 0.1 (gm)   Chol: 3 (mg)

Ingredients

  1 CUP PLAIN LOW-FAT YOGURT
½ CUP LOW-FAT COTTAGE CHEESE
¼ MINCED GREEN PEPPER
  1 TABLESPOON CATSUP
1½ TEASPOONS PREPARED HORSERADISH
  1 TEASPOON WORCESTERSHIRE SAUCE
⅛ TEASPOON MINCED GARLIC
½ TEASPOON DRY MUSTARD

Method

1. Mix yogurt and cottage cheese.
2. Stir in remaining ingredients.
3. Cover and chill 2 hours to blend flavors.
4. Serve as a dip for crackers, chips, or raw vegetable pieces. Or serve as dressing for lettuce wedge or green salad.

Horseradish Dip

Yield: 1 cup
Serving Size: $1\frac{1}{3}$ tablespoons
Exchange List Approximation:
    Free food

Nutrient Content Per Serving:
CAL: 17   PRO: 0.7 (gm)
FAT: 1.1 (gm)   CHO: 1 (gm)
Na: 16.6 (mg)   K: 33.9 (mg)
Fiber: 0.1 (gm)   Chol: 2 (mg)

Ingredients

1 8-OUNCE CONTAINER PLAIN LOW-FAT YOGURT
1 TABLESPOON MAYONNAISE
2 TEASPOONS PREPARED HORSERADISH

Method

1. Mix well and serve as dip for raw vegetables.

Spinach Dip for Raw Vegetables

Yield: 16 servings
Serving Size: $2\frac{1}{2}$ tablespoons
Exchange List Approximation:
    Vegetable $\frac{1}{2}$
    Fat 1

Nutrient Content Per Serving:
CAL: 62   PRO: 1.1 (gm)
FAT: 5.8 (gm)   CHO: 1.8 (gm)
Na: 66.6 (mg)   K: 73.4 (mg)
Fiber: 0.3 (gm)   Chol: 5 (mg)

Ingredients

1 10-OUNCE PACKAGE FROZEN CHOPPED SPINACH
½ CUP MAYONNAISE
1 CUP LOW-FAT YOGURT
¼ CUP CHOPPED PARSLEY OR 2 TABLESPOONS
    PARSLEY FLAKES
¼ CUP FINELY CHOPPED ONION
    PINCH DILL WEED
    PINCH SALT

Method

1. Thaw spinach and drain thoroughly.
2. Combine with remaining ingredients.
3. Cover and chill to let blend.

Black-Eye Pea Dip

Yield: 10 servings
Serving Size: $\frac{1}{4}$ cup
Exchange List Approximation:
    Starch/Bread 1
    Fat $\frac{1}{2}$

Nutrient Content Per Serving:
CAL: 113   PRO: 5.4 (gm)
FAT: 3.4 (gm)   CHO: 16.2 (gm)
Na: 94.5 (mg)   K: 319.9 (mg)
Fiber: 6.1 (gm)   Chol: 0

Ingredients

  3 CUPS COOKED, DRY BLACK-EYE PEAS
½ CUP CHOPPED ONION
½ CUP CHOPPED GREEN PEPPER
½ CUP TOMATO SAUCE
¼ CUP VINEGAR
  2 TABLESPOONS VEGETABLE OIL
  2 PACKETS SUGAR SUBSTITUTE
  1 TABLESPOON WORCESTERSHIRE SAUCE
¼ TEASPOON PEPPER
¼ TEASPOON GARLIC POWDER

Method

1. Place all ingredients in blender or food processor. Blend for 2 to 3 seconds. Pieces of pea should be present.

Variation: For relish, combine ingredients and add 1 small jalapeno pepper, chopped.

Garbanzo Spread

Yield: 6 servings
Serving Size: $\frac{1}{4}$ cup
Exchange List Approximation:
    Starch/Bread 1
    Fat $\frac{1}{2}$

Nutrient Content Per Serving:
CAL: 112   PRO: 5.4 (gm)
FAT: 4 (gm)   CHO: 14.9 (gm)
Na: 50.8 (mg)   K: 208.2 (mg)
Fiber: 3.7 (gm)   Chol: 0

Ingredients

1¾ CUPS GARBANZO BEANS, DRAINED (ABOUT 15 OUNCES)
¼ CUP TOASTED SESAME SEEDS
4 TABLESPOONS LEMON JUICE
2 TABLESPOONS CHOPPED ONION
¼ TEASPOON MINCED GARLIC
¾ TEASPOON BASIL
⅛ TEASPOON PEPPER
⅛ TEASPOON SALT

Method

1. Drain beans and reserve liquid.
2. Place all ingredients in blender or food processor.
3. Blend to a smooth paste. Add a little bean liquid (about 1 Tablespoon) to get desired consistency.
4. Serve on lettuce with wedge of onion and whole wheat toast or crackers. Also can be served as dip for raw vegetables.

Note: If your diet permits, sprinkle a little olive oil over spread.

Chick Peas and
Sesame-Seed-Paste Dip

Yield: 6 servings
Serving Size: $\frac{1}{4}$ cup
Exchange List Approximation:
    Starch/Bread 1
    Fat 1

Nutrient Content Per Serving:
CAL: 133   PRO: 6.9 (gm)
FAT: 3.7 (gm)   CHO: 19.4 (gm)
Na: 9.3 (mg)   K: 261.8 (mg)
Fiber: 4.7 (gm) Chol: 0

Ingredients

1¾ CUPS CHICK PEAS (GARBANZO BEANS, ABOUT 1 15-OUNCE CAN)
  2 TABLESPOONS TAHINI (SESAME SEED PASTE)
  2 TABLESPOONS LEMON JUICE
  1 SMALL GARLIC CLOVE
 ½ TEASPOON GROUND CORIANDER
 ¼ TEASPOON CUMIN
¹⁄₁₆ TEASPOON CAYENNE PEPPER

Method

1. Place all ingredients in blender or food processor. Blend to a smooth paste.
2. Serve as a vegetable dip or sandwich spread.

Ranch Salad Dressing

Yield: 32 servings
Serving Size: 1 tablespoon
Exchange List Approximation:
Fat $\frac{1}{2}$

Nutrient Content Per Serving:
CAL: 20   PRO: 0.7 (gm)
FAT: 1.6 (gm)   CHO: 0.9 (gm)
Na: 31.1 (mg)   K: 30 (mg)
Fiber: 0   Chol: 2 (mg)

Ingredients

1¾ CUPS PLAIN LOW-FAT YOGURT
¼ CUP MAYONNAISE
1 TEASPOON DRIED PARSLEY FLAKES
1 TEASPOON DRIED MINCED ONION
½ TEASPOON ONION POWDER
½ TEASPOON GARLIC POWDER
½ TEASPOON DILL WEED
¼ TEASPOON PAPRIKA
¼ TEASPOON PEPPER
¼ TEASPOON CELERY SALT
⅛ TEASPOON MONOSODIUM GLUTAMATE

Method

1. Place ingredients in mixing bowl. Stir until blended and smooth.
2. Pour into container and refrigerate 1 hour to blend flavors. Can be stored for several weeks.
3. Use on salad greens or as dip for raw vegetables.

*Exchanges for less than 1 Tablespoon serving are Free.

Mock French Dressing

Yield: 8 servings
Serving Size: 2 tablespoons
Exchange List Approximation:
    Free food

Nutrient Content Per Serving:

CAL: 18	PRO: 0
FAT: 0	CHO: 4.7 (gm)
Na: 66.7 (mg)	K: 7.5 (mg)
Fiber: 0	Chol: 0

Ingredients

1½ TABLESPOONS CORNSTARCH
  2 TABLESPOONS SUGAR
  1 CUP WATER
 ¼ CUP VINEGAR
 ¼ TEASPOON SALT
 ½ TEASPOON DRY MUSTARD
 ½ TEASPOON PAPRIKA
 ⅛ TEASPOON ONION POWDER
   DASH GARLIC POWDER

Method

1. Mix cornstarch and sugar in saucepan; stir in water.
2. Cook over low heat, stirring constantly, until thickened.
3. Cool slightly.
4. Add remaining ingredients. Mix thoroughly.
5. Chill.

Note: One serving contains ¾ teaspoon sugar (12 calories).

Yogurt-Dill Dressing

Yield: 8 servings
Serving Size: 2 tablespoons
Exchange List Approximation:
    Free food

Nutrient Content Per Serving:
CAL: 18   PRO: 1.5 (gm)
FAT: 0.4 (gm)   CHO: 2.1 (gm)
Na: 20 (mg)   K: 68.2 (mg)
Fiber: 0   Chol: 2 (mg)

Ingredients

1   8-OUNCE CARTON PLAIN LOW-FAT YOGURT
2   TEASPOONS VERY FINELY CHOPPED ONION
1   TEASPOON LEMON JUICE
½   TEASPOON CRUSHED DILL WEED
¼   TEASPOON DRY MUSTARD
⅛   TEASPOON GARLIC POWDER

Method

1. Mix all ingredients thoroughly.
2. Chill until served.
3. Serve over tossed green salad.

Condiments, Spreads, Sauces, Toppings

California Salad Seasoning

Yield: 24 servings (1 cup)
Serving Size: 2 teaspoons
Exchange List Approximation:
    Free food

Nutrient Content Per Serving:

CAL: 12	PRO: 1.1 (gm)
FAT: 0.8 (gm)	CHO: 0.1 (gm)
Na: 91 (mg)	K: 3.2 (mg)
Fiber: 0	Chol: 2 (mg)

Ingredients

¾ CUP GRATED PARMESAN CHEESE
¼ CUP PARSLEY FLAKES
1 TEASPOON GARLIC POWDER
½ TEASPOON FRESHLY GROUND PEPPER
1 TEASPOON CHIVES
1 TEASPOON BELL PEPPER FLAKES
1 TEASPOON BASIL
½ TEASPOON SALT

Method

1. Mix all ingredients together.
2. Sprinkle on salad and garlic bread.

Diet Catsup
(from Tomato Juice)

Yield: 48 servings

Serving Size: 1 tablespoon

Exchange List Approximation:

    Free food

Nutrient Content Per Serving:

CAL: 5	PRO: 0.2 (gm)
FAT: 0	CHO: 1.3 (gm)
Na: 105.7 (mg)	K: 65.5 (mg)
Fiber: 0	Chol: 0

Ingredients

- 1 46-OUNCE CAN TOMATO JUICE
- ¼ CUP VINEGAR
- ⅛ TEASPOON EACH: DRY MUSTARD, ALLSPICE, CINNAMON, CELERY SEED
- 1 TEASPOON ONION POWDER
- 6 PACKETS SUGAR SUBSTITUTE

Method

1. Combine all ingredients except sweetener in large, shallow saucepan. Simmer about 1½ hours until thickened.
2. Remove from heat. Stir in substitute sweetener. Store in refrigerator.

Diet Catsup
(from Tomato Sauce)

Yield: 1½ cups
Serving Size: 1 tablespoon
Exchange List Approximation:
    Free food

Nutrient Content Per Serving:

CAL: 6	PRO: 0.2 (gm)
FAT: 0	CHO: 1.5 (gm)
Na: 114.4 (mg)	K: 72.6 (mg)
Fiber: 0.2 (gm)	Chol: 0

Ingredients

2 8-OUNCE CANS TOMATO SAUCE WITHOUT
  DEXTROSE OR OTHER SUGARS
¼ CUP VINEGAR
⅛ TEASPOON EACH: DRY MUSTARD, ALLSPICE,
  CINNAMON, AND CELERY SEED
1 TEASPOON ONION POWDER
  DASH CAYENNE PEPPER
6 PACKETS SUGAR SUBSTITUTE

Method

1. Combine all ingredients except sugar substitute in saucepan.
2. Simmer 30 minutes until thickened.
3. Remove from heat. Stir in sugar substitute. Store in refrigerator.

Texas-Style Barbecue Sauce

Yield: 6 servings
Serving Size: 3 tablespoons
Exchange List Approximation:
    Free food

Nutrient Content Per Serving:

CAL: 11	PRO: 0.5 (gm)
FAT: 0.1 (gm)	CHO: 2.5 (gm)
Na: 453.7 (mg)	K: 111.2 (mg)
Fiber: 0	Chol: 0

Ingredients

- 4 TABLESPOONS TOMATO PASTE
- 1 TABLESPOON DEHYDRATED ONION FLAKES
- 1 TEASPOON WORCESTERSHIRE SAUCE
- 1 TEASPOON LEMON JUICE
- 1 TEASPOON SALT
- 1 TEASPOON MINCED GARLIC CLOVE
- DASH CAYENNE PEPPER
- 1 CUP SUGAR-FREE COLA

Method

1. In a small saucepan, mix ingredients in order listed.
2. Bring to a boil, reduce heat, and simmer for 5 minutes.
3. Serve over grilled chicken, beef, pork, or frankfurters.

Texas Picante Sauce (Fresh or Canned)

Yield: 6 servings
Serving Size: 1 tablespoon
Exchange List Approximation:
    Free food

Nutrient Content Per Serving:
CAL: 4   PRO: 0.2 (gm)
FAT: 0   CHO: 0.9 (gm)
Na: 11.4 (mg)   K: 35.1 (mg)
Fiber: 0.2 (gm) Chol: 0

Ingredients

    5   POUNDS RIPE TOMATOES (ABOUT 9 TO 10 LARGE)
    1   LARGE ONION (ABOUT 10 OUNCES)
    ½   CUP CHOPPED CARROTS (ABOUT 1 SMALL)
    ½   CUP CHOPPED JALAPENO PEPPER, DISCARD SEEDS
        (ABOUT 3)
    ½   CUP CHOPPED CHILI PEPPERS, DISCARD SEEDS
    ¼   TEASPOON PEPPER
    ¾   TEASPOON PICKLING SALT
    2   TEASPOONS MINCED GARLIC CLOVE (ABOUT 2)

Method

1. Cut tomatoes, onion, and carrot. Place in food processor
    and blend until chunky. Place in cooking pot.
2. Handle peppers carefully when chopping. Cut off stem,
    slit, remove seeds, and chop into large pieces.
3. Place in processor and blend to small chunks.
4. Add peppers, pepper, pickling salt, and garlic to tomatoes.
    Bring to boil and cook slowly 30 minutes.
5. Fill into clean, sterile jars (4 1-pint). Leave ½ inch head
    space. Cap and seal.
6. Process in water bath for 15 minutes. (Place in large pot
    with rack, fill with hot water to cover, bring to boil, and
    boil 15 minutes.)

Green Chilies Sauce

Yield: 20 servings (2½ cups)
Serving Size: 2 tablespoons
Exchange List Approximation:
    Free food

Nutrient Content Per Serving:
CAL: 7   PRO: 0.3 (gm)
FAT: 0.1 (gm)   CHO: 1.7 (gm)
Na: 37.1 (mg)   K: 56.8 (mg)
Fiber: 0.4 (gm)   Chol: 0

Ingredients

½ CUP CHOPPED ONION
1 16-OUNCE CAN TOMATOES
1 4-OUNCE CAN GREEN CHILIES
2 TEASPOONS CHILI POWDER
½ TEASPOON GARLIC POWDER
¼ TEASPOON GROUND CUMIN
¼ TEASPOON GROUND OREGANO

Method

1. Spray saucepan with vegetable pan spray.
2. Add onions and saute until tender, about 5 minutes.
3. Add tomato juice. Chop tomatoes and add.
4. Add green chilies and spices. Stir.
5. Bring to a boil, cover, and simmer 10 minutes.
6. Pour into clean jar and store in refrigerator. Use to season beans and other foods such as eggs and hamburgers where catsup might otherwise be used.

Earle's Fire Sauce (Hot Sauce)

Yield: 16 servings (4 cups)
Serving Size: 4 tablespoons
Exchange List Approximation:
    Vegetable 1

Nutrient Content Per Serving:
CAL: 24   PRO: 1 (gm)
FAT: 0.2 (gm)   CHO: 5.4 (gm)
Na: 187.5 (mg)   K: 220 (mg)
Fiber: 1.2 (gm)   Chol: 0

Ingredients

- 6 JALAPENO PEPPERS*, ENDS CUT OFF AND QUARTERED
- 4 TABLESPOONS WATER
- 2 CUPS TOMATO SAUCE, SPANISH STYLE (ABOUT 1 16-OUNCE CAN)
- 2 TOMATOES, MEDIUM, CHOPPED
- 1 WHITE ONION, LARGE, DICED
- 1 TEASPOON MINCED GARLIC CLOVE (ABOUT 1)
- 1 TEASPOON MEXICAN CHILI POWDER
- 1 TEASPOON LEMON JUICE
- ½ TEASPOON BLACK PEPPER

Method

1. Exercising caution, cut ends off jalapeno peppers, quarter, and remove seeds. Place in blender or food processor, add water, and liquefy. Pepper juice may burn unless well washed off hands.
2. Add tomato sauce, chopped tomatoes, diced onion, minced garlic clove, and remaining ingredients.
3. Gently blend for *short* period. Sauce should have small pieces of tomato and onion in it.

*This sauce is hot. For a milder version, use only 4 peppers.

Dried Fruit Spread(s)

Yield = number of 1-Tablespoon servings in fruit recipe selected.
Exchanges are based upon 1-Tablespoon serving for each fruit spread.

Fruit	APPLE	APRICOT	PEACH	PRUNE
Yield	32	20	24	16
CAL	17	26	31	34
FAT (gm)	0	0	0.1	0.1
Na (mg)	6.3	0.9	1.0	0.6
Fiber (gm)	1.0	2.7	2.3	2.3
PRO (gm)	0.1	0.4	0.5	0.4
CHO (gm)	4.7	6.9	7.9	8.8
K (mg)	32.0	153.7	128.1	104.6
Chol (mg)	0	0	0	0
Exchanges	½ Fruit	½ Fruit	½ Fruit	½ Fruit

Ingredients

1 8-OUNCE PACKAGE OF THE DRIED FRUIT SELECTED
   (APPLE OR APRICOT OR PEACH OR PRUNES, pitted)
2–6 PACKETS SUGAR SUBSTITUTE

Method

1. Select the dried fruit for the spread desired.
2. Cover dried fruit with water and simmer until soft and most of water is absorbed.
3. Put in blender and blend until smooth. Add more water if needed to get spreading consistency.
4. Add sweetener to taste.
5. Store in covered container in refrigerator.

Variation: For spiced spread, add ½ teaspoon mace or nutmeg.

Apple Butter

Yield: 10 servings
Serving Size: 2 tablespoons
Exchange List Approximation:
    Fruit $\frac{1}{2}$

Nutrient Content Per Serving:

CAL: 36	PRO: 0.1 (gm)
FAT: 0.1 (gm)	CHO: 9.4 (gm)
Na: 1.7 (mg)	K: 72.2 (mg)
Fiber: 1.1 (gm)	Chol: 0

Ingredients

- 1 20-OUNCE JAR UNSWEETENED APPLESAUCE
- 1 CUP SWEET CIDER (NO SUGAR ADDED)
- 1 TEASPOON GROUND CINNAMON
- ½ TEASPOON GROUND CLOVES
- ½ TEASPOON ALLSPICE
- 2 PACKETS SUGAR SUBSTITUTE

Method

1. Combine applesauce, cider, and spices in electric frying pan, or in iron or cast aluminum skillet or pot.
2. Simmer slowly, stirring frequently, 2 to 3 hours until spreading consistency is reached.
3. Cool and sweeten to taste.
4. Store in covered container in refrigerator.

Sugarless Grape Jam

Yield: 2⅔ cups
Serving Size: 1 tablespoon
Exchange List Approximation:
    Free food

Nutrient Content Per Serving:
CAL: 13   PRO: 0.1 (gm)
FAT: 0   CHO: 3.2 (gm)
Na: 0.5 (mg)   K: 16.3 (mg)
Fiber: 0   Chol: 0

Ingredients

2 CUPS UNSWEETENED GRAPE JUICE
1 CUP WATER
½ CUP QUICK TAPIOCA
   SUGAR SUBSTITUTE EQUIVALENT TO 3 CUPS SUGAR

Method

1. Combine grape juice, water, and tapioca in saucepan. Let set 5 minutes to soften tapioca.
2. Add sweetener. Bring to a boil and boil hard for 1 minute.
3. Pour into clean jars, seal, and store in refrigerator.

Strawberry Jam

Yield: 1¼ cups
Serving Size: 1 tablespoon
Exchange List Approximation:
　　Free food

Nutrient Content Per Serving:
CAL: 4　　　　　PRO: 0.2 (gm)
FAT: 0　　　　　CHO: 0.5 (gm)
Na: 12.9 (mg)　　K: 12.4 (mg)
Fiber: 0.2 (gm)　　Chol: 0

Ingredients

1　CUP SLICED STRAWBERRIES UNSWEETENED (ABOUT 5 TO 6 OUNCES)
¾　CUP SUGAR-FREE STRAWBERRY SODA
1　PACKAGE STRAWBERRY LOW-CALORIE GELATIN DESSERT
3　PACKETS SUGAR SUBSTITUTE

Method

1. Mash strawberries. Add soda and bring to a boil. Cook 1 minute.
2. Remove from heat. Stir in gelatin dessert until dissolved. Stir in sweetener.
3. Pour into clean hot jars, seal, and store in refrigerator.

Mock Sour Cream

Yield: 5 servings ($\frac{2}{3}$ cup)
Serving Size: 2 tablespoons
Exchange List Approximation:
   Meat, medium-fat $\frac{1}{2}$

Nutrient Content Per Serving:
CAL: 44   PRO: 2.9 (gm)
FAT: 3.2 (gm)   CHO: 0.9 (gm)
Na: 66.1 (mg)   K: 24.2 (mg)
Fiber: 0   Chol: 1 (mg)

Ingredients

½ CUP COTTAGE CHEESE, UNCREAMED (DRY)
¼ CUP BUTTERMILK
1 TABLESPOON OIL
1 TEASPOON LEMON JUICE
⅛ TEASPOON SALT

Method

1. Put all ingredients into blender container; cover. Blend until smooth.
2. Serve over baked potatoes or other vegetables.

Low-Calorie Whipped Topping

Yield: 8 servings
Serving Size: ¼ cup
Exchange List Approximation:
    Free food

Nutrient Content Per Serving:
CAL: 20   PRO: 1.5 (gm)
FAT: 0   CHO: 3.4 (gm)
Na: 20.1 (mg)   K: 69.9 (mg)
Fiber: 0   Chol: 1 (mg)

Ingredients

- 1 TEASPOON UNFLAVORED GELATIN
- 2 TEASPOONS WATER
- ¼ CUP INSTANT NONFAT DRY MILK
- ½ CUP SKIM MILK
- ½ TEASPOON VANILLA
- 1 TABLESPOON SUGAR

Method

1. Soften gelatin in water for 5 minutes.
2. Stir nonfat dry milk into skim milk in saucepan. Heat to simmering. Add softened gelatin. Stir until gelatin is dissolved.
3. Add vanilla and sugar.
4. Chill until mixture begins to thicken.
5. Beat with electric mixer or rotary beater until very thick and light.
6. Serve on fresh fruit.

Note: Less than ½ teaspoon sugar per serving (6 calories).

Whipped Topping

Yield: 12 servings (1½ cups)
Serving Size: 2 tablespoons
Exchange List Approximation:
  Meat, lean ½

Nutrient Content Per Serving:
CAL: 21   PRO: 1.7 (gm)
FAT: 0.8 (gm)   CHO: 1.6 (gm)
Na: 21.3 (mg)   K: 20.5 (mg)
Fiber: 0   Chol: 3 (mg)

Ingredients

  2 EGG WHITES
  ¼ TEASPOON CREAM OF TARTAR
  1 TABLESPOON SUGAR
  ½ CUP PART SKIM RICOTTA CHEESE
  ½ TEASPOON VANILLA

Method

1. Whip egg whites until foamy, add cream of tartar, and whip until peaks fold over.
2. Gradually add sugar while whipping. Whip until stiff peaks are formed.
3. Add vanilla to Ricotta cheese and whip until smooth.
4. Fold whites into cheese. Keep refrigerated until served.

Note: This topping tastes like cheesecake. Serve on blueberry-banana bread.

Dream Desserts

Wheat-Germ Gems

Yield: 60 cookies (1-inch
　diameter, approximately)
Serving Size: 2 cookies
Exchange List Approximation:
　Starch/Bread 1
　Fat $\frac{1}{2}$

Nutrient Content Per Serving:
CAL: 104　　　PRO: 2.2 (gm)
FAT: 5.5 (gm)　CHO: 12 (gm)
Na: 38.2 (mg)　K: 46.2 (mg)
Fiber: 1 (gm)　Chol: 9 (mg)

Ingredients

　2　CUPS FLOUR
　1　CUP TOASTED WHEAT GERM
　¾　CUP SHORTENING
　½　CUP SUGAR
　1　EGG
　1　TEASPOON GRATED ORANGE RIND
　1　TEASPOON VANILLA
　½　TEASPOON SALT

Method

1. Combine all ingredients in mixing bowl. Repeat at low
   speed until well mixed.
2. Chill dough. Roll into 1-inch balls. Roll in wheat germ.
3. Place on cookie sheet and bake at 350° F for 12 to 15
   minutes.

Note: Approximately ¾ teaspoon sugar (13 to 14 calories) per 2-
cookie serving.

Date Cookies

Yield: 48 cookies (2-inch diameter) Nutrient Content Per Serving:
Serving Size: 2 cookies

CAL: 72   PRO: 1.4 (gm)

Exchange List Approximation:

FAT: 2.5 (gm)   CHO: 11.7 (gm)

    Fruit 1   Na: 62.9 (mg)   K: 80.1 (mg)

    Fat $\frac{1}{2}$ Fiber: 0.9 (gm) Chol: 23 (mg)

Ingredients

- 1 CUP RAISINS
- ½ CUP CHOPPED DATES
- 1 CUP WATER
- 2 EGGS
- ¼ CUP MARGARINE
- 1 TABLESPOON LIQUID SUGAR SUBSTITUTE
- 1 TEASPOON VANILLA
- ¼ TEASPOON CINNAMON
- 1 CUP FLOUR
- 1 TEASPOON BAKING SODA

Method

1. Combine in saucepan raisins, dates, and water. Boil 3 minutes, stirring constantly. Cool.
2. Cream together eggs, margarine, liquid sugar substitute, and vanilla.
3. Sift together cinnamon, flour, and soda.
4. Add dry ingredients to creamed mixture alternately with date mixture. Beat well. Chill several hours.
5. Drop from teaspoon onto greased baking pan. Bake at 350° F for 10 to 12 minutes.

Chewy Cookies

Yield: 24 cookies
Serving Size: 1 cookie
Exchange List Approximation:
   Starch/Bread $\frac{1}{2}$
   Fat $\frac{1}{2}$

Nutrient Content Per Serving:
CAL: 61   PRO: 0.9 (gm)
FAT: 3.7 (gm)   CHO: 6.4 (gm)
Na: 50 (mg)   K: 38 (mg)
Fiber: 0.5 (gm)   Chol: 11 (mg)

Ingredients

- ⅓ CUP VEGETABLE OIL
- 2 PACKETS SUGAR SUBSTITUTE
- BROWN SUGAR SUBSTITUTE FOR ¾ CUP BROWN SUGAR
- 1 TEASPOON VANILLA
- 1 EGG
- 1 CUP WHEAT-FLAKE CEREAL
- ½ CUP ALL-PURPOSE FLOUR
- ¼ CUP WHOLE-WHEAT FLOUR
- ½ TEASPOON BAKING POWDER
- 2 TABLESPOONS WHEAT GERM
- ½ CUP CHOPPED RAISINS
- ½ TEASPOON BAKING SODA
- 1 TABLESPOON WATER

Method

1. Mix ingredients in order given, adding soda that has been dissolved in water last.
2. Drop by teaspoon on ungreased cookie sheet.
3. Bake in 350° F oven 8 to 12 minutes.

Sugarless Raisin Cookies

Yield: 24 cookies
Serving Size: 2 cookies
Exchange List Approximation:
    Starch/Bread 1
    Fat $\frac{1}{2}$

Nutrient Content Per Serving:

CAL: 93	PRO: 2 (gm)
FAT: 2.5 (gm)	CHO: 15.9 (gm)
Na: 99.4 (mg)	K: 85.2 (mg)
Fiber: 1 (gm)	Chol: 23 (mg)

Ingredients

¾ CUP RAISINS
⅔ CUP WATER
1 TABLESPOON LIQUID SUGAR SUBSTITUTE
1 TEASPOON CINNAMON
¼ TEASPOON NUTMEG
2 TABLESPOONS MARGARINE
1 EGG
1 CUP FLOUR
1 TEASPOON BAKING POWDER
¼ TEASPOON SALT

Method

1. Combine raisins, water, sweetener, spices, and margarine in saucepan. Bring to a boil and cook 3 minutes. Cool.
2. Stir in egg.
3. Mix flour, baking powder, and salt. Add to fruit mixture and mix well.
4. Drop by teaspoon onto a lightly greased baking sheet. Bake in 350° F oven for 9 to 10 minutes until light brown.

Date Prune Bars

Yield: 18 servings
Serving Size: 1 bar
Exchange List Approximation:
    Starch/Bread 1
    Fat 1

Nutrient Content Per Serving:

CAL: 124	PRO: 2.2 (gm)
FAT: 5.4 (gm)	CHO: 17.9 (gm)
Na: 113.4 (mg)	K: 144.2 (mg)
Fiber: 2.4 (gm)	Chol: 30 (mg)

Ingredients

½ CUP QUARTERED DATES
½ CUP PITTED CHOPPED PRUNES (ABOUT 16)
½ CUP RAISINS
1 CUP WATER
¼ CUP MARGARINE
1 CUP FLOUR
1 TEASPOON BAKING SODA
¼ TEASPOON SALT
½ TEASPOON CINNAMON
¼ TEASPOON NUTMEG
2 EGGS
2 TEASPOONS LIQUID SUGAR SUBSTITUTE
1 TEASPOON VANILLA
½ CUP CHOPPED PECANS

Method

1. Combine dates, prunes, raisins, and water in saucepan. Simmer for 5 minutes, stirring occasionally. Stir in margarine. Cool.
2. Mix flour, soda, salt, and spices until blended.
3. Add fruit mixture, eggs, sugar substitute, and vanilla. Stir until blended. Stir in pecans.
4. Spread in lightly greased 9- by 13-inch pan. Bake in 350° F oven for 15 to 20 minutes. Cool and cut into bars.

Fresh-Fruit Parfait

Yield: 6 or 2 servings
Serving Size: $\frac{3}{4}$ cup
Exchange List Approximation:
    Meat, medium-fat $\frac{1}{2}$
    Fruit $1\frac{1}{2}$

Nutrient Content Per Serving:
CAL: 131   PRO: 5.7 (gm)
FAT: 3.7 (gm)   CHO: 20.7 (gm)
Na: 54.5 (mg)   K: 332.7 (mg)
Fiber: 2.3 (gm)   Chol: 13 (mg)

Ingredients

Six Servings		*Two Servings*
1	CUP PART SKIM-MILK RICOTTA CHEESE	⅓ CUP
2	PACKETS SUGAR SUBSTITUTE	2 TEASPOONS
½	TEASPOON ALMOND EXTRACT	2 DROPS
1	TABLESPOON MILK	1 TEASPOON
1	CUP SLICED ORANGES	⅓ CUP
1	CUP SLICED STRAWBERRIES	⅓ CUP
1	CUP DICED APPLES	⅓ CUP
1½	CUPS SLICED BANANAS	⅔ CUP

Method

1. Place cheese in mixing bowl. Whip cheese, sugar substitute, and almond extract together. Gradually whip in milk. Chill.
2. Prepare fruits to make 4½ cups.
3. Prepare in parfait glass. Place 2 teaspoons cheese in glass, layer of fruit, 1 tablespoon cheese, layer of fruit, 1 tablespoon cheese, layer of fruit.

Variation: Use other available fruits such as blueberries, seedless grapes, sliced peaches, or melon balls.

Seasonal Fruit Salad with Cardamom

Yield: 6 servings
Serving Size: ⅙ recipe
Exchange List Approximation:
    Fruit 2

Nutrient Content Per Serving:
CAL: 117   PRO: 1.1 (gm)
FAT: 0.6 (gm)   CHO: 30.1 (gm)
Na: 2.6 (mg)   K: 372.8 (mg)
Fiber: 3.1 (gm)   Chol: 0

Ingredients

1⅓ CUPS SLICED ORANGES
2½ CUPS SLICED, UNPEELED APPLES
  2 CUPS SLICED BANANAS
  6 MARASCHINO CHERRIES, QUARTERED
  1 TABLESPOON CHERRY JUICE
  2 TABLESPOONS LEMON JUICE
  2 TABLESPOONS WATER
1⁄16 TEASPOON CARDAMOM, GROUND (OR 1 POD, CRUSHED)

Method

1. Place fruits in salad bowl.
2. Combine lemon juice, cherry juice, and water. Pour over fruit.
3. Sprinkle with cardamom and mix lightly.
4. Cover, chill about an hour before serving.

Variation: When available, substitute 1 cup of following fruits for 1 cup bananas: red grapes, sliced strawberries, green grapes, or melon balls.

Note: One packet of sugar substitute may be added to marinade.

Marinated Fruit Bowl

Yield: 12 or 4 servings
Serving Size: $\frac{1}{2}$ cup
Exchange List Approximation:
    Fruit 1

Nutrient Content Per Serving:
CAL: 61   PRO: 0.6 (gm)
FAT: 0.3 (gm)   CHO: 15.4 (gm)
Na: 4.5 (mg)   K: 194.5 (mg)
Fiber: 1.4 (gm)   Chol: 0

Ingredients

Twelve Servings	*Four Servings*
1 CUP UNPEELED, SLICED APPLE (ABOUT 1 MEDIUM)	⅓ CUP
¾ CUP SEEDLESS GREEN GRAPES (ABOUT ¼ POUND)	¼ CUP
1 CUP SLICED ORANGE (ABOUT 1 LARGE)	⅓ CUP
¾ CUP HONEYDEW-MELON BALLS	¼ CUP
1 CUP SLICED BANANA (ABOUT 1 LARGE)	⅓ CUP
1 CUP SLICED STRAWBERRIES (ABOUT ½ PINT)	⅓ CUP
½ CUP SLICED KIWI (ABOUT 1 LARGE)	⅓ KIWI
6 MARASCHINO CHERRIES	3
3 TABLESPOONS CHERRY JUICE	1½ TABLESPOONS
2 TABLESPOONS WATER	2 TEASPOONS
1 TABLESPOON LIME JUICE FRESH MINT LEAVES	1 TEASPOON

Method

1. Mix fruits, except bananas, in large bowl.

2. Mix cherry juice, water, and lime juice. Add bananas and stir carefully to coat slices.
3. Add to fruit, stir lightly; cover and chill about 2 hours.
4. Garnish each serving with mint leaves.

Orangesicles

Yield: 8 or 2 popsicles	Nutrient Content Per Serving:
Serving Size: 1 popsicle	CAL: 60 PRO: 3.5 (gm)
Exchange List Approximation:	FAT: 1 (gm) CHO: 9.4 (gm)
Milk, low-fat $\frac{1}{2}$	Na: 43.4 (mg) K: 233.1 (mg)
	Fiber: 0 Chol: 4 (mg)

Ingredients

Eight Popsicles
  1 PINT PLAIN LOW-FAT YOGURT
  6 TABLESPOONS FROZEN ORANGE JUICE CONCENTRATE
  1 TEASPOON VANILLA
 30 DROPS LOW CALORIE SWEETENER (1 TABLESPOON SUGAR EQUIVALENT)

Two Popsicles
  ½ CUP
  1½ TABLESPOONS

  ¼ TEASPOON
  8 DROPS (¾ TEASPOON)

Method

1. Stir together all ingredients and freeze in popsicle molds or paper cups. Insert sticks when partially frozen.

Light and Luscious Orange Bars

Yield: 12 sandwiches
Serving Size: 1 sandwich
Exchange List Approximation:
    Starch/Bread 1

Nutrient Content Per Serving:

CAL: 84	PRO: 2.7 (gm)
FAT: 1.3 (gm)	CHO: 16.1 (gm)
Na: 110.4 (mg)	K: 159.2 (mg)
Fiber: 1.4 (gm)	Chol: 1 (mg)

Ingredients

  1 TEASPOON UNFLAVORED GELATIN
¼ CUP FROZEN CONCENTRATED ORANGE JUICE, THAWED
  2 TABLESPOONS SUGAR
½ TEASPOON VANILLA EXTRACT
½ CUP INSTANT NONFAT DRY-MILK POWDER
½ CUP COLD WATER
  1 TABLESPOON LEMON JUICE
24 GRAHAM CRACKERS

Method

1. Chill small mixing bowl and beaters.
2. In the top section of a double boiler, soften the gelatin in the concentrated orange juice. Place over hot water and stir until the gelatin is completely dissolved.
3. Remove from heat; stir in the sugar and vanilla extract.
4. Using cold bowl and beaters, beat dry milk and water until soft peaks form. Add lemon juice and beat until stiff. Fold in orange juice mixture.
5. Spread on 12 graham crackers. Top with remaining crackers.
6. Wrap individually in aluminum foil; freeze until firm (about 2 hours).

Note: Approximately ½ teaspoon sugar (8 calories) per serving.

Cocoa Ice Milk

Yield: 8 servings (4 cups)
Serving Size: ½ cup
Exchange List Approximation:
    Milk, skim 1

Nutrient Content Per Serving:
CAL: 64   PRO: 6.1 (gm)
FAT: 0.4 (gm)   CHO: 9.8 (gm)
Na: 160.1 (mg)   K: 437.9 (mg)
Fiber: 0   Chol: 1 (mg)

Ingredients

2½ CUPS SKIM MILK
1 ENVELOPE PLAIN GELATIN
3 OUNCES SUGAR-FREE HOT COCOA MIX (SUCH AS 4½ PACKAGES ALBA HOT COCOA OR 6 PACKAGES SWISS MISS)
1 TEASPOON VANILLA

Method

1. Add gelatin to 1 cup milk, stir, heat until gelatin is dissolved.
2. Add cocoa mix, stir until dissolved. Add remaining milk and vanilla.
3. Pour into shallow pan. Place in freezer until firm, about 4 hours.
4. Break into pieces and place in electric mixer or food processor. Whip until smooth.
5. Spoon into 8 individual containers. Serve immediately as soft ice milk or place in freezer to harden.

Peach Cobbler

Yield: 6 servings
Serving Size: $\frac{2}{3}$ cup
Exchange List Approximation:
    Starch/Bread 1
    Fruit $\frac{1}{2}$

Nutrient Content Per Serving:
CAL: 126   PRO: 2.1 (gm)
FAT: 3.9 (gm)   CHO: 21.6 (gm)
Na: 222.2 (mg) K: 197.2 (mg)
Fiber: 2.1 (gm)   Chol: 1 (mg)

Ingredients

  3 CUPS FRESH PEACHES (PEELED AND SLICED)
  ½ CUP WATER
  ¼ TEASPOON NUTMEG
  ¾ CUP BAKING MIX (BISQUICK TYPE)
  2 TEASPOONS SUGAR
  ¼ CUP SKIM MILK
  1 TABLESPOON MARGARINE
  3 PACKETS SUGAR SUBSTITUTE

Method

1. Bring peaches, water, and nutmeg to a boil. Pour one third into 2-quart casserole.
2. Combine baking mix, sugar, and milk. Stir to form a dough, turn out on floured board, roll out in rectangle ⅛-inch thick and cut into 6 strips.
3. Place 3 strips evenly over peaches. Add remaining peaches. Cover with 3 strips of dough.
4. Pour juice over dough and dot with margarine.
5. Bake in 400° F oven for 30 minutes until brown and bubbly.
6. Remove from oven and sprinkle with 3 packets of sugar substitute.

Pear Crisp

Yield: 6 servings (3 cups)
Serving Size: $\frac{1}{2}$ cup
Exchange List Approximation:
    Starch/Bread 1
    Fruit 1
    Fat 1

Nutrient Content Per Serving:
CAL: 191   PRO: 1.7 (gm)
FAT: 6.2 (gm)   CHO: 33.6 (gm)
Na: 239 (mg)   K: 189.4 (mg)
Fiber: 4.9 (gm) Chol: 1 (mg)

Ingredients

  3 CUPS PEAR SAUCE (SEE FOLLOWING RECIPE)
¾ CUP BAKING MIX (BISQUICK TYPE)
  1 TABLESPOON BROWN SUGAR SUBSTITUTE
½ TEASPOON CINNAMON
  2 TABLESPOONS MARGARINE
  2 PACKETS SUGAR SUBSTITUTE

Method

1. Pour pear sauce into shallow 2-quart casserole or 8- by 8- by 2-inch pan.
2. Mix baking mix, brown sugar substitute, and cinnamon together. Add softened margarine and mix until crumbly.
3. Sprinkle mixture evenly over sauce.
4. Bake in 400° F oven about 30 minutes until top is brown.
5. Remove from oven and sprinkle with sugar substitute.

Variation: Three cups of cooked chopped apples may be used.

Pear Sauce

Yield: 6 servings (3 cups)
Serving Size: $\frac{1}{2}$ cup
Exchange List Approximation:
    Fruit $1\frac{1}{2}$

Nutrient Content Per Serving:
CAL: 83   PRO: 0.5 (gm)
FAT: 0.5 (gm)   CHO: 21.1 (gm)
Na: 0   K: 175.4 (mg)
Fiber: 4.2 (gm)   Chol: 0

Ingredients

2 POUNDS UNPEELED, CHOPPED PEARS
⅓ CUP WATER
1½ TEASPOONS GROUND CINNAMON
½ TEASPOON GROUND NUTMEG
1 TABLESPOON VANILLA EXTRACT

Method

1. Mix ingredients together in saucepan. Cover and cook until pears are tender. Then mash.
2. Serve by itself, or take 2 Tablespoons and serve hot over banana bread. (Two Tablespoons count as a free food.)

Variation: Omit cinnamon, nutmeg, and vanilla; use 1 teaspoon fresh, chopped ginger root and then add 2 packets sugar substitute after cooking.

Date Drops

Yield: 42 cookies
Serving Size: 2 cookies
Exchange List Approximation:
    Fruit ½
    Fat 1

Nutrient Content Per Serving:
CAL: 78   PRO: 1.1 (gm)
FAT: 4.6 (gm)   CHO: 9 (gm)
Na: 56.8 (mg)   K: 83.1 (mg)
Fiber: 1 (gm)   Chol: 23 (mg)

Ingredients

  2 EGGS, BEATEN
 ⅓ CUP MARGARINE
 ½ POUND DATES, FINELY CUT
1½ CUPS CRISP RICE CEREAL
 ½ CUP NUTS, CHOPPED
  1 TEASPOON VANILLA

Method

1. Combine eggs, margarine, and dates. Cook over low heat, stirring constantly.
2. Boil 2 minutes. Remove from heat and add cereal, nuts, and vanilla.
3. Cool; shape into little balls.

Oatmeal Cake

Yield: 9 servings
Serving Size: $\frac{1}{9}$ recipe
Exchange List Approximation:
    Starch/Bread 1
    Fruit 1
    Fat 1

Nutrient Content Per Serving:
CAL: 173   PRO: 4.6 (gm)
FAT: 5.5 (gm)   CHO: 26.4 (gm)
Na: 104.9 (mg)   K: 159.8 (mg)
Fiber: 1.9 (gm)   Chol: 61 (mg)

Ingredients

1½ CUPS OATMEAL
3 TABLESPOONS BROWN SUGAR SUBSTITUTE
3 TABLESPOONS NONFAT DRY MILK
4 TABLESPOONS FLOUR
2 TEASPOONS BAKING POWDER
⅛ TEASPOON BAKING SODA
1 TEASPOON CINNAMON
2 CUPS CRUSHED PINEAPPLE, IN OWN JUICE
2 EGGS
2 TABLESPOONS CORN OIL

Method

1. Combine all ingredients in a large bowl. Mix well.
2. Place in 8- by 8-inch baking pan sprayed with vegetable pan spray.
3. Bake in 375° F oven for 25 minutes.

Low-Calorie Pumpkin Pie

Yield: 8 servings
Serving Size: $\frac{1}{8}$ recipe
Exchange List Approximation:
   Starch/Bread $1\frac{1}{2}$

Nutrient Content Per Serving:
CAL: 114   PRO: 6.3 (gm)
FAT: 1.9 (gm)   CHO: 18.5 (gm)
Na: 174.9 (mg) K: 304.2 (mg)
Fiber: 1.4 (gm)   Chol: 37 (mg)
Key Source Nutrients:
   Vitamin A: 13668 (IU)

Ingredients

  1 16-OUNCE CAN SOLID-PACK PUMPKIN
  1 13-OUNCE CAN EVAPORATED SKIM MILK
  1 EGG
  2 EGG WHITES
 ½ CUP BISCUIT MIX (BISQUICK TYPE)
  2 TABLESPOONS SUGAR
  8 PACKETS SUGAR SUBSTITUTE
  2 TEASPOONS PUMPKIN PIE SPICE
  2 TEASPOONS VANILLA

Method

1. Heat oven to 350° F. Lightly grease or spray 9-inch pie pan with vegetable pan spray.
2. Place all ingredients in blender, food processor, or mixing bowl. Blend 1 minute or beat 2 minutes with mixer.
3. Pour into pie pan and bake for 50 minutes or until center is puffed up.

Peachy Pie

Yield: 6 servings
Serving Size: 5 ounces
Exchange List Approximation:
    Starch/Bread 1
    Fruit $\frac{1}{2}$
    Fat $1\frac{1}{2}$

Nutrient Content Per Serving:
CAL: 179   PRO: 3.3 (gm)
FAT: 10 (gm)   CHO: 19.6 (gm)
Na: 189.3 (mg)   K: 156.5 (mg)
Fiber: 1.6 (gm)   Chol: 0

Ingredients

1 ENVELOPE UNFLAVORED GELATIN
¼ CUP WATER
1 12-OUNCE CAN DIET GINGER ALE
2 CUPS SLICED, FRESH, RIPE PEACHES OR UNSWEETENED FROZEN PEACHES
1 READY-TO-FILL GRAHAM-CRACKER CRUST OR PREBAKED 9-INCH PIE SHELL

Method

1. Sprinkle gelatin over water in small mixing bowl. Place in pan of hot water, heat until dissolved.
2. Add diet ginger ale, stir. Add peaches and juice. Chill until thickened.
3. Spoon into prepared crust and chill until firm.
4. May be served with Low-Calorie Whipped Topping (refer to page 329).

Variation: 2 packets of sugar substitute may be added to peaches. 1 package of orange or raspberry flavored low-calorie gelatin dessert and 1¾ cups water may be used with peaches.

Fruit Yogurt Freeze

Yield: 8 servings (4 cups)
Serving Size: $\frac{1}{2}$ cup
Exchange List Approximation:
    Milk, low-fat $\frac{1}{2}$

Nutrient Content Per Serving:

CAL: 60	PRO: 4.3 (gm)
FAT: 1 (gm)	CHO: 9.1 (gm)
Na: 43.9 (mg)	K: 249.7 (mg)
Fiber: 0.7 (gm)	Chol: 4 (mg)

Ingredients

2 CUPS UNSWEETENED PEACHES
2 CUPS PLAIN LOW-FAT YOGURT
1 PACKAGE UNFLAVORED GELATIN
6 PACKETS SUGAR SUBSTITUTE
¼ CUP HOT WATER

Method

1. Place peaches and yogurt in blender or food processor. Blend until smooth.
2. Mix gelatin and sweetener, add hot water, stir until dissolved. Add to peach mixture. Blend about 1 minute.
3. Pour into metal container, place in freezer for 1 hour until partially frozen.
4. Put back in blender or processor. Blend until smooth.
5. Immediately pour into 8 individual serving containers or pan. Cover and place in freezer until ready to serve. If frozen hard, let sit in refrigerator about an hour before serving.

Whipped Chocolate Cream

Yield: 6 servings (3 cups)
Serving Size: $\frac{1}{2}$ cup
Exchange List Approximation:
    Milk, skim $\frac{1}{2}$
    Fat 2

Nutrient Content Per Serving:

CAL: 134	PRO: 5 (gm)
FAT: 11.9 (gm)	CHO: 3.5 (gm)
Na: 44.6 (mg)	K: 154.6 (mg)
Fiber: 0	Chol: 119 (mg)

Ingredients

 1 OUNCE UNSWEETENED CHOCOLATE (ABOUT 1 SQUARE)
¾ CUP SKIM MILK
 1 ENVELOPE UNFLAVORED GELATIN
½ CUP WATER
 2 EGG YOLKS
½ CUP WHIPPING CREAM
 2 TEASPOONS VANILLA
 2 EGG WHITES
 3 PACKETS SUGAR SUBSTITUTE

Method

1. Melt chocolate with milk in top of double boiler over simmering water; stir occasionally.
2. Sprinkle gelatin over water and let stand about 1 minute. Add to chocolate mixture and stir until completely dissolved.
3. Beat egg yolks until lemon colored. Stir part of hot mixture into egg yolks, then add back to hot mixture. Cook over low heat until mixture begins to thicken.
4. Remove from heat. Add vanilla and chill until mixture begins to thicken.

5. Whip cream and fold into chocolate mixture.
6. Beat egg whites until peaks begin to form, add sugar substitute, and beat until stiff. Gently fold into chocolate.
7. Spoon into dessert dishes. Chill until set.

Note: Cream may be used as a cake frosting. Also, you can break a sponge cake (see Volume I for recipe) into pieces, pour the cream over it, and chill for a surprising dessert.

Party-Time
Special Effects

Eggplant Appetizers

Yield: 6 servings (24 slices)
Serving Size: 4 slices
Exchange List Approximation:
    Vegetable 1
    Fat $\frac{1}{2}$

Nutrient Content Per Serving:
CAL: 53   PRO: 1.3 (gm)
FAT: 3.6 (gm)   CHO: 4.9 (gm)
Na: 64 (mg)   K: 181.2 (mg)
Fiber: 1.5 (gm)   Chol: 2 (mg)

Ingredients

- 1 POUND EGGPLANT (ABOUT 2 SMALL OR 2 JAPANESE)
- 2 TEASPOONS VEGETABLE OIL
- 2 TEASPOONS MAYONNAISE
- ⅛ TEASPOON EACH: GARLIC SALT, PAPRIKA, BASIL, PEPPER
- ¼ TEASPOON OREGANO
- 2 TABLESPOONS GRATED PARMESAN CHEESE

Method

1. Trim ends from eggplant and cut in ⅜-inch slices.
2. Place slices on oiled sheet pan and brush with oil.
3. Spread top with small amount of mayonnaise.
4. Sprinkle evenly with garlic salt, paprika, basil, pepper, oregano, and cheese.
5. Bake in 425° F oven until lightly browned, about 10 minutes. May be browned under broiler. Do not burn.
6. Serve as appetizer or vegetable.

Guacamole (Avocado Dip)

Yield: 6 servings ($\frac{3}{4}$ cup)
Serving Size: 2 tablespoons
Exchange List Approximation:
    Fat 1

Nutrient Content Per Serving:
CAL: 35   PRO: 0.5 (gm)
FAT: 3.2 (gm)   CHO: 2 (gm)
Na: 24.7 (mg)   K: 138.5 (mg)
Fiber: 0.5 (gm)   Chol: 0

Ingredients

1 LARGE RIPE AVOCADO (ABOUT 6 OUNCES)
1 TABLESPOON LEMON JUICE
1 TABLESPOON FINELY CHOPPED GREEN ONION
2 TABLESPONS DICED TOMATO PIECES, FRESH OR
  CANNED
  DASH SALT

Method

1. Peel avocado, cut in half, and remove pit.
2. Place avocado halves in bowl, add lemon juice, and mash with fork.
3. Add onion, tomato, and salt. Mix lightly. Cover tightly and use as soon as possible as it will darken.

Note: The above is a basic guacamole to be served with lettuce and highly seasoned Mexican dishes. To make dip, add hot sauce, picante sauce, chili powder, or chopped green chilies to taste.

Soy Nuts

Yield: 12 servings ($1\frac{1}{2}$ cups)
Serving Size: $\frac{1}{12}$ recipe
Exchange List Approximation:
    Starch/Bread $\frac{1}{2}$
    Meat, lean 1

Nutrient Content Per Serving:
CAL: 88   PRO: 7.5 (gm)
FAT: 3.9 (gm)   CHO: 7.3 (gm)
Na: 1.1 (mg)   K: 366.9 (mg)
Fiber: 3.1 (gm)   Chol: 0

Ingredients

1¼ CUPS SOYBEANS (ABOUT ½ POUND)
4 CUPS WATER

Method

1. Soak soybeans for 12 hours. Remove excess moisture on paper towel.
2. Place on baking sheet and toast in oven for 2 or more hours at 250° F until crisp all the way through.

Note: May be used whole or ground in salads, sandwiches, snacks, dessert toppings, breads, quick breads, etc.

Build-a-Burrito

Select one or more items from each category to match your meal pattern.

Yield: Varies
Exchanges and estimated nutrients per one serving in each category. Nutritional analyses are *averages* of the alternative items listed in each category.

Category	CAL	FAT (gm)	Na (mg)	Fiber (gm)	PRO (gm)	CHO (gm)	K (mg)	Chol (mg)
Bread	74	1.0	73.3	0.9	2.7	13.9	28.7	0
Bean	82	1.0	4.2*	3.6	5.6	13.3	235.5	0
Meat/Cheese	76	4.8	130.2	0	7.2	0.5	67.4	24
Vegetable	28	0.1	314.7	0.9	1.3	5.9	258.9	0
Fat	45	4.5	98.3	0.7	.06	1.2	63.3	3

Exchanges
Bread   1 Starch/Bread
Bean   1 Starch/Bread
Meat/Cheese   1 Meat, medium-fat
Vegetable   1 Vegetable
Fat   1 Fat

Ingredients

Bread Category
   1 6-INCH DIAMETER FLOUR TORTILLA (MADE WITH OIL OR SHORTENING—NOT LARD)
   1 6-INCH DIAMETER CORN TORTILLA
   1 6-INCH DIAMETER WHOLE-WHEAT FLOUR TORTILLA
   ½ SMALL (6-INCH-DIAMETER) POCKET BREAD (WHOLE-WHEAT, RYE, OR WHITE)

Bean Category
¼ CUP COOKED, FORK-MASHED BEANS: PINTO, OR GARBANZO, OR RED, OR WHITE, OR NAVY, OR LENTILS, OR SPLIT PEAS, OR SOY, OR REFRIED (RECIPE, PAGE 254)

Meat/Cheese Category
1 OUNCE COOKED, DRAINED GROUND ROUND
1 OUNCE COOKED, SHREDDED CHICKEN BREAST (WITHOUT SKIN)
1 OUNCE COOKED, LEAN SHREDDED PORK (OMIT ½ FAT EXCHANGE)
1 OUNCE GRATED, SHARP CHEDDAR CHEESE (OMIT 1 FAT EXCHANGE)**
1 OUNCE GRATED, LOW-FAT CHEESE

Vegetable Category (Optional)
½ CUP CHOPPED TOMATO
½ CUP CHOPPED GREEN PEPPER
½ CUP ENCHILADA SAUCE (OMIT 1 FAT EXCHANGE)
½ CUP TOMATO SAUCE

Fat Category
⅛ RIPE AVOCADO, MASHED
2 TABLESPOONS SOUR CREAM**
5 SMALL, BLACK, RIPE OLIVES, SLICED OR CHOPPED

Free Exchange Category
1 TABLESPOON† CHOPPED TOMATO, OR CHOPPED GREEN PEPPER, OR CHOPPED ONION, OR CHOPPED JALAPENO PEPPER, OR SALSA, OR PLAIN LOW-FAT YOGURT
CILANTRO TO TASTE
CUMIN TO TASTE
CHILI POWDER TO TASTE
TABASCO SAUCE TO TASTE

Method

1. Select one or more items from each category to match your meal pattern.
2. Fill the item(s) from the Bread Category with items from the other categories to match your meal pattern. Best if served warm.

Example: One 6-inch flour tortilla (1 Starch/Bread exchange) filled with ¼ cup pinto beans (1 Starch/Bread); 1 ounce shredded chicken breast (1 Medium-Fat Meat); ⅛ ripe avocado, mashed (1 Fat exchange); 1 Tablespoon salsa (Free exchange); 1 Tablespoon chopped onion (Free exchange); cilantro and cumin to taste (Free exchanges). Total exchanges per meal used from this recipe:

1 Medium-Fat Meat
2 Starch/Bread
1 Fat

*Beans are cooked or canned without salt.
**Limit to 1 serving per meal; high in cholesterol and saturated fat.
†Limit to 2 servings per meal.

Tofu Pizza

Yield: 6 or 2 servings
Serving Size: $\frac{1}{2}$ muffin
Exchange List Approximation:
    Starch/Bread 1
    Meat, medium-fat 1
    Vegetable 1

Nutrient Content Per Serving:
CAL: 183   PRO: 9.9 (gm)
FAT: 6.8 (gm)   CHO: 21 (gm)
Na: 478 (mg)   K: 348 (mg)
Fiber: 0.8 (gm)   Chol: 11 (mg)

Ingredients

Six Servings		Two Servings	
3	ENGLISH MUFFINS	1	
1	CUP PIZZA SAUCE	⅓	CUP
6	OUNCES TOFU	2	OUNCES
⅜	TEASPOON OREGANO	⅛	TEASPOON
⅜	TEASPOON GARLIC POWDER	⅛	TEASPOON
4	OUNCES SHREDDED PART-SKIM MOZZARELLA CHEESE	1⅓	OUNCES

Method

1. Cut English muffins in half.
2. Spread each half with 2½ Tablespoons sauce.
3. Crumble tofu and mix with oregano and garlic powder. Spread evenly over sauce.
4. Cover with shredded cheese, about 3 Tablespoons per pizza.
5. Bake in 350° F oven until cheese melts and starts to brown, about 15 minutes.

Fruit Pizzas
with Apple Juice Glaze

Yield: 6 servings (3- by 4-inch pieces)
Exchanges and estimated nutrients per 1 serving:

	OATMEAL CRUST		CHEESE CRUST	
	Apple-Raisin	-Blueberry	Apple-Raisin	-Blueberry
CAL	185	164	245	224
FAT (gm)	3.3	3.3	6.0	6.0
Na (mg)	206.4	207.8	82.4	83.8
Fiber (gm)	3.1	3.2	3.0	3.2
PRO (gm)	3.7	3.5	6.3	6.2
CHO (gm)	36.7	31.1	42.8	37.1
K (mg)	191.4	128.8	194.7	132.1
Chol (mg)	0	0	9	9
Exchanges	Starch/	Starch/	Starch/	Starch/
	Bread 1	Bread 1	Bread 1½	Bread 1½
	Fruit 1½	Fruit 1	Fruit 1½	Fruit 1
	Fat ½	Fat ½	Fat 1	Fat 1

Ingredients

Oatmeal Crust
- 1 CUP LESS 1 TABLESPOON ALL-PURPOSE FLOUR
- ¾ CUP QUICK OATMEAL
- 1 TABLESPOON OIL
- ½ CUP WARM WATER
- ½ PACKAGE DRY YEAST
- ½ TEASPOON SALT
- ½ TEASPOON BAKING POWDER

Cheese Crust
- 1⅓ CUPS PLUS 2 TABLESPOONS ALL-PURPOSE FLOUR
- 1 TABLESPOON OIL
- ½ CUP WARM WATER
- ½ PACKAGE DRY YEAST

½ TEASPOON BAKING POWDER
⅓ CUP PLUS 2 TABLESPOONS GRATED, SHARP
   CHEDDAR CHEESE

Apple-Raisin Topping
3½ CUPS PARED AND SLICED APPLES
 1 PACKET SUGAR SUBSTITUTE
¾ TEASPOON CINNAMON
⅓ CUP PLUS 1 TABLESPOON SEEDLESS RAISINS

Apple-Blueberry Topping
2¼ CUPS PARED AND SLICED APPLES
1½ CUPS BLUEBERRIES, UNSWEETENED
1¼ PACKETS SUGAR SUBSTITUTE
¾ TEASPOON CINNAMON
 2 TEASPOONS LEMON JUICE

Method

1. Gather together ingredients to make the fruit pizza crust and topping desired.
2. Make the crust. Combine flour, oatmeal, salt, and baking powder together in a bowl. (Add cheese if making cheese crust and omit oatmeal and salt.) Blend oil in with a fork.
3. Dissolve yeast in water and add to the flour mixture. Stir with a wooden spoon until all ingredients are combined. Cover and let rise 1 hour.
4. Stir down dough and pat into 9- by 8-inch rectangle. Combine topping ingredients and arrange over crust.
5. Bake 30 to 40 minutes at 375° F.
6. *Glaze:* Make apple juice glaze. Combine ⅔ cup unsweetened apple juice and 1½ teaspoons cornstarch in small saucepan. Cook over medium heat until thickened. Remove from heat. Spread over fruit pizzas during last 15 minutes of baking. Cut 2 by 3 into 6 pieces.

Basic Chocolate Milkshake

Yield: 1 serving
Serving Size: $1\frac{3}{4}$ cup
Exchange List Approximation:
    Meat, lean 2
    Milk, skim 2

Nutrient Content Per Serving:
CAL: 298   PRO: 40.2 (gm)
FAT: 5.5 (gm)   CHO: 22.8 (gm)
Na: 1046 (mg)   K: 704 (mg)
Fiber: 0.3 (gm)   Chol: 24 (mg)

Ingredients

1 TABLESPOON COCOA
1 TABLESPOON WATER
1 CUP FROZEN SKIM MILK
1 CUP FROZEN LOW-FAT COTTAGE CHEESE
2 PACKETS SUGAR SUBSTITUTE

Method

1. Boil cocoa and water together for ½ minute.
2. Put cocoa mixture, milk, cottage cheese, and sweetener in blender and blend until well blended, about 3 minutes.

Variations: Chocomint Shake uses recipe as above with a drop of peppermint extract. Cocoa-Coconut Shake uses recipe as above with ¼ teaspoon coconut extract.

Milkshake with Variations

Yield: 1 serving (1¾ cups for plain; 2 cups for variation)
Exchanges and Estimated nutrients are per ½-recipe serving.

Variation	CAL	FAT (gm)	Na (mg)	Fiber (gm)	PRO (gm)	CHO (gm)	K (mg)	Chol (mg)
Plain	188	2.6	586.0	0	24.0	15.9	514.0	14
Banana	240	2.9	587.0	1.1	24.6	29.3	740.0	14
Banana and peanut butter	430	19.3	737.0	3.5	33.8	34.3	960.0	14
Peanut butter	378	19.0	736.0	2.4	33.2	20.9	734.0	14
Unsweetened peach	245	2.7	586.0	2.1	24.9	30.6	774.0	14
Pineapple	238	2.7	587.0	0.7	24.3	29.0	615.0	14
Strawberry	244	3.3	588.0	4.1	25.1	29.0	823.0	14

Exchanges

Plain	2 Meat, lean + 1 Milk, skim
Banana	2 Meat, lean + 1 Fruit + 1 Milk, skim
Banana and peanut butter	4 Meat, medium-fat + 1 Fruit + 1 Milk, skim
Peanut butter	4 Meat, medium-fat + 1 Milk, skim
Peach	2 Meat, lean + 1 Fruit + 1 Milk, skim
Pineapple	2 Meat, lean + 1 Fruit + 1 Milk, skim
Strawberry	2 Meat, lean + 1 Fruit + 1 Milk, skim

Ingredients

Plain

   1 CUP SKIM MILK
   ½ CUP LOW-FAT COTTAGE CHEESE
   ¼ TEASPOON VANILLA
2-3 PACKETS SUGAR SUBSTITUTE

Variation

   ½ BANANA, OR
   ½ BANANA AND 2 TABLESPOONS PEANUT BUTTER, OR
   2 TABLESPOONS PEANUT BUTTER, OR
   ½ CUP UNSWEETENED PEACHES, OR
   ⅓ CUP CRUSHED PINEAPPLE IN OWN JUICE, OR
   ¾ CUP FRESH STRAWBERRIES OR FROZEN
     UNSWEETENED STRAWBERRIES

Method

1. Combine ingredients to make Plain Milkshake, place in
   metal pan, and freeze.
2. Break up mixture and blend or process until smooth.
3. To make a variation, add one of the variations and blend
   until smooth.

Wine Spritzer

Yield: 8 servings
Serving Size: 8 ounces
Exchange List Approximation:
    Fat 2

Nutrient Content Per Serving:

CAL: 84	PRO: 0.4 (gm)
FAT: 0	CHO: 2 (gm)
Na: 33 (mg)	K: 134 (mg)
Fiber: 0	Chol: 0

Ingredients

1 QUART CLUB SODA
1 QUART DRY WHITE OR RED WINE
   ICE CUBES
   LIME OR LEMON WEDGES

Method

1. Mix soda and wine.
2. Add ice and garnish with lime or lemon wedges.

Note: May be served in pitcher or punch bowl, as well as 8-ounce glass.

12 □ FAST FOOD (HOW TO BYPASS THE BOOBY TRAPS)

Move over, Mom's apple pie. Hamburgers and french fries are giving the old favorite mean competition for first place in Americans' stomachs, if not their hearts. If you're like most Americans, you probably find yourself in line at fast food restaurants 9 to 10 times a month and spend close to a third of your total food budget on meals away from home.

Having diabetes doesn't make you immune to the attractions of quick service and reasonable prices. Fortunately, if you follow a few guidelines, you can usually eat wherever you want without seriously compromising on nutrition.

KNOW YOUR MEAL PLAN and choose foods that fit it as closely as possible. For example, if you're on an exchange diet and are allowed 2 Starch/Bread exchanges and 2 Medium-Fat Meat exchanges during lunch, you would steer clear of the double cheeseburger (which is 2 Starch/Bread exchanges, 3 Medium-Fat Meat exchanges, and 3 Fat exchanges) and instead order a single hamburger.

AVOID SUGAR, FAT, AND SALT. You already know to avoid such obvious "no-nos" as milkshakes, apple pie, and gooey sundaes. But spotting other diet disasters can be tricky. Many

367

fast foods contain "hidden" salt as well as saturated fat, cholesterol, and calories. Salt can be harmful to people who have high
blood pressure, and cholesterol is believed to contribute to cor-
onary artery disease. To avoid unhealthy foods, you need to be
armed with information about the makeup of fast foods. The
accompanying chart will give you specifics about the fat, calorie,
and salt content of many popular fast foods, but here are some
general tips.

Items that tend to be high in fat and cholesterol are dairy
products, meats, and fried foods (which are almost always cooked
in saturated fat). Of course, these are the mainstays of many fast
food places, so if you must have fast foods, sometimes the best
you can do is to get rid of some excess fat (and calories!) by
choosing small portions, scraping away greasy breadings, and
draining excess oils. Also, be wary of sauces containing mayonnaise. They're high in fat.

Avoiding high-salt foods can be difficult because you can't
always taste the salt. For example, who would suspect that a
Whopper with Cheese has 1,435 milligrams of sodium, or that a
12-inch pizza may contain 2,700 milligrams of sodium? (The suggested maximum sodium allowance for an entire day is 3,000
milligrams.) Catsup, pickles, mustard, tartar sauce, and salad
dressing all have added salt, too, so tell the counter-person to
cancel the condiments.

KNOW THE NUTRITIVE VALUES OF FAST FOODS. The
nutritional worth of your meal depends on how good your choices
are. Fast foods are often low in vitamins A, C, and D, as well as
folic acid, fiber, and certain minerals. However, if properly selected,
fast food meals *can* give you adequate amounts of protein, thia-
mine, riboflavin, and calcium. Reasonable choices, in addition to
hamburgers (without condiments), are plain roast beef sandwiches, chili, and fresh salads. Fortunately, many fast food restaurants provide salad bars these days. If you miss out on some
essential nutrients, vitamins, and minerals in your fast food meal,
eat a variety of vegetables, fruits, milk, and whole-grain foods in

your other meals and snacks during the day to make up for the lack.

PORTION PREDICAMENTS. Portion sizes are usually standard in fast food restaurant chains across the country, which makes estimating fairly easy once you familiarize yourself with a given chain's menu. But among independent establishments, such as delicatessens and sandwich shops, contents and portions can differ dramatically. When selecting from these menus, you'll need to do some quick calculating on your own.

Begin by breaking down the selection you want into its separate ingredients, noting the *kinds* and *amounts* of ingredients used. Then, see if it fits into your meal plan. If you follow an "exchange" meal plan, try to estimate the proper exchange for each ingredient, taking care not to *underestimate.* For example, a deli-bought turkey sandwich might calculate like this:

Turkey (approx. 3 oz. meat) = 3 Lean-Meat exchanges; tomatoes and lettuce = 1 Vegetable exchange; 1 teaspoon mayonnaise = 1 Fat exchange; 2 slices French bread = 2 Starch/Bread exchanges. (The sandwich would give you 395 calories, with 35 grams carbohydrate, 29 grams protein, and 14 grams fat.)

If you have trouble "guesstimating," train yourself to judge portions by eye. Practice measuring foods at home with your food scale, measuring cups, and spoons. Remind yourself what half a cup of milk looks like; see how many slices of cheese are in one ounce.

CHECK OUT THE CHART. The following chart is included to show you the nutritive values of selected fast foods, so you can make informed choices. It is not meant as an endorsement of fast foods, or any restaurant in particular. Remember, some of the foods listed here may not be appropriate for your meal plan.

If your favorite food isn't here, compare it to a similar food. Be sure to gauge portions accurately. Your diet counselor should be able to help calculate exchanges and determine whether or not the food has a place in your diet.

FAST FOOD EXCHANGES*

	SERVING SIZE	CALORIES (1 SERVING)	CARB. (GM.)	PRO (GM.)	FAT (GM.)	SODIUM (MG.)	EXCHANGES (1 SERVING)
ARBY'S							
Roast Beef Sandwich	5 oz.	350	32	22	15	880	2 Bread, 2 Med.-Fat Meat, 1 Fat
Junior Roast Beef Sandwich	3 oz.	220	21	12	9	530	1½ Bread, 1 Med.-Fat Meat, 1 Fat
Turkey Sandwich	6 oz.	410	36	24	19	1,060	2½ Bread, 2 Med.-Fat Meat, 2 Fat
ARTHUR TREACHER'S							
Fish	2 pieces	355	25	19	20	450	2 Bread, 2 Med.-Fat Meat, 2 Fat
Fish	3 pieces	533	38	29	30	675	2 Bread, 3 Med.-Fat Meat, 3 Fat
Fish Sandwich	1	440	39	16	24	836	3 Bread, 1 Med.-Fat Meat, 4 Fat
Chips	4 oz.	276	35	4	13	393	2 Bread, 3 Fat
Cole Slaw	3 oz.	123	11	1	8	266	1 Bread, 1 Fat
Chowder	1 bowl	112	11	5	5	835	1 Bread, 1 Fat
BURGER KING							
Hamburger	3.9 oz.	290	29	15	13	525	2 Bread, 1 Med.-Fat Meat, 2 Fat
Cheeseburger	4.4 oz.	350	30	18	17	730	2 Bread, 2 Med.-Fat Meat, 1 Fat
Whopper	9.2 oz.	630	50	26	36	990	3½ Bread, 2 Med.-Fat Meat, 5 Fat
Whopper Jr.	5.1 oz.	370	31	15	20	560	2 Bread, 1 Med.-Fat Meat, 3 Fat

Item	Portion	Calories	Carb	Protein	Fat	Sodium	Exchanges
French Fries	2.4 oz.	210	25	3	11	230	1½ Bread, 2 Fat
Onion Rings	2.7 oz.	270	29	3	16	450	2 Bread, 3 Fat

DAIRY QUEEN

Item	Portion	Calories	Carb	Protein	Fat	Sodium	Exchanges
Single Hamburger	5 oz.	360	33	21	16	630	2 Bread, 2 Med.-Fat Meat, 1 Fat
Hot Dog	3.5 oz.	280	21	11	16	830	1½ Bread, 1 Med.-Fat Meat, 2 Fat
French Fries (Regular)	2.5 oz.	200	25	2	10	115	1½ Bread, 2 Fat
Cone (Small)**	3 oz.	140	22	3	4	45	1 Bread, 1 Fat
Chocolate Sundae (Small)**	3.7 oz.	190	33	3	4	75	2 Bread, 1 Fat
"Dilly" Bar**	3 oz.	210	21	3	13	50	1½ Bread, 3 Fat
"DQ" Sandwich**	2 oz.	140	24	3	4	40	1½ Bread, 1 Fat

KENTUCKY FRIED CHICKEN

Original Recipe Chicken (Edible Portion)

Item	Portion	Calories	Carb	Protein	Fat	Sodium	Exchanges
Wing (one piece)	1.5 oz.	136	4	10	9	302	1½ Med.-Fat Meat
Drumstick	1.6 oz.	117	3	12	7	207	1½ Lean Meat
Side Breast	2.4 oz.	199	7	16	12	558	½ Bread, 2 Med.-Fat Meat
Thigh	3 oz.	257	7	18	18	556	½ Bread, 2½ Med.-Fat Meat, 1 Fat
Keel	3.3 oz.	236	7	24	12	631	½ Bread, 3 Med.-Fat Meat

(Extra crispy has more fat and approx. 50 cal. extra per piece.)

Item	Portion	Calories	Carb	Protein	Fat	Sodium	Exchanges
Chicken Breast Sandwich	5.5 oz.	436	34	25	23	1,093	2 Bread, 3 Med.-Fat Meat, 2 Fat
Mashed Potatoes	3 oz.	64	12	2	1	268	1 Bread
Gravy	2 Tbsp.	46	2	–	4	57	1 Fat
Roll	0.7 oz.	61	11	2	1	118	1 Bread
Cole Slaw	¾ Cup	121	13	1	7	225	1 Bread, 1 Fat
Kentucky Fries	3.4 oz.	184	28	3	7	174	2 Bread, 1 Fat

FAST FOOD EXCHANGES*

	SERVING SIZE	CALORIES (1 SERVING)	CARB. (GM.)	PRO. (GM.)	FAT (GM.)	SODIUM (MG.)	EXCHANGES (1 SERVING)
LONG JOHN SILVER'S							
Chicken Planks	4	457	35	27	23	NA	2 Bread, 3 Med.-Fat Meat, 2 Fat
Seafood Platter							
Fish	1	183	11	11	11	NA	1Bread, 1 Med.-Fat Meat, 1 Fat
Scallops	2	94	10	4	5	NA	½ Bread, 1 Fat
Shrimp	2	89	10	3	4	NA	½ Bread, 1 Fat
Hush Puppies	2	102	13	2	4	NA	1 Bread, 1 Fat
Fryes	3 oz.	288	33	4	16	NA	2 Bread, 3 Fat
Cole Slaw	4 oz.	138	16	1	8	NA	1 Bread (or 3 Vegetable,) 2 Fat
Total		894	93	25	48	NA	6 Bread, 1 Vegetable, 1 Med.-Fat Meat, 8 Fat
Clams on Clam Dinner	5 oz.	465	46	13	25	NA	3 Bread, 1 Med.-Fat Meat, 4 Fat
Clam Chowder	8 oz.	107	15	5	3	NA	1 Bread, 1 Fat
McDONALD'S							
Hamburger	3.5 oz.	255	30	12	10	520	2 Bread, 1 Med.-Fat Meat, 1 Fat
Cheeseburger	4 oz.	307	30	15	14	767	2 Bread, 1 Med.-Fat Meat, 2 Fat
Big Mac	7 oz.	563	41	26	33	1,010	3 Bread, 3 Med.-Fat Meat, 3 Fat
Quarter Pounder	5.8 oz.	424	33	24	22	735	2 Bread, 3 Med.-Fat Meat, 1 Fat

Item	Serving	Calories				Sodium	Exchanges
Filet-O-Fish	4.8 oz.	432	37	14	25	781	2½ Bread, 1 Med.-Fat Meat, 4 Fat
French Fries (Regular)	2.4 oz.	220	26	3	12	109	2 Bread, 2 Fat
Egg McMuffin	4.8 oz.	327	31	19	15	885	2 Bread, 2 Med.-Fat Meat, 1 Fat
Scrambled Eggs (1 Order)	3.4 oz.	180	2	13	13	205	2 Med.-Fat Meat, 1 Fat
Hash Brown Potatoes (1 Order)	2 oz.	125	14	2	7	325	1 Bread, 1 Fat

PIZZA HUT

Thin 'N Crispy Pizza

Item	Serving	Calories				Sodium	Exchanges
Beef	½ 10" Pizza (3 Slices)	490	51	29	19	NA	3 Bread, 3 Med.-Fat Meat, 1 Fat
Pork	"	520	51	27	23	NA	3 Bread, 3 Med.-Fat Meat, 2 Fat
Cheese	"	450	54	25	15	NA	3½ Bread, 2 Med.-Fat Meat, 1 Fat
Pepperoni	"	430	45	23	17	NA	3 Bread, 2 Med.-Fat Meat, 1 Fat
Supreme	"	510	51	27	21	NA	3½ Bread, 2 Med.-Fat Meat, 2 Fat

Thick 'N Chewy Pizza

Item	Serving	Calories				Sodium	Exchanges
Beef	½ 10" Pizza (3 Slices)	620	73	38	20	NA	5 Bread, 3 Med.-Fat Meat, 1 Fat
Pork	"	640	71	36	23	NA	5 Bread, 3 Med.-Fat Meat, 1 Fat
Cheese	"	560	71	34	14	NA	5 Bread, 3 Med.-Fat Meat
Pepperoni	"	560	68	31	18	NA	4½ Bread, 3 Med.-Fat Meat, 1 Fat
Supreme	"	640	74	36	22	NA	5 Bread, 3 Med.-Fat Meat, 1 Fat

FAST FOOD EXCHANGES*

215	SERVING SIZE	CALORIES (1 SERVING)	CARB. (GM.)	PRO (GM.)	FAT (GM.)	SODIUM (MG.)	EXCHANGES (1 SERVING)
TACO BELL							
Beef Burrito	6.5 oz.	466	37	30	21	327	2½ Bread, 3 Med.-Fat Meat, 1 Fat
Beefy Tostada	6.5 oz.	291	21	19	15	138	1½ Bread, 2 Med.-Fat Meat, 1 Fat
Enchirito	7 oz.	454	42	25	21	1,175	3 Bread, 3 Med.-Fat Meat, 2 Fat
Taco	3 oz.	186	14	15	8	79	1 Bread, 2 Med.-Fat Meat
WENDY'S							
Hamburger	7 oz.	470	34	26	26	774	2 Bread, 3 Med.-Fat Meat, 2 Fat
Cheeseburger	8.5 oz.	580	34	33	34	1,085	2 Bread, 4 Med.-Fat Meat, 3 Fat
French Fries	4.2 oz.	330	41	5	16	112	2½ Bread, 3 Fat
Chili	8.8 oz.	230	21	19	8	1,065	1½ Bread, 1½ Med.-Fat

Adapted from *Fast Food Facts*, a 1983 publication of the International Diabetes Center, 4959 Excelsior Blvd., Minneapolis, MN 55436.
*Nutritive values are supplied by companies. Some foods here also appear in *Family Cookbook* Volume I. Where there is a discrepancy, use the figures in this, the more current, chart.
**For occasional use *only*, preferably before exercise.
NA = not available.

13 □ INTRODUCING TOFU

You're tired of chicken but you want to cook with a food that's equally versatile, is high in protein, has no saturated fat, and is low in calories? Consider tofu, otherwise known as bean curd— a staple of Oriental cooking that is gaining increasing popularity in America's health-conscious homes.

Tofu is derived from pureed soybeans and is pressed into white cakes with a custardlike texture. This inexpensive protein source can be served raw (uncooked) or used in many other ways: boiled, steamed, stir-fried, baked, marinated, or deep-fried. Its natural taste is subtle, but when prepared with other ingredients it absorbs and complements the stronger flavors around it, mixing well with most foods.

Tofu can be "counted" in a few different ways, each of them equally acceptable.

3 oz. = 1 Lean Meat
Estimated nutrients per serving = CAL 61
                                    PRO   7 gm.
                                    FAT   4 gm.
                                    CHO 2 gm.
4 oz. = 1½ Lean Meat or 1 Medium-Fat Meat
Estimated nutrients per serving = CAL 82
                                    PRO   9 gm.
                                    FAT   5 gm.
                                    CHO 3 gm.

For anyone new to the delights of tofu, here is some advice for buying, storing, and preparing it.

BUYING TOFU

1. Buy only fresh tofu, which has by far the best flavor.
2. Check the date stamped on the package. For best results, serve before that date, which is usually seven days after the tofu was made.
3. If the store sells tofu in a large container filled with water, make sure the container has a lid on top. Tofu must be kept in clean water, and an open lid is an invitation for contaminants to drop in.
4. When the water in the container looks somewhat yellow, yet the date shows that the tofu is not out of date, you can generally assume that the color is from the soybean protein and that you do not necessarily need to worry about the tofu's freshness. However, put tofu in fresh water if storing it.
5. Read the label on the container to make sure the tofu is made without any preservatives or chemical additives.

STORING TOFU

1. Tofu should be kept in a sealed container in a refrigerator at all times; do not let it freeze.
2. Change the water daily until the tofu is used. In summer, tofu will last three to four days beyond the date stamped on the package. In winter, however, it will last up to seven days. Keep in mind, though, that tofu loses its flavor as the days go by.
3. Particularly in hot weather when you plan to serve tofu raw (uncooked), place it in a strainer and rinse with boiling water before using. This eliminates bacteria that may be present. Then put the tofu in cold water, cover, and refrigerate until used.
4. You may refresh old or leftover tofu by rinsing with boiling

water as described above; however, such tofu should be used within a day.

DRAINING TOFU

It is very important to drain tofu very well before cooking, otherwise it becomes somewhat watery and loses flavor. The following two methods of draining are most popular.

1. At least an hour before cooking, wrap the tofu with a clean dish towel. Place the tofu on something flat, such as a large plate or a chopping board, next to the sink. Raise one end of the board or plate several inches so that any liquid will go into the sink. Put another board or something flat on top of the tofu to act as a press. You can also put another weight, such as a plate on top of this, if necessary.
2. You may drain the tofu gradually in the refrigerator overnight. In this case, wrap the tofu with a clean dish towel in several layers; place on a large, flat plate. Just before using, dry the tofu well with either a paper towel or another clean dish towel.

Tofu
Recipes

Sprouts Salad with Low-Calorie Tofu Dressing

Yield: 4 servings
Serving Size: $\frac{1}{4}$ recipe
Exchange List Approximation:
    Meat, medium-fat $1\frac{1}{2}$
    Vegetable 2

Nutrient Content Per Serving:
CAL: 158   PRO: 13.6 (gm)
FAT: 6.8 (gm)   CHO: 14.4 (gm)
Na: 182 (mg)   K: 456.5 (mg)
Fiber: 2.6 (gm)   Chol: 68 (mg)

Ingredients

- 1 POUND TOFU, TOWEL-DRIED
- ½ MEDIUM ONION, CHOPPED
- 3 TABLESPOONS TOMATO PASTE
- 1 TABLESPOON APPLE-CIDER VINEGAR OR LEMON JUICE
- ¼ TEASPOON DRY MUSTARD
- 2 TABLESPOONS TOMATO JUICE
- 1 HARD-BOILED EGG, CHOPPED FINE
- 3 TEASPOONS SWEET RELISH
- 1 CUP SHREDDED CABBAGE
- ½ CUCUMBER, THINLY SLICED
- 1 LARGE (OR 2 SMALL) TOMATOES, CUT INTO 8 WEDGES
- 1 CUP BEAN SPROUTS
- 1 CUP ALFALFA SPROUTS
- LETTUCE LEAVES

Method

1. Combine tofu, onion, tomato paste, vinegar, mustard, and tomato juice; blend thoroughly.
2. Add chopped egg and relish; mix well.
3. Arrange vegetables and sprouts on lettuce in a salad bowl. Serve the dressing separately.

Fruit Salad with Tofu Dressing

Yield: 4 servings
Serving Size: $\frac{1}{4}$ recipe
Exchange List Approximation:
    Meat, medium-fat 1
    Fruit 1
    Fat 2

Nutrient Content Per Serving:
CAL: 223   PRO: 6.5 (gm)
FAT: 16.3 (gm)   CHO: 16.2 (gm)
Na: 66.2 (mg)   K: 308.7 (mg)
Fiber: 2.6 (gm)   Chol: 1 (mg)
Key Source Nutrients:
    Ascorbic acid: 54 (mg)

Ingredients

3	CUPS MIXED FRESH FRUIT (SUCH AS ORANGES, GRAPEFRUIT, APPLES, BANANAS, STRAWBERRIES, PINEAPPLE, AND GRAPES)
½	STALK CELERY, THINLY SLICED CROSSWISE
½	CAKE (8 OUNCES) TOFU, TOWEL-DRIED
1	TABLESPOON APPLE-CIDER VINEGAR OR LEMON JUICE
3½	TABLESPOONS VEGETABLE OIL
½	TEASPOON SOY SAUCE
3½	TABLESPOONS PLAIN YOGURT
	LETTUCE
	WATERCRESS

Method

1. Soak celery in cold water for 1 to 2 minutes. Drain well.
2. Combine tofu, vinegar, oil, soy sauce, and yogurt in blender. Blend thoroughly for about 2 minutes.
3. Mix together fruit and celery. Arrange on lettuce leaf. Garnish with watercress.
4. Serve the dressing separately. If it separates, stir before serving.

Eggplant-and-Tofu Casserole

Yield: 4 servings
Serving Size: $\frac{1}{4}$ recipe
Exchange List Approximation:
    Starch/Bread 1
    Meat, medium-fat 1$\frac{1}{2}$
    Vegetable 2
    Fat 1$\frac{1}{2}$

Nutrient Content Per Serving:
CAL: 300   PRO: 17.3 (gm)
FAT: 16.2 (gm)   CHO: 28 (gm)
Na: 925.2 (mg)   K: 1141.2 (mg)
Fiber: 5.2 (gm)   Chol: 137 (mg)
Key Source Nutrients:
    Ascorbic acid: 59 (mg)
    Folacin: 463 (mcg)

Ingredients

- 1 POUND TOFU, TOWEL-DRIED
- 2 TEASPOONS MINCED PARSLEY
- 2 EGGS, BEATEN
- 2 TEASPOONS UNBLEACHED FLOUR
- 2 SMALL EGGPLANTS, SLICED ½" THICK
- 1 MEDIUM ONION, THINLY SLICED
- 1 MEDIUM-SIZED, RIPE TOMATO, QUARTERED, THINLY SLICED
- ½ MEDIUM-SIZED GREEN PEPPER, HALVED, THINLY SLICED
- 8 PIECES FRESH MUSHROOM, THINLY SLICED
- 1 CLOVE GARLIC, MINCED OR CRUSHED
- 1 TEASPOON OREGANO
- 2 TABLESPOONS VEGETABLE OIL
- 4 TABLESPOONS TOMATO PASTE
- 2 CUPS TOMATO JUICE
- 3-4 TEASPOONS SOY SAUCE
  GRATED CHEESE (OPTIONAL)
  MINCED PARSLEY

Method

1. Combine tofu, minced parsley, eggs, and flour in a bowl.
   Mix until well blended.
2. Boil eggplant slices for 7 to 8 minutes until tender.
3. Heat oil in large frying pan, saute garlic briefly, then add
   remaining vegetables. Cook for 2 minutes over medium-
   high heat, stirring constantly.
4. Add tomato paste, tomato juice, soy sauce, and oregano
   and bring to boil. Reduce heat and add eggplant slices.
   Simmer for another 2 to 3 minutes.
5. Spread tofu mixture evenly over the vegetables. Cover and
   cook over low heat for another 5 minutes.
6. Sprinkle the top with grated cheese. Remove from heat.
   Leave covered another 5 minutes or until cheese melts.
   Garnish with minced parsley.
7. If a crispy top is preferred, bake in a preheated hot oven
   for 5 minutes.

Tofu-Stuffed Rolled Cabbage

Yield: 4 servings
Serving Size: ¼ recipe
Exchange List Approximation:
    Meat, lean 2
    Vegetable 2
    Fat 1

Nutrient Content Per Serving:
CAL: 192   PRO: 17 (gm)
FAT: 11 (gm)   CHO: 8.3 (gm)
Na: 608.9 (mg) K: 281.4 (mg)
Fiber: 1.5 (gm) Chol: 92 (mg)

Ingredients

  4 LARGE OR 8 SMALL CABBAGE LEAVES
  ½ CAN (6½-OUNCE SIZE) WATER-PACKED TUNA FISH OR CRAB MEAT, DRAINED
  ½ MEDIUM ONION, MINCED
  1 POUND TOFU, WELL DRAINED
  2 TEASPOONS MINCED PARSLEY
  ¼ MEDIUM-SIZED GREEN PEPPER, MINCED
  ¼ STALK CELERY, MINCED
  1 TABLESPOON UNBLEACHED FLOUR
  1 EGG, BEATEN
1½-2 CUPS SOUP STOCK: 2 HEAPING TEASPOONS SOUP MIX TO 1½-2 CUPS WATER
  1 TABLESPOON VEGETABLE OIL

Method

1. Steam cabbage leaves in boiling water for 1 minute. Drain.
2. Preheat oven to 350° F.
3. Heat oil in frying pan, saute onion, green pepper, and celery over medium-high heat for 1 minute.
4. In a mixing bowl, crumble tofu; add parsley, tuna fish, flour, and beaten egg. Mix well.
5. Add the vegetables and mix thoroughly.

6. Spread equal amounts of the mixture on top of each cabbage leaf. Roll tightly.
7. Put the cabbage rolls in a single layer in a large casserole. Add soup stock and cover the casserole with foil.
8. Bake for 25 minutes.
9. Cooking may be finished on top of stove by covering pan and simmering over low heat for 25 minutes.

Tofu Salad with Garlic Dressing

Yield: 4 servings
Serving Size: $\frac{1}{4}$ recipe
Exchange List Approximation:
    Meat, medium-fat 1
    Vegetable 2
    Fat* 5

Nutrient Content Per Serving:
CAL: 345   PRO: 11.5 (gm)
FAT: 30.2 (gm)*   CHO: 12.1 (gm)
Na: 107 (mg)   K: 325.1 (mg)
Fiber: 1.7 (gm)   Chol: 0

Ingredients

1   POUND TOFU, WELL DRAINED
1   MEDIUM-SIZED TOMATO, QUARTERED
½   CUCUMBER, PEELED, QUARTERED LENGTHWISE
½   STALK CELERY, CUT LENGTHWISE, SLICED INTO ½-INCH PIECES
¼   CUP WALNUTS, CHOPPED
2   TABLESPOONS RAISINS
2   TABLESPOONS APPLE-CIDER VINEGAR OR LEMON JUICE
5½   TABLESPOONS VEGETABLE OIL

1 TEASPOON SOY SAUCE
1 CLOVE GARLIC, MINCED OR CRUSHED
  LETTUCE LEAVES

Method

1. Cut the well-drained tofu into ½-inch cubes.
2. Soften the raisins in warm water for 5 minutes; drain and towel-dry.
3. Quarter the tomato; slice into ½-inch thickness.
4. Peel and quarter cucumber lengthwise; then slice into ½-inch thickness.
5. Halve the celery lengthwise; then slice into ½-inch thickness.
6. Mix together vinegar, oil, soy sauce, and garlic.
7. Arrange all the vegetables on lettuce in a salad bowl. Sprinkle with walnuts and raisins. Serve dressing separately.

*Note recipe is high in fat and may be more acceptable if divided into eight servings.

Marinated Tofu Salad

Yield: 4 servings
Serving Size: $\frac{1}{4}$ recipe
Exchange List Approximation:
    Meat, medium-fat 1
    Vegetable 1
    Fat 3

Nutrient Content Per Serving:
CAL: 236   PRO: 10.2 (gm)
FAT: 20.3 (gm)   CHO: 6.9 (gm)
Na: 99.7 (mg)   K: 209.5 (mg)
Fiber: 1.6 (gm)   Chol: 0

Ingredients

1 POUND TOFU, WELL-DRAINED
4 LARGE RED RADISHES, MINCED
1 MEDIUM GREEN PEPPER, MINCED
½ MEDIUM ONION, MINCED

Marinade
2 TABLESPOONS APPLE-CIDER VINEGAR OR LEMON JUICE
4 TABLESPOONS VEGETABLE OIL
1 TEASPOON SOY SAUCE
LETTUCE LEAVES
MINCED PARSLEY

Method

1. Cut tofu into 1-inch cubes.
2. Mix vinegar, oil, and soy sauce. Add the vegetables and mix well.
3. Pour mixture over tofu cubes in covered container and chill for at least 1 hour before serving.
4. Arrange on lettuce leaves and garnish with minced parsley.

*Fat is reduced if marinade is drained off before serving. Measure the amount drained.

14 □ HEALTHFUL HINTS

The practical aspects of preparing and choosing healthful foods are sometimes the most challenging part of meal planning. But there's a lot you can do fairly easily to enhance the value and variety of your meals, reduce kitchen costs, increase your food sense, and prepare for special events (such as that camping or canoeing vacation you've always wanted to take). And if these tips don't tell you all you need to know, the chapter also includes advice on how to find a Registered Dietitian (R.D.) who should be able to help you with just about anything else you need to know about food!

SUBSTITUTE WITH SPICE

Most of us relish a touch of the exotic in our lives. By rediscovering herbs and spices used by creative cooks for thousands of years, you can add a dash of the exotic to otherwise ordinary meals. Try rubbing rosemary on chicken before baking to transport yourself to the sea-sprayed cliffs of the Mediterranean, where rosemary, which means, "dew of the sea," was given its name. Use basil in a cucumber salad to conjure up visions of Italy and of glowing girls wearing sprigs of basil to show they are in love. Or, add a pinch of saffron to bread to feel as if you are sprinkling gold on dough. The thread-like stigmas of 70,000 crocus blooms are collected in southern Europe and western Asia to make just one pound of saffron powder!

But the best news is that sweet-tasting (but sugar-free) spices and some flavoring extracts can be used to sweeten foods without sugar. (See the heading "Ways to Cut Back on Sugar" for a list of spices.)

If you're concerned about high blood pressure, you will find using herbs and spices useful here too. They do such a wonderful job of flavoring food that you may be able to skip the salt, which can aggravate high blood pressure. And, a dash of the right spice can add zest to a dish without adding a single calorie!

Be sure your herbs and spices are as fresh as possible. It's best to buy in small quantities to keep infrequently-used spices, such as cardamom, at the peak of potency. Buy just a few tablespoons at a time and check freshness by looking for rich color and a full aroma. Or grow your own and dry them yourself.

Store your dried herbs and spices in airtight glass or tin containers in a cool, dry, dark location. (Paper is not airtight, and cardboard and plastic can absorb flavors.) Never keep your spices over the stove. Also, be sure to date each container; ground spices and dried herbs lose much of their flavor after six months.

Some herbs are better frozen than dried. These include chives, fennel leaves, parsley, winter savory, and tarragon. To prepare for storing, wash the fresh herbs and pat dry. Mince with kitchen shears or a knife, spread on a cookie sheet and freeze, then transfer to a plastic bag. This way, the minced herbs and spices will stay in separate easy-to-measure pieces.

When you are ready to use any herb or spice, give it the sniff test. If it doesn't have a strong aroma, it's best to discard it. Heat brings out the flavor of fresh herbs and spices. Rubbing them between warm fingers before adding to a recipe draws out the best flavor. For long-cooking dishes, most cooks recommend waiting until the last 30 to 45 minutes before adding the herbs. This prevents the flavoring oils from evaporating.

When doubling a recipe, add only 1½ times the amount of herbs and spices. If tripling a recipe, add twice the amount. When substituting use the following guide:

1 Tablespoon fresh herb =
1 teaspoon dried = ⅓ teaspoon ground

Use a light hand when trying out a new herb or spice. Start out with about ¼ teaspoon for four servings, adding more later if needed. To get started in the exotic world of spices, experiment with these suggestions:

DILL WEED: Sprinkle on fish, potatoes, or cucumbers.

CUMIN: Sprinkle on cheese when grilling a sandwich. Add 1 teaspoon to cornbread batter.

MARJORAM: Add to egg or tomato dishes, using ½ teaspon for four servings.

FENNEL SEED: Crush one teaspoon and add to a pound of hamburger when browning to give a taste similar to Italian sausage.

CILANTRO: Its leaves are known as Chinese parsley. Its seeds are called coriander. Try this herb in tomato sauce to give it a truly Mexican flavor. Also good in curries.

To avoid the salt found in many prepackaged herb mixtures, combine herbs and spices to make your own tasty blends. Try the following instead of salt on vegetables, meats, eggs, and in soups (calories and sodium content are negligible):

HERB BLEND 1 (RED)

Ingredients

- ½ TEASPOON EACH DRIED THYME LEAVES, DRIED MARJORAM LEAVES, CELERY SEED, GARLIC POWDER
- ¼ TEASPOON EACH ONION POWDER, CURRY POWDER, AND DRIED DILL WEED
- 3 TEASPOON PAPRIKA

HERB BLEND 2 (GREEN)

Ingredients

- 1 TEASPOON THYME
- 1½ TEASPOON SAVORY

1   TEASPOON SAGE
1½   TEASPOON MARJORAM
1   TEASPOON ROSEMARY
1   TEASPOON TARRAGON

WAYS TO CUT BACK ON SUGAR

You have many options for cutting back on sugar:

INSTEAD OF:	USE MORE:
Soft drinks/fruit drinks	Diet soft drinks
	Seltzer
	Juices mixed with seltzer/carbonated water
	Herb teas
	Water
Super-sweet desserts	Desserts that use fruit
	Desserts that use sweet spices (see section following)
Sugar or honey in coffee or tea	Dash of vanilla or cinnamon in coffee
	Lemon in tea
	Herb teas
Sugar-coated cereals	Low-sugar cereals
Candy	Nuts
	Seeds
	Popcorn
Canned fruit in heavy syrup	Canned fruit in its own juice or fruit juice
Sweet rolls	Fruited muffins
	Bagels
	English muffins

SWEET SPICES*

CINNAMON: Bark of true cinnamon tree that grows in Ceylon. Mild in flavor. Used to flavor pickles, preserves, fruits, hot drinks, and as "spoons" for after-dinner coffee. When ground, used in baked goods, puddings, cake, mincemeat.

CLOVES: Nail-shaped dried flower bud of the clove tree. Rich and pungent in flavor. Used whole in baked ham, pickling, and drinks. Used ground in cakes, cookies, conserves, desserts.

NUTMEG: Kernel of fruit of the nutmeg tree. One of the oldest known spices. Used as traditional flavoring for baked custard and other desserts. Also used in cream soups, sauces, stews, and vegetables such as spinach.

ALLSPICE: Dried berry with a flavor resembling a blend of cinnamon, nutmeg, and cloves. Used whole in stews, soups, gravy, preserved fruit, boiled fish, and for spicing meat. The ground form is used to season pot roast, baked goods, catsup, mincemeat.

ANISE: Seed of herbaceous plant of Mediterranean regions, has subtle licorice overtones. Used in cookies. Oil used in spongecake. Chinese star anise used in watermelon-rind pickle.

CARDAMOM: The aromatic seed capsule of a plant native to tropical Asia. Used in cakes, cookies, and bread. Delicious in coffee. Smaller type is used whole in barbecue and basting sauces, and pickles.

CORIANDER: Seed or seedlike fruit of the coriander plant. Used in gingerbread, apple pie, or as an ingredient of curry. Fresh leaves of plant is Chinese parsley. Use leaves only, no stems, and do not chop. Float leaves in pea or chicken soup and in stews.

GINGER: Dried root of a subtropical plant. Warm in flavor. Cracked root used in pickles, preserves, chutney. Ground root used in cake, gingerbread, cookies, puddings, soups, pot roasts.

*Adapted from *Nutritious and Delicious,* by the Greater Cincinnati Dietetic Association and the Greater Cincinnati Nutrition Council, Joerger-Vetter Printing, Cincinnati, OH, 1982.

MACE: Lace covering on inner shell holding nutmeg. Flavor more delicate than nutmeg. Used in pound and yellow cake, oyster stew, spinach. Used whole in pickling, preserving, and fish sauces.

PUMPKIN PIE SPICE: Blend of cinnamon, nutmeg, ginger, and cloves. Used in pumpkin pie, on fruit desserts, apple pie, and on sweet yellow vegetables such as squash, sweet potatoes, and carrots. Also used in cookies, gingerbread, and breakfast buns.

Note: Even without using spices, you can usually cut back ¼ to ⅓ on the sweetener (and oil) called for in many recipes.

USING EGG WHITES
FOR WHOLE EGGS

The American Diabetes Association recommends a moderate intake of dietary cholesterol, which would be less than 300 milligrams per day. Since one egg yolk contains more than 250 milligrams, egg yolks should be limited to three a week. This prudent recommendation for cholesterol intake is consistent with the recommendations of the American Heart Association and other health groups.

What can you do if a recipe calls for eggs and you've already eaten your allotment of eggs for the week? Egg white can be substituted for whole eggs in most recipes. Most recipes listing eggs as an ingredient assume you will use a large egg, which is a 2-ounce egg (this weight includes the weight of the shell). You can use 2 egg whites (1½ fluid ounces) for each egg listed in a recipe. If you prefer to measure in tablespoons and teaspoons, you can use 3 Tablespoons + 1 teaspoon of egg white for one whole egg. If the recipe calls for 2 whole eggs you can use 3 egg whites.

Remember that egg yolks are not only high in cholesterol but also contain most of the calories in an egg. The yolk of one large egg contains about 64 calories, and the white contains only about 16 calories, so you not only decrease cholesterol consumption but save calories as well. The commercially available egg substitutes use 2 Tablespoons of egg white and 1 teaspoon of vegetable oil for each whole egg. If you are preparing an omelet or scrambled eggs, you may want to add similar amounts of vegetable oil for flavoring and yellow coloring to egg white. To achieve the yellow color of the egg yolk, you can also use ⅛ teaspoon saffron with your egg white mixture.

DECREASING CALORIES IN FAMILY MEAL PLANNING AND PREPARATION

To save calories, the most important food item to trim or delete from the family's meals is fat. Remember that fat is 2¼ times higher in calories than carbohydrate or protein foods. Simply pouring oil into a skillet unmeasured can increase the calories of the completed dish by several hundred. By making some permanent changes in your cooking techniques and learning to modify recipes, you can save thousands of calories per year.

Learn to "saute" or "brown" food using nonstick skillets or pans sprayed with a nonstick spray. Or try using a measured amount of oil or margarine, while cooking at a bit lower temperature than usual. You'll be surprised at how little fat you need.

You can easily get by without using any fat at all—instead use beef, chicken, or vegetable broth, lime juice, wine, or water. Add a couple of tablespoons of the liquid to the heated pan and allow it to reduce somewhat. Then add your items to be sauteed or browned and add more broth or water as needed. Mushrooms are a very low-calorie food—½ cup cooked contains fewer than 25 calories. They are often served as a side dish and are usually laden with butter, margarine, or oil used for cooking. This makes a low-calorie, nutritious dish very high in calories. Cooking them in a few tablespoons of chicken broth (or even wine), however, adds negligible calories. Otherwise, every teaspoon of fat in a serving raises the calories by 45. (Alcohol is safe in cooking because most of the calories burn off, leaving primarily good flavor behind.)

If you normally put a chunk of butter or margarine on all of your cooked vegetables, begin experimenting with spices and herbs instead. In fact, once your palate has become used to much less fat you will be surprised how good the vegetables taste all by themselves—especially if fresh or fresh-frozen and steamed until just crisp-tender.

When using milk in cooking, always use nonfat or low-fat, never whole milk. You will get the same nutritional value minus the fat calories (low-fat milk—2%—contains about the equivalent of one teaspoon of fat per 8-ounce glass, and nonfat milk contains a negligible amount). You may find it convenient to use powdered low-fat or non-fat milk, and don't forget to keep a few cans of evaporated skim milk on hand. It has many uses including as a luscious low-calorie topping when chilled and whipped.

Be sure to switch to low-calorie salad dressing whether homemade or store-bought, and not just for salads. For example, use a low-calorie Italian dressing as a marinade for chicken or fish. Brush it on while broiling or barbecueing instead of using heavy, calorie-laden sauces. Marinate crisp-cooked and cooled vegetables for a different type of salad or side dish.

Sour cream has fewer calories than butter, margarine, mayonnaise, or oil per tablespoon, and plain nonfat or low-fat yogurts have even less than sour cream. Try yogurt instead of mayonnaise as a base for salad dressings or for use in sauces and baking. Mix yogurt with chives and a touch of garlic powder for a delicious topping on baked potatoes.

Be sure to "de-fat" all of your soups, stocks, and stews. Let the dish chill and lift the chilled fat off the top. Remember that each teaspoon you skim off is 45 calories less. Make tasty gravies or sauces by using de-fatted drippings thickened with flour, cornstarch, or arrowroot. Remember that the majority of the calories in sauces and gravies are not in the thickener used but, rather, in the fat. Keep canned broth and soups (except creamed) in the refrigerator for easy use.

Just using some of these simple techniques will help you and your family save a significant number of fat calories.

FREEZING IN INDIVIDUAL PORTIONS

Fruits can be frozen in individual portion sizes to allow you to enjoy the taste of products from gardens and orchards year-round. Choose fruits that are in their prime—ripe, and firm. Prepare fruits for the way you plan to use them, such as peeled or diced. For fruits that tend to discolor you can add lemon juice, ascorbic acid, or a compound containing ascorbic acid, such as Fruit Fresh.

Fruits are sometimes packed with sugar or syrups when frozen to add texture and flavor. This is not necessary to prevent spoilage. Fruits can be packed unsweetened. Some fruits can also be packed dry without adding liquid. A syrup for freezing may be made from an artificial sweetener and water. The syrup should completely cover the fruit when used. Freeze in individual portions.

Fruits and vegetables stored at 0° F or below will maintain high quality for 8 to 12 months. However, unsweetened fruit may lose quality more rapidly.

CUTTING KITCHEN COSTS

With the rising costs of food, utilities, and medication, making ends meet is becoming more and more difficult. You may be tempted to try to save money by scrimping on food, but eating a well-balanced diet is an important part of controlling diabetes. Here are some ways to keep down food and energy costs and stay within your diet.

Efficiency can save you money. When cooking small amounts of food, save energy by using a small appliance such as a grill, toaster oven, slow-cooking pot, or frying pan instead of the oven.

When using the oven, make the most of its heat by planning complete oven meals so that all foods are baked at once (for instance, chicken, potato, squash, and custard), or by making many casseroles at once and freezing them for future use. To save oven time, be sure to thaw all frozen foods. Also, try not to open the door often, since every time you do, the temperature drops 25 degrees. Cooking temperature also drops when lids are lifted off pots. Check the heat in your oven with a thermometer to be sure you're not losing heat because of a faulty temperature gauge.

Preheating is necessary only for cakes and pastries, not roasts and casseroles. Overcooking shrinks foods and destroys many vitamins. Set a timer so you don't forget to turn off the oven on time.

Use pans with flat bottoms, straight sides, and tight-fitting covers for range-top cooking; they cook food more quickly and uniformly. Bring food to cooking temperature on high heat, then reduce to complete cooking.

If you use electric appliances, check with the electric company to find out which hours are off-peak in your area. Try to plan cooking times around these hours because the rate charged for electricity is lower.

Because electrical cooking units retain heat, you can turn off an electric "burner" or the oven 2 to 5 minutes before you expect the item cooking to be done.

Smart shopping and storage can also stretch your food dollars:

☐ Plan your menus for a week at a time to make the most of leftovers and save trips to the store.
☐ Do use a list and stick to it.
☐ Don't go shopping hungry.
☐ Don't let attractive displays entice you into buying on impulse.
☐ Take a calculator with you. That way you can figure costs per serving or keep a running total of your bill.
☐ When buying inexpensive cuts of meat, avoid those with

a lot of fat, gristle, or bone. Pressure cookers or slow-cooking pots are best for cooking "thrifty" cuts of meat, since such meats should be cooked at a low temperature for a long time (to avoid shrinkage and to lock in vitamins). Don't be deceived by low prices. Though some cuts of meat are a few cents more a pound, they are better buys because they include more meat.

- ☐ Make full use of bones (beef, chicken, and ham) by making broth, soups, or stews from them.
- ☐ Use all your leftovers! Try putting them into soup (if necessary freeze leftovers until you have enough), spaghetti sauce, pita (pocket) bread sandwiches, tortillas with a touch of cheese melted on top, or casseroles.
- ☐ Chicken is still one of the best buys around. Save money by cutting up whole chickens instead of buying parts. Sometimes there are good sales on fowl (mature female birds). Fowl may be tough, so use it for boiling, roasting, and making soups.
- ☐ Use dry beans and peas as protein source (see chart).
- ☐ When buying cheese, remember that domestic is less expensive than imported, and mild is less expensive than sharp.
- ☐ Powdered nonfat or low-fat milk is as nutritious as nonfat or low-fat liquid milk, and less expensive. Use powdered skim milk in cooking.
- ☐ "Day-old" bread is not necessarily stale. Enriched or whole wheat is best and can be used for toast or stuffing.
- ☐ Freeze breads and other baked goods that you will not eat within a day or two. Bread becomes moldy easily at room temperature (especially during hot weather) and becomes stale when refrigerated. These foods are easily defrosted.
- ☐ In addition to meat and bread, save room in your freezer for a large bag of frozen vegetables. They have less salt than canned vegetables and usually taste better. You can also freeze most fresh vegetables if you submerge them

first in boiling water for a few seconds. This is called "blanching" and will keep the vegetables from turning tough later on.

☐ When storing fresh produce in the refrigerator, keep it unwashed in plastic bags until you use it.

☐ If your orange juice often becomes sour in the refrigerator, buy frozen concentrate in cans. To save money, cut cans into halves and store the parts in aluminum foil in your freezer. Defrost one at a time. Or prepare the full container and then freeze small portions of the reconstituted juice.

☐ Hot cereals cost less per serving than ready-to-eat cereals. Small boxes may cost as much as three times more per serving than large "economy" boxes.

☐ Remember that in most cases plain is cheaper. For example, saltines and graham crackers cost less than fancy, filled, or flavored cookies and crackers. Long-cooking white rice or brown rice is cheaper than precooked or seasoned rice mixes. Precooked, convenience, and snack foods are always more expensive. Read the labels and avoid expensive, nutrition-poor foods whenever possible.

☐ Check unit prices.

☐ Generic labels may be a good buy depending on use. For instance, "generic" canned tomatoes can be cheaper for use in casseroles or spaghetti sauce than national brands.

WAYS TO MAKE COMPLETE PROTEINS FROM VEGETABLE COMBINATIONS

COMBINE THIS:	WITH THIS:
Rice	Legumes
	Cheese
	Sesame seeds
Wheat	Legumes
	Peanuts and milk
	Sesame seeds and soybeans

Corn	Legumes
Beans	Wheat or corn
Soybeans	Rice and wheat
	Corn and milk
	Wheat and sesame seeds
	Peanuts and sesame seeds
	Peanuts and wheat and rice
Sesame seeds	Beans or peanuts, and soybeans
	Soybeans and wheat
Peanuts	Sunflower seeds

MAKING SENSE OF FOOD CLAIM NONSENSE

Looking for straightforward nutrition advice? Good luck! Now that health has become a national obsession, con artists eager to make big money are competing with truly knowledgeable diet counselors for your attention. And you are left trying to sift the sound advice from the abounding fads and fallacies! Don't despair; here are some pointers:

MAKE SURE THE SOURCE IS UP-TO-DATE. New nutrition discoveries are being made all the time. If an article is more than a year old, be suspicious. It may be outdated.

SEEK RELIABLE SOURCES. This may be difficult because so many authors claim to be nutrition experts. Generally, however, you can trust nutrition textbooks or publications put out by reputable organizations, such as the American Diabetes Association, The American Dietetic Association, government agencies, and some popular sports, fitness, and women's magazines. Recognized nutrition experts include registered dietitians (R.D.s). A number of doctors (M.D.s and Ph.D.s), although not all, are also experts. If an author has a degree or claims to be a nutritionist, note whether he or she is affiliated with a hospital, a university medical or nutrition program, or some other accredited health institution.

GET ALL SIDES OF THE STORY. When reading about

controversial nutrition topics, such as the role of vitamin E, look for fair treatment of all sides of the issue. Try to differentiate between opinion and fact. Does the author back up his or her theories with confirmation by respected doctors and other officials? Is the information supported by research data? Also, who did the research? For example, a study that said cholesterol was great for you sponsored by someone interested in selling eggs may well be biased. (Eggs are high in cholesterol.)

DON'T BE DUPED BY UNSUPPORTED CLAIMS. One favorite selling tactic in advertising is to have celebrities endorse a product. But, what's good for a star might not shine for you. Another promotion technique is to call a product the "Newest Vitamin." In truth, no new vitamins have been uncovered since vitamin B_{12} was discovered in 1948. In addition, steer clear of products that promise overnight success or miracle cures. Just because a product is marketed doesn't mean it works.

DIETERS, BEWARE! People who are trying to lose weight are particularly vulnerable to sensational advertising. Watch out for illogical claims, such as "Lose 15 pounds a week eating all you want." They sound tempting, but the safest rate of weight loss for most people is 1 to 1½ pounds a week (unless you are on an unusually strict diet that is closely monitored by a doctor familiar with your health history). Also, approach with caution any diet that focuses on one particular food or nutrition. These diets are unbalanced and unhealthy and can have harmful side effects.

For more sound nutrition know-how, contact your local American Diabetes Association; local registered dietitian; city, county, or state health department; local or county Agriculture Extension Service; local community college or university.

FOR OUTDOOR ENTHUSIASTS

Camping, backpacking, canoeing. There's nothing like them— but to enjoy them safely, you will want to take some precautions.

These sports are so physically demanding that most people

need to take in many more calories than usual. On strenuous days of backpacking or canoeing, you may need as many as 1,000 extra calories a day. Enjoy the extra food, being sure that you eat enough to cover any insulin you take. (Also see Chapter 9, on exercise.) Snacks are always important for insulin users, but even more so with increased activity.

If you do any type of camping, pack enough food for the duration of the trip. It's helpful to plan daily menus in advance and then to pack foods for each meal together. Label each packet accordingly. Include extra food, too, in case a pack is lost or damaged. Remember to include plenty of food for snacks as well.

For canoeing and backpacking, choose compact, light-weight, nonperishable foods that are filling yet provide a concentrated source of nutrients. You'll be glad you packed compactly when that pack starts to feel heavier as the hiking goes on.

For people who take insulin, lunch should be an all-day meal during days of hard hiking or canoeing, and should be consumed in small and frequent feedings to provide a steady flow of fuel without overloading the stomach. Weariness tends to kill the appetite, but keep your food needs in mind.

You may use freeze-dried and other dried (dehydrated) foods. Freeze-dried foods are usually the best choice because their flavor is more like fresh foods, and freeze-dried items are virtually foolproof to prepare. Just add water and serve. (They also last indefinitely when kept dry.)

Be sure to take more than enough insulin and other medical supplies to last the duration of the trip. Divide your supplies between packs in case one pack gets lost or damaged and keep insulin well-cushioned and out of direct sunlight, although it does not need to be refrigerated unless you are on the trail for three months or more. To be sure that diabetes is kept in good control, test blood glucose regularly. This is not the time for a vacation from testing! Also be sure to wear your medical identification at all times.

MENU IDEAS FOR HIKERS AND CAMPERS

Be sure to include foods from all four major food groups: milk, fruit, bread, and meat. Also, drink enough liquid to avoid dehydration. Exchanges for common portion sizes accompany the suggested menu items here, but work out other menu ideas and the amounts you are likely to need with your diet counselor.

Note 1: Instant cocoa, instant oatmeal, peanut butter, granola, and Cheddar, Edam, Gouda, and provolone cheeses all keep well if wrapped in cellophane and kept out of the sun. See recipe section, Chapter 11, for granola recipes.

Note 2: Single serving packets of a sugar substitute can be carried for sweetening cocoa, cereal, beverages, and such.

BREAKFAST:
Fruit	Fruit juices (½ cup = 1 Fruit) or
	Dried fruit (see Fruit Exchange list in Appendix I)
Meat	Eggs (2 Tbsp. dried = 1 Med.-Fat Meat) or
	Canned meats (1 oz. = 1 High-Fat Meat)
Bread	Cooked cereal (½ cup = 1 Starch/Bread), or
	Biscuits (2-inch square = 1 Starch/Bread, 1 Fat) or
	Pancakes (3–4-inch = 2 Starch/Bread, 1 Fat), or
	French toast (1 = 1 Starch/Bread, 1 Med.-Fat Meat)
Milk	Cocoa (cocoa, artificially sweetened; instant dried skim milk) (1 cup = 1 Skim Milk)

A.M. SNACK
Bread	Granola (¼ c. = 1 Starch/Bread, 1 Fat)

TRAIL LUNCH
Fruit	Raisins (2 Tablespoons = 1 Fruit)
Bread	Ry Krisp (4 triple crackers = 1 Starch/Bread)
Meat	Hard salami (1 slice, ¼-inch thick = 1 High-Fat Meat), or
	Cheese (1 oz. = 1 High-Fat Meat), or

| | Peanut butter (1 Tablespoon = 1 High-Fat Meat) |
| Beverage | Artificially sweetened Kool-Aid |

AFTERNOON SNACK

Bread	Graham crackers (3 squares = 1 Starch/Bread), or
	Trail mix (without chocolate candy) (⅓ cup = 1 Starch/Bread, 1 Fat), or
	Granola bar (1 small bar = 1 Starch/Bread, 1 Fat)
Fruit	Fruit jerky (1 strip = 1 Fruit) or
	Dried fruit (¼ cup = 1 Fruit)
Beverage	Artificially sweetened Kool-Aid

DINNER

| Bread and Meat | Casserole (1 cup = 2 Starch/Bread, 2 Med.-Fat Meat, 1 Fat) |

Examples:
Macaroni and cheese
Spaghetti and meat sauce
Chicken and dumplings
Tuna and noodle
Spam and potatoes

Bread	Biscuits or cornbread (2-inch square = 1 Starch/Bread, 1 Fat)
Vegetable	Dried vegetables (1 ounce dried weight = 1 Vegetable)
Fruit	Dried fruit (¼ cup = 1 Fruit)

EVENING SNACK

Bread	Soda crackers (4–5) = 1 Starch/Bread, 1 Fat) or
	Popcorn (3 cups = 1 Starch/Bread)
Meat	Sunflower or pumpkin seeds (¼ Tablespoon = 1 Med.-Fat Meat) or
	Peanut butter (1 Tablespoon = 1 High-Fat Meat, 2 Fat)
Fruit	Marshmallows (2 large = 1 Fruit)
Milk	Cocoa (as above, 1 cup = 1 Skim Milk)

Recipes

Meat

Meat □ 151

Beef Burgundy

Yield: 4 servings
Exchanges per
1 cup serving:
  2 Lean Meat
  3 Vegetable
  1 Bread

Estimated nutrients
per serving:
CAL 211 Na 346
CHO 19   K 645
PRO 21 Fiber 3
FAT 4

Ingredients

3/4 POUND BEEF ROUND, WELL-TRIMMED
1/2 TEASPOON SALT
1/8 TEASPOON PEPPER
1 BAY LEAF
1/8 TEASPOON THYME LEAVES
1 1/2 CUPS WATER
1 1/2 CUPS DICED POTATOES
1 CUP SLICED CARROTS
1/2 CUP DICED CELERY
1/3 CUP CH
1 CUP SL
3 TABL
1/4 CUP
1/3 CUP
PARSLEY

THYME

Summersausage

Yield: 80 slices (¼-inch thick)
Serving Size: 3 slices
Exchange List Approximation:
    Meat, medium-fat 1

Nutrient Content per Serving:
CAL: 65   PRO: 5.4 (gm)
FAT: 4.7 (gm)   CHO: 0
Na: 255.8 (mg) K: 65.5 (mg)
Fiber: 0   Chol: 21 (mg)

Ingredients

2   POUNDS HAMBURGER
2   TABLESPOONS TENDERIZER
1   TEASPOON ONION POWDER
½   TEASPOON GARLIC POWDER
1   CUP WATER

Method

1.   Hickory smoke if desired.
2.   Roll into two rolls, each about 12 inches long.
3.   Refrigerate 24 hours.
4.   Bake on rack, after piercing with fork, at 150° F for at least 8 hours.

Beef Jerky

Yield: 8 servings
Serving Size: 1 ounce
Exchange List Approximation:
    Meat, lean 2

Nutrient Content per Serving:
CAL: 119   PRO: 10 (gm)
FAT: 8.6 (gm) CHO: 0.1 (gm)
Na: 40.6 (mg) K: 118.7 (mg)
Fiber: 0   Chol: 69 (mg)

Ingredients

1 POUND HAMBURGER, BEEF, OR CHICKEN
1 EGG
SPICES, SEASON TO TASTE

Method

1. Roll out as thinly as possible.
2. Place on cookie sheet and bake at 150° F for at least 8 hours.
3. Cut or break into 8 equal pieces.

Biscuits

Yield: 4 biscuits
Serving Size: 1 biscuit
Exchange List Approximation:
    Starch/Bread 1

Nutrient Content per Serving:
CAL: 92   PRO: 2.4 (gm)
FAT: 1.2 (gm) CHO: 17.5 (gm)
Na: 95 (mg)   K: 22.6 (mg)
Fiber: 0.8 (gm) Chol: 0

Ingredients

2 PINCHES SALT
2 FISTFULS FLOUR
3 PINCHES BAKING POWDER
1 TEASPOON FAT

Method

1. Add water until dough is formed.
2. Place in aluminum foil and roll edges of foil tightly.
3. Bake on hot coals for 15 to 20 minutes, turning once after 7 to 10 minutes.

Gorp

Yield: 20 servings
Serving Size: ⅓ cup
Exchange List Approximation:
    Starch/Bread 1
    Fat 1½

Nutrient Content per Serving:
CAL: 135   PRO: 3.7 (gm)
FAT: 8 (gm)   CHO: 14.6 (gm)
Na: 151 (mg)   K: 188.5 (mg)
Fiber: 2.6 (gm) Chol: 0

Ingredients

1 CUP SALTED PEANUTS
1 CUP RAISINS
1 CUP COCONUT
1 CUP SALTED SUNFLOWER SEEDS
1 CUP OF EACH CEREAL: BRAN, WHEAT, CORN CHEX

Method

1. Mix all ingredients together.

HOW TO CHOOSE
A DIET COUNSELOR

The cornerstone of good diabetes management is good nutrition. And to meet your particular lifestyle and medical needs you should have individual counseling. Good counseling includes more than a preprinted meal plan with a list of foods to eat or avoid. It includes personal talks even after you leave the hospital to insure that the meal plan you receive is one you can live with.

THE COUNSELING PROCESS

What can you expect when you go to a dietitian or other diet counselor? Often, good counseling consists of three phases. During the first phase, the dietitian gets to know you by asking questions about your lifestyle and your diabetes treatment program. Do you take insulin and, if so, how much? Are you trying to lose or gain weight? Do you have any food allergies? What foods do you like or dislike? Who prepares your meals, and where do you usually eat them? If you eat in a restaurant every day, you probably have less control over calories than if you prepare your meals at home. And if you frequently eat with a lot of people, you might be overinfluenced by what others are eating.

Once these questions are answered, your counseling moves into the second phase. You and your diet counselor prepare a meal plan listing foods you can eat and foods you usually cannot. You will probably be advised to try your new meal plan for a week to a month, depending on your condition and the diet counselor's judgment. After the trial period, you will visit the dietitian again (phase three) to review the plan's success and make any needed adjustments.

FINDING A DIET COUNSELOR

Now that you know what good counseling involves, where do you find a good dietitian? Almost anyone can hang a shingle in front of his or her home proclaiming, "Nutritionist." But the most qualified ones are registered dietitians (R.D.). To become an R.D., a person must have a bachelor's degree with an emphasis in nutrition, plus qualifying experience in an American Dietetic Association accredited or approved program. In addition, the candidate must pass an examination given by the Commission on Dietetic Registration. Once someone becomes a registered dietitian, he or she may work in a hospital or go into private practice as a consulting dietitian. To keep "registered" status, the dietitian must have continuing education, which assures the public of the person's continuing competence to practice.

You can find a consulting or registered dietitian in several ways. One, ask your doctor for recommendations. Two, check your local American Diabetes Association affiliate or American Heart Association chapter. They may have a referral service or offer some counseling themselves. Three, see if any hospital outpatient clinics in your area offer nutrition counseling for diabetics. Four, write to The American Dietetic Association. Five, telephone or write to government health agencies, such as your county or state health department or the nutrition division of the Agriculture Extension Service. Their numbers can be found in the telephone white pages under "Government."

WHAT TO LOOK FOR

Once you find the name of a registered dietitian who counsels diabetics, how do you know you'll receive the best care possible? Call several dietitians and ask questions to find out which are most thorough and compatible with you. For example:

- □ Will he or she ask questions about your diabetes history?
- □ Will the diet be tailored specifically to you, or will it be a general meal plan? Of course, you'll want an individual diet.
- □ Will you be asked to keep a diary of what you eat? Dietitians usually like to see a record of what you've eaten.
- □ Will you have to go back for follow-up visits? At least one should be recommended to check the progress of the diet.

□　Does the dietitian require a medical examination? Many dietitians want you to have a physical no more than two months prior to your visit because such disorders as high blood pressure or high cholesterol levels can affect diet. If no medical examination is required, you might be better off with someone else.

Dietitians can be thorough but still work in different styles. Some like to conduct a long first visit, lasting up to an hour. Others may prefer to have a longer second visit to check on your progress. Either way is all right as long as you receive complete, personal attention.

Dietitians also differ in their fees, usually charging from $25 to $60 per hour. Sometimes a less expensive fee means inferior service, but it can also mean that the dietitian has fewer overhead expenses to meet. Don't judge a dietitian solely by price. Remember, too, that these fees are sometimes covered by medical insurance, depending on the state where you live and the type of insurance you have.

Once you've found a suitable dietitian, don't go to him or her expecting miracles. Good nutrition counseling will help you control your diabetes, but only if you stay on your prescribed diet. By taking the responsibility for following your meal plan, you'll be helping yourself live a comfortable, healthy life.

APPENDIX I: MEAL PLANNING USING EXCHANGE LISTS*

A widely used guide to meal planning for people with diabetes and for others who want a healthful diet is the *Exchange Lists for Meal Planning. The Exchange Lists* enable people to include a wide variety of foods in what they eat each day, without having to calculate calories and balance nutrients. There are six Exchange Lists, or food classes:

1. Starch/Bread
2. Meat (Lean, Medium-Fat, High-Fat)

*The Exchange Lists are the basis of a meal-planning system designed by a committee of the American Diabetes Association and The American Dietetic Association. While designed primarily for people with diabetes and others who must follow special diets, the Exchange Lists are based on principles of good nutrition that apply to everyone. Copyright © 1986 American Diabetes Association, Inc., The American Dietetic Association.

This appendix is adapted from the book *The American Diabetes Association/The American Dietetic Association Family Cookbook* by the American Diabetes Association/The American Dietetic Association, copyright © 1980 by The American Diabetes Association/The American Dietetic Association. Published by Prentice Hall Press, New York, NY 10023.

3. Vegetable
4. Fruit
5. Milk (Skim, Low-Fat, Whole)
6. Fat

Think of exchanges as trades or options. A food within a particular Exchange List can be substituted, traded, or exchanged for another food within the same list. Specific serving sizes are indicated for each food and must be substituted in the amounts specified. Trading one food for another within one Exchange List does not significantly alter the calorie, protein, fat, and carbohydrate content of your meal plan, although foods do vary slightly. To ensure that all your nutrient needs are met, choose a variety of foods even *within* lists.

When prescribing a meal plan for treatment of diabetes, a diet counselor considers an individual's nutritional status, weight, age, sex, daily activity, and whether or not medication is needed to help control diabetes. If insulin is taken, the counselor will also take into account the type and the number and timing of injections daily. (See Chapter 15 for advice on how to choose a dietitian.)

The diet is prescribed in terms of the number of calories and amounts of carbohydrate, protein, and fat for each day. These can be translated into a variety of meals and snacks. A daily meal plan can be tailored to suit the individual's lifestyle, tastes, and budget. It can be altered from time to time even if the basic diet prescription remains the same.

A SAMPLE MEAL PLAN

A sample meal-planning pattern similar to one a registered dietitian might help you develop is shown in the following table. *Note: Do not use this for your meal plan.* Each person who has diabetes should have an individual plan that he or she works out with a diet counselor.

YOUR MEAL PLAN IN EXCHANGES

Must be planned with the assistance of your diet counselor

Meal plan for _____ John Doe _____
                            (name)

Carbohydrate	274 grams	Protein	88 grams	Fat	57 grams	Calories 1961

	1 Starch/ Bread	2 Med.- Fat Meat	3 Veg.	4 Fruit	5 Milk	6 Fat
Breakfast Time 8:00 AM	3	—	—	2	1 skim	2
Snack Time none	—	—	—	—	—	—
Lunch or Dinner Time 12:30 PM	4	2	1	1	—	2
Snack Time none	—	—	—	—	—	—
Dinner or Supper Time 6:00 PM	3	3	1	1	—	2
Bedtime Snack Time 9:30 PM	1	—	—	1	1 skim	1

The numbers 1 to 6 across the top of the table above refer to specific numbered Exchange Lists at the end of this chapter. Meals and snacks are identified in the left margin. The number in the box indicates how many choices to make from the specified Exchange List.

For example, follow across the middle of the chart and see what's for lunch: One Vegetable (list 3) and a serving of fruit or juice (list 4). The four choices from the Starch/Bread list (1) will permit two sandwiches, each made with two slices of whole-grain bread, 1 ounce of meat (list 2), and 1 teaspoon of mayonnaise-type dressing (list 6). A noncaloric beverage of choice can be added. This is just one possible menu; your imagination is the limit.

The reason for dividing food into six different groups is that foods vary in their carbohydrate, protein, fat, and calorie content. Each Exchange List contains foods that are alike — each choice contains about the same amount of carbohydrate, protein, fat, and calories.

The following chart shows the amount of these nutrients in one serving from each Exchange List.

EXCHANGE LIST	CHO (grams)	PRO (grams)	FAT (grams)	CALORIES
Starch/Bread	15	3	trace	80
Meat				
Lean	—	7	3	55
Medium-Fat	—	7	5	75
High-Fat	—	7	8	100
Vegetable	5	2	—	25
Fruit	15	—	—	60
Milk				
Skim	12	8	trace	90
Low-Fat	12	8	5	120
Whole	12	8	8	150
Fat	—	—	5	45

As you read the Exchange Lists, you will notice that one choice often is a larger amount of food than another choice from the same list. Because foods are so different, each food is measured or weighed so the amount of carbohydrate, protein, fat, and calories is the same in each choice.

You will notice footnotes on some foods in the exchange groups. For example, foods that are high in fiber (3 grams or more per normal serving). High-fiber foods are good for you. It is important to eat more of these foods.

Foods that are high in sodium (400 milligrams or more of sodium per normal serving) are also footnoted. It's a good idea to limit your intake of high-salt foods, especially if you have high blood pressure.

If you have a favorite food that is not included in any of these groups, ask your dietitian about it. That food can probably be worked into your meal plan, at least now and then.

LIST 1   STARCH/BREAD EXCHANGES

Each item in this list contains about 15 grams of carbohydrate, 3 grams of protein, a trace of fat, and 80 calories.

Whole grain products average about 2 grams of fiber per serving. Some foods are higher in fiber.

You can choose your starch servings from any of the items on this list. If you want to eat a starch food that is not on this list, the general list is:

- ½ cup of cereal, grain, or pasta is one serving
- 1 ounce of a bread product is one serving

Your dietitian can help you be more exact.

CEREALS/GRAINS/PASTA

Bran cereals*, concentrated (such as
Bran Buds®, All Bran®)

*3 grams or more of fiber per serving.

Bran cereals, flaked	½ cup
Bulgur (cooked)	½ cup
Cooked cereals	½ cup
Cornmeal (dry)	2½ tablespoons
Grape nuts®	3 tablespoons
Grits (cooked)	½ cup
Other ready-to-eat unsweetened cereals	¾ cup
Pasta (cooked)	½ cup
Puffed cereal	1½ cups
Rice, white or brown (cooked)	⅓ cup
Shredded wheat	½ cup
Wheat germ*	3 tablespoons

DRIED BEANS, PEAS/LENTILS

Beans* and peas* (cooked), such as kidney, white, split, blackeye	⅓ cup
Baked beans*	¼ cup
Lentils* (cooked)	⅓ cup

STARCHY VEGETABLES

Corn*	½ cup
Corn on cob, 6 inches long	1
Lima beans*	½ cup
Peas, green* (canned or frozen)	½ cup
Plantain*	½ cup
Potato, baked	1 small (3 ounces)
Potato, mashed	½ cup
Squash, winter* (acorn, butternut)	¾ cup
Yam, sweet potato, plain	⅓ cup

BREAD

Bagel	½ (1 ounce)

*3 grams or more of fiber per serving.

Bread sticks, crisp, 4 inches long x ½ inch wide	2 (⅔ ounce)
Croutons, low-fat	1 cup
English muffin	½
Frankfurter or hamburger bun	½ (1 ounce)
Pita, 6 inches across	½
Plain roll, small	1 (1 ounce)
Raisin, unfrosted	1 slice (1 ounce)
Rye*, pumpernickel*	1 slice (1 ounce)
Tortilla, 6 inches across	1
White (including French, Italian)	1 slice (1 ounce)
Whole wheat	1 slice (1 ounce)

CRACKERS/SNACKS

Animal crackers	8
Graham crackers, 2½-inch square	3
Matzo	¾ ounce
Melba toast	5 slices
Oyster crackers	24
Popcorn (popped, no fat added)	3 cups
Pretzels	¾ ounce
Rye crisp, 2 inches x 3½ inches	4
Saltine-type crackers	6
Whole wheat crackers, no fat added (crisp breads, such as Finn®, Kavli®, Wasa®)	2-4 slices (¾ ounce)

STARCH FOODS PREPARED WITH FAT
(Count as 1 Starch/Bread serving, plus 1 Fat serving)

Biscuit, 2½ inches across	1
Chow mein noodles	½ cup
Corn bread, 2-inch cube	1 (2 ounces)
Cracker, round butter type	6

*3 grams or more of fiber per serving.

French fried potatoes, 2 to 3½ inches long	10 (1½ ounces)
Muffin, plain, small	1
Pancake, 4 inches across	2
Stuffing, bread (prepared)	¼ cup
Taco shell, 6 inches across	2
Waffle, 4½-inch square	1
Whole wheat crackers, fat added (such as Triscuits®)	4-6 (1 ounce)

LIST 2   MEAT EXCHANGES

Each serving of meat and substitutes on this list contains varying amounts of fat and calories. The list is divided into three parts based on the amount of fat and calories: Lean Meat, Medium-Fat Meat, and High-Fat Meat. One ounce (1 Meat Exchange) of each of these includes:

	Carbohydrate (grams)	Protein (grams)	Fat (grams)	Calories
Lean	0	7	3	55
Medium-Fat	0	7	5	75
High-Fat	0	7	8	100

You are encouraged to use more lean and medium-fat meat, poultry, and fish in your meal plan. This will help decrease your fat intake, which may help decrease your risk for heart disease. The items from the high-fat group are high in saturated fat, cholesterol, and calories. You should limit your choices from the high-fat group to three times per week. Meat and substitutes do not contribute any fiber to your meal plan.

Tips:

• Bake, roast, broil, grill, or boil these foods rather than frying them with added fat.

- Use a nonstick pan spray or a nonstick pan to brown or fry these foods.
- Trim off visible fat before and after cooking.
- Do not add flour, bread crumbs, coating mixes, or fat to these foods when preparing them.
- Weigh meat after removing bones and fat, and after cooking. Three ounces of cooked meat is about equal to 4 ounces of raw meat. Some examples of meat portions are:

2 ounces meat (2 Meat = 1 small chicken leg or thigh
    Exchanges   ½ cup cottage cheese or tuna

3 ounces meat (3 Meat = 1 medium pork chop
    Exchanges   1 small hamburger
                         ½ chicken breast (1 side)
                         1 unbreaded fish fillet
                         cooked meat, about the size of a deck of cards

- Restaurants usually serve prime cuts of meat, which are high in fat and calories.

LEAN MEAT AND SUBSTITUTES
(One Exchange is equal to any one of the following items.)

Beef:	USDA good or choice grades of lean beef, such as round, sirloin, flank steak, tenderloin, chipped beef*.	1 ounce
Pork:	Lean pork, such as fresh ham; canned, cured or boiled ham*; Canadian bacon*; tenderloin.	1 ounce
Veal:	All cuts are lean except for veal cutlets (ground or cubed). Examples of lean veal are chops and roasts.	1 ounce

*400 milligrams or more of sodium per serving.

Poultry:	Chicken, turkey, Cornish hen (without skin)	1 ounce
Fish:	All fresh and frozen fish	1 ounce
	Crab, lobster, scallops, shrimp, clams* (fresh, or canned in water)	1 ounce (¼ cup)
	Oysters	3 ounces (5 to 7 medium)
	Tuna* (canned in water)	¼ cup
	Herring (uncreamed or smoked)	1 ounce
	Sardines (canned)	2 medium
Wild Game:	Venison, rabbit, squirrel	1 ounce
	Pheasant, duck, goose (without skin)	1 ounce
Cheese:	Any cottage cheese	¼ cup
	Grated parmesan	2 tablespoons
	Diet cheeses* with less than 55 calories per ounce	1 ounce
Other:	95 percent fat-free luncheon meat*	1 ounce
	Egg whites	3 whites
	Egg substitutes with less than 55 calories per ¼ cup	¼ cup

MEDIUM-FAT MEAT AND SUBSTITUTES
(One exchange is equal to any one of the following items.)

Beef:	Most beef products fall into this category. Examples are: all ground beef, roast (rib, chuck, rump), steak (cubed, Porterhouse, T-bone), and meatloaf	1 ounce
Pork:	Most pork products fall into this category. Examples are: chops, loin roast, Boston butt, cutlets	1 ounce

*400 milligrams or more of sodium per serving.

Lamb:	Most lamb products fall into this category. Examples are: chops, leg, and roast.	1 ounce
Veal:	Cutlet (ground or cubed, un-breaded)	1 ounce
Poultry:	Chicken (with skin), domestic duck or goose (well-drained of fat), ground turkey	1 ounce
Fish:	Tuna* (canned in oil and drained), salmon* (canned)	¼ cup
Cheese:	Skim or part-skim milk cheeses, such as:	
	Ricotta	¼ cup
	Mozzarella	1 ounce
	Diet cheeses* with 56–80 calories per ounce	1 ounce
Other:	86 percent fat-free luncheon meat*	1 ounce
	Egg (high in cholesterol, limit to 3 per week)	1
	Egg substitutes with 56–80 calories per ¼ cup	¼ cup
	Tofu (2½ x 2¾ x 1 inches)	4 ounces
	Liver, heart, kidney, sweetbreads (high in cholesterol)	1 ounce

HIGH-FAT MEAT AND SUBSTITUTES

Remember, these items are high in saturated fat, cholesterol, and calories, and should be used only three times per week. One exchange is equal to any one of the following items.

Beef:	Most USDA prime cuts of beef, such as ribs, corned beef*	1 ounce

*400 milligrams or more of sodium per serving.

Pork:	Spareribs, ground pork, pork sausage* (patty or link)	1 ounce
Lamb:	Patties (ground lamb)	1 ounce
Fish:	Any fried fish product	1 ounce
Cheese:	All regular cheeses*, such as American, Blue, Cheddar, Monterey, Swiss	1 ounce
Other:	Luncheon meat*, such as bologna, salami, pimento loaf	1 ounce
	Sausage*, such as Polish, Italian, knockwurst, smoked	1 ounce
	Bratwurst*	1 ounce
	Frankfurter* (turkey or chicken)	1 frank (10 per pound)
	Peanut Butter (contains unsaturated fat)	1 tablespoon

Count as one High-Fat Meat plus one Fat Exchange:

	Frankfurter* (beef, pork, or combination)	1 frank (10 per pound)

LIST 3   VEGETABLE EXCHANGES

Each vegetable serving on this list contains about 5 grams of carbohydrate, 2 grams of protein, and 25 calories. Vegetables contain 2 to 3 grams of dietary fiber.

Vegetables are a good source of vitamins and minerals. Fresh and frozen vegetables have more vitamins and less added salt. Rinsing canned vegetables will remove much of the salt.

Unless otherwise noted, the serving size for vegetables is:

*400 milligrams or more of sodium per serving.

• ½ cup of cooked vegetables or vegetable juice
• 1 cup of raw vegetables

Artichoke	Cauliflower	Rutabaga
(½ medium)	Eggplant	Sauerkraut*
Asparagus	Greens (collard,	Spinach, cooked
Beans (green,	mustard, turnip)	Summer squash
wax, Italian)	Kohlrabi	(crookneck)
Bean sprouts	Leeks	Tomato (one large)
Beets	Mushrooms, cooked	Tomato/vegetable
Broccoli	Okra	juice*
Brussels sprouts	Onions	Turnips
Cabbage, cooked	Pea pods	Water chestnuts
Carrots	Peppers (green)	Zucchini, cooked

Starchy vegetables such as corn, peas, and potatoes are found on the Starch/Bread List.

For free vegetables, see Free Food List on pages 429–432.

LIST 4   FRUIT EXCHANGES

Each item on this list contains about 15 grams of carbohydrate, and 60 calories. Fresh, frozen, and dry fruits have about 2 grams of fiber per serving. Fruit juices contain very little dietary fiber.

The carbohydrate and calorie content for a fruit serving are based on the usual serving of the most commonly eaten fruits. Use fresh fruits, or fruits frozen or canned without sugar added. Whole fruit is more filling than fruit juice, and may be a better choice for those who are trying to lose weight. Unless otherwise noted, the serving size for fruit is:

• ½ cup of fresh fruit or fruit juice
• ¼ cup of dried fruit

*400 milligrams or more of sodium per serving.

FRESH, FROZEN, AND UNSWEETENED CANNED FRUIT

Apple (raw, 2 inches across)	1 apple
Applesauce (unsweetened)	½ cup
Apricots (medium, raw)	4 apricots
Apricots (canned)	½ cup, or 4 halves
Banana (9 inches long)	½ banana
Blackberries* (raw)	¾ cup
Blueberries* (raw)	¾ cup
Cantaloupe (cubed)	1 cup
Cantaloupe (5 inches across)	⅓ melon
Cherries (large, sweet, raw)	12 cherries
Cherries (canned)	½ cup
Figs (raw, 2 inches across)	2 figs
Fruit cocktail (canned)	½ cup
Grapefruit (medium)	½ grapefruit
Grapefruit (segments)	¾ cup
Grapes (small)	15 grapes
Honeydew melon (medium)	⅛ melon
Honeydew melon (cubed)	1 cup
Kiwi (large)	1 kiwi
Mandarin oranges	¾ cup
Mango (small)	½ mango
Nectarine* (1½ inches across)	1 nectarine
Orange (2½ inches across)	1 orange
Papaya	1 cup
Peach (2¾ inches across)	1 peach, or ¾ cup
Peaches (canned)	½ cup, or 2 halves
Pear	½ large, 1 small
Pears (canned)	½ cup, or 2 halves
Persimmon (medium, native)	2 persimmons
Pineapple (raw)	¾ cup
Pineapple (canned)	⅓ cup
Plum (raw, 2 inches across)	2 plums

*3 grams or more of fiber per serving.

Pomegranate*	½ pomegranate
Raspberries* (raw)	1 cup
Strawberries* (raw, whole)	1¼ cup
Tangerine* (2½ inches across)	2 tangerines
Watermelon (cubes)	1¼ cups

DRIED FRUIT

Apples*	4 rings
Apricots*	7 halves
Dates	2½ medium
Figs*	1½
Prunes*	3 medium
Raisins	2 tablespoons

FRUIT JUICE

Apple juice/cider	½ cup
Cranberry juice cocktail	⅓ cup
Grapefruit juice	½ cup
Grape juice	⅓ cup
Orange juice	½ cup
Pineapple juice	½ cup
Prune juice	⅓ cup

LIST 5   MILK EXCHANGES

Each serving of milk or milk products on this list contains about 12 grams of carbohydrate and 8 grams of protein. The amount of fat in milk is measured in percent of butterfat. The calories vary, depending on what kind of milk you choose. The list is divided into three parts based on the amount of fat and calories: skim/very low-fat milk, low-fat milk, and whole milk. One serving (1 Milk Exchange) of each of these includes:

*3 grams or more of fiber per serving.

	Carbohydrate (grams)	Protein (grams)	Fat (grams)	Calories
Skim/Very Low-Fat	12	8	trace	90
Low-Fat	12	8	5	120
Whole	12	8	8	150

Milk is the body's main source of calcium, the mineral needed for growth and repair of bones. Yogurt is also a good source of calcium. Yogurt and many dry or powdered milk products have different amounts of fat. If you have questions about a particular item, read the label to find out the fat and calorie content.

Milk is good to drink, but it can also be added to cereal, and to other foods. Many tasty dishes such as sugar-free pudding are made with milk. Plain yogurt is delicious with one of your fruit servings mixed with it.

SKIM AND VERY LOW-FAT MILK

1 cup skim milk
1 cup ½ percent milk
1 cup 1 percent milk
1 cup low-fat buttermilk
½ cup evaporated skim milk
⅓ cup dry nonfat milk
8-ounce carton plain nonfat yogurt

LOW-FAT MILK

1 cup fluid 2 percent milk
8-ounce carton plain low-fat yogurt (with added nonfat milk solids)

WHOLE MILK

The whole milk group has much more fat per serving than the skim and low-fat groups. Whole milk has more than 3¼ percent butterfat. Try to limit your choices from the whole milk group as much as possible.

1 cup whole milk
½ cup evaporated whole milk
8-ounce carton whole plain yogurt

LIST 6   FAT EXCHANGE

Each serving on the fat list contains about 5 grams of fat and 45 calories.

The foods on the fat list contain mostly fat, although some items may also contain a small amount of protein. All fats are high in calories, and should be carefully measured. Everyone should modify fat intake by eating unsaturated fats instead of saturated fats. The sodium content of these foods varies widely. Check the label for sodium information.

UNSATURATED FATS

Avocado	⅛ medium
Margarine	1 teaspoon
Margarine, diet*	1 tablespoon
Mayonnaise	1 teaspoon
Mayonnaise, reduced-calorie*	1 tablespoon
Nuts and Seeds:	
Almonds, dry roasted	6 whole
Cashews, dry roasted	1 tablespoon
Pecans	2 whole
Peanuts	20 small, 10 large
Walnuts	2 whole
Other nuts	1 tablespoon
Seeds, pine nuts, sunflower (without shells)	1 tablespoon
Pumpkin seeds	2 teaspoons
Oil (corn, cottonseed, safflower, soybean, sunflower, olive, peanut)	1 teaspoon

*If more than one or two servings are consumed, sodium levels will equal or exceed 400 milligrams.

Olives*	10 small, 5 large
Salad dressing, mayonnaise-type	2 teaspoons
Salad dressing, mayonnaise-type, reduced-calorie	1 tablespoon
Salad dressing (all varieties)*	1 tablespoon
Salad dressing, reduced-calorie†	2 tablespoons

(Two tablespoons of low-calorie salad dressing is a Free food.)

SATURATED FATS

Butter	1 teaspoon
Bacon*	1 slice
Chitterlings	½ ounce
Coconut, shredded	2 tablespoons
Coffee whitener, liquid	2 tablespoons
Coffee whitener, powder	4 teaspoons
Cream (light, coffee, table)	2 tablespoons
Cream, sour	2 tablespoons
Cream (heavy, whipping)	1 tablespoon
Cream cheese	1 tablespoon
Salt pork*	¼ ounce

FREE FOODS

A free food is any food or drink that contains 20 calories or less per serving. You can eat as much as you want of those items that have no serving size specified. You may eat two or three servings per day of those items that have a specific serving size. Be sure to spread them out through the day.

Drinks

Bouillon,† or broth without fat

Bouillon, low-sodium

*If more than one or two servings are consumed, sodium levels will equal or exceed 400 milligrams.

†400 milligrams or more of sodium per serving.

Carbonated drinks, sugar-free
Carbonated water
Club soda
Cocoa powder, unsweetened
  (1 tablespoon)
Coffee/Tea
Drink mixes, sugar-free
Mineral water
Tonic water, sugar-free

Nonstick pan spray

Fruit
Cranberries, unsweetened
  (½ cup)
Rhubarb, unsweetened (½ cup)

Vegetables (raw, 1 cup)
Cabbage
Celery
Chinese cabbage*
Cucumber
Green onion
Hot peppers
Mushrooms
Radishes
Zucchini*
Salad greens:
  Endive
  Escarole
  Lettuce
  Romaine
  Spinach

*3 grams or more of fiber per serving.

Sweet Substitutes

Candy, hard, sugar-free
Gelatin, sugar-free
Gum, sugar-free
Jam/jelly, sugar-free
  (2 teaspoons)
Pancake syrup, sugar-free
  (¼ cup)
Sugar substitutes
  (saccharin, Equal)
Whipped topping,
  low-calorie

Condiments

Catsup (1 tablespoon)
Horseradish
Mustard
Pickles*, dill, unsweetened
Salad dressing, low-calorie
  (2 tablespoons)
Taco sauce (1 tablespoon)

Seasonings can be very helpful in making food taste better. Be careful of how much sodium you use. Read the label, and choose seasonings that do not contain sodium or salt.

Basil (fresh)	Flavoring extracts	Herbs
Celery seeds	(vanilla, lemon,	Hot pepper
Cinnamon	almond, walnut,	sauce
Chili powder	peppermint, butter,	Lemon
Chives	and the like)	Lemon juice
Curry	Garlic	Lemon pepper
Dill	Garlic powder	Lime

*400 milligrams or more of sodium per serving.

Lime juice

Mint

Onion powder

Oregano

Paprika

Pepper

Pimento

Spices

Soy sauce*

Soy sauce, low
   sodium

Wine, used in
   cooking (¼ cup)

Worcestershire sauce

COMBINATION FOODS

Much of the food we eat is mixed together in various combinations. These combination foods do not fit into only one Exchange List. It can be quite hard to tell what is in a certain casserole dish or baked food item. This is a list of average values for some typical combination foods. This list will help you fit these foods into your meal plan. Ask your dietitian for information about any other foods you'd like to eat.

FOOD	AMOUNT	EXCHANGES
Casseroles, homemade	1 cup (8 ounces)	2 Starch, 2 Medium-Fat Meat, 1 Fat
Cheese pizza*, thin crust	¼ of 15 ounces or ¼ of 10 inches	2 Starch, 1 Medium-Fat Meat, 1 Fat
Chili with beans*†, (commercial)	1 cup (8 ounces)	2 Starch, 2 Medium-Fat Meat, 2 Fat
Chow mein*†, (without noodles or rice)	2 cups (16 ounces)	1 Starch, 2 Vegetable, 2 Lean Meat
Macaroni and cheese*	1 cup (8 ounces)	2 Starch, 1 Medium-Fat Meat, 2 Fat

*400 milligrams or more of sodium per serving.
†3 grams or more of fiber per serving.

FOOD	AMOUNT	EXCHANGES
Soup:		
Bean*†	1 cup (8 ounces)	1 Starch, 1 Vegetable, 1 Lean Meat
Chunky, all varieties*	10¾-ounce can	1 Starch, 1 Vegetable, 1 Medium-Fat Meat
Cream* (made with water)	1 cup (8 ounces)	1 Starch, 1 Fat
Vegetable* or broth-type*	1 cup (8 ounces)	1 Starch
Spaghetti and meatballs* (canned)	1 cup (8 ounces)	2 Starch, 1 Medium-Fat Meat, 1 Fat
Sugar-free pudding (made with skim milk)	½ cup	1 Starch
If beans are used as a meat substitute:		
Dried beans†, peas†, lentils†	1 cup (cooked)	2 Starch, 1 Lean Meat

FOODS FOR OCCASIONAL USE

Moderate amounts of some foods can be used in your meal plan, in spite of their sugar or fat content, as long as you can maintain blood-glucose control. The following list includes average exchange values for some of these foods. Because they are concentrated sources of carbohydrate, you will notice that the portion sizes are very small. Check with your dietitian for advice on how often and when you can eat them.

*400 milligrams or more of sodium per serving.
†3 grams or more of fiber per serving.

FOOD	AMOUNT	EXCHANGES
Angel food cake	¹⁄₁₂ cake	2 Starch
Cake, no icing	¹⁄₁₂ cake, or a 3-inch square	2 Starch, 2 Fat
Cookies	2 small (1¾ inches across)	1 Starch, 1 Fat
Frozen fruit yogurt	⅓ cup	1 Starch
Gingersnaps	3	1 Starch
Granola	¼ cup	1 Starch, 1 Fat
Granola bars	1 small	1 Starch, 1 Fat
Ice cream, any flavor	½ cup	1 Starch, 2 Fat
Ice milk, any flavor	½ cup	1 Starch, 1 Fat
Sherbet, any flavor	¼ cup	1 Starch
Snack chips*, all varieties	1 ounce	1 Starch, 2 Fat
Vanilla wafers	6 small	1 Starch, 1 Fat

*If more than one serving is consumed, sodium levels will equal or exceed 400 milligrams.

APPENDIX II: ETHNIC EXCHANGES FOR EXTRA FREEDOM IN MEAL PLANNING

Do you love ethnic foods but have no idea how to fit your favorite dishes into your meal plan? For those of you who use the *Exchange Lists for Meal Planning,* here are additional exchanges for Black American, Indian, Jewish, Mexican, and Oriental cuisines.* Because some foods here are high in salt and fat, check with your diet counselor before including them in your meal plan.

Note: This book contains several ethnic recipes. Each one of the recipes includes exchanges for one serving.

FOOD ITEM	SIZE OF SERVING	EXCHANGE VALUES
BLACK AMERICAN Chicken and dumplings	3 oz. chicken and 1 large or 2 small dumplings	3 Lean Meat, 1 Vegetable, 1 Starch/ Bread, 1 Fat

*The Indian, Jewish, Oriental, and many of the Black American food exchanges appear courtesy of the American Diabetes Association, Washington, D.C. Area Affiliate, Inc., and the Mexican food exchanges are from Loma Linda University Medical Center, in California.

435

Chitterlings	¼ cup	2 Fat
	2 ounces	1 Fat
Coo coo (cornmeal, ochra, butter, salt, water)	¾ cup	1 Starch/Bread, 1 Vegetable, ½ Fat
Fatback	1 slice	1 Fat
Hog mow	¾ cup	2 Lean Meat
Pig's ear	3 ounces	2 Lean Meat
Pig's feet	4 ounces (1 inch × 1 inch × ¼ inch)	1 High-Fat Meat
Smothered chicken (chicken, flour, milk)	¼ broiler	4 Lean Meat, ½ Starch/Bread
Steamed fish (cooked with a dab of butter)	4 ounces	4 Lean Meat, ½ Fat
Turnip greens (cooked with fat back)	½ cup	1 Vegetable, 2 Fat

INDIAN

Alu mattar (curried potatoes and peas)	1 cup	1½ Starch/Bread, 1 Vegetable, 3 Fat
Alu paratha (flat whole wheat bread with spiced potato filling)	1 6-inch bread	½ Starch/Bread, 6 Fat
Chana dal (curried chick peas)	½ cup	2 Lean Meat, 2 Fat
Kheema do pyaza (curried ground lamb with onions)	1 cup	3 Lean Meat, 2 Vegetable, 3 Fat

Kofta (ground lamb meatballs stuffed with almonds in curry sauce)	3 balls (approx.1½ inches)	3 Lean Meat, 7 Fat
Machli aur tamatar (curried halibut)	3 ounces fish	3 Meat, ½ Vegetable, 1½ Fat
Masala dosa* (crepelike pancake with spiced potato filling)	1	2 Starch/Bread, 4 Fat
Mattar pannir	½ cup	1 High-Fat Meat, 1 Starch/Bread, 1 Vegetable, 3 Fat
Murg kari (chicken curry)	3 ounces chicken	3 Lean Meat, ½ Vegetable, 2 Fat
Pakoras (deep-fried potato and chick-pea flour balls)	2 1-inch balls	1 Lean Meat, 5 Fat
Samosas (deep-fried filled pastries)		
with potato filling	1 large or 3 small	1 Starch/Bread, 2 Fat
with lamb filling	1 large or 3 small	1 Starch/Bread, ½ Lean Meat, 2½ Fat
JEWISH		
Bialy	½ of 1	1 Starch/Bread
Borscht, no sugar	½ cup	1 Vegetable
Challah	1 slice	1 Starch/Bread
Chopped liver, (homemade)	1 ounce	1 High-Fat Meat
Flanken	1 ounce	1 High-Fat Meat, 1 Fat

Gefilte fish	1 ounce	1 Lean Meat
Kippered herring	1 ounce	1 Lean Meat
Lox (smoked salmon)	1 ounce	1 Lean Meat
Matzoh meal	2½ Tablespoons	1 Starch/Bread
Pastrami	1 ounce	1 High-Fat Meat
Pickled Herring*	1 ounce	1 Lean Meat
Pot cheese	½ cup	1 Lean Meat
Potato knish	3-inch round (2)	1 Starch/Bread, 2 Fat
Sablefish	2 ounce	1 High-Fat Meat
Sorrel (Schav)	½ cup	1 Vegetable

*If in sour cream, omit 1 Fat from meal plan.

ORIENTAL

These figures do not include the rice usually served with these dishes.

Chicken with nuts	1 cup	2 Medium-Fat Meat, 1 Starch/Bread 3 Fat
Beef chow mein with	1½ cups	3 Medium-Fat Meat, 1 Starch/Bread, 2 Fat
chow mein noodles	½ cup	1 Starch/Bread, 1 Fat
Chicken chow mein with	1½ cups	3 Medium-Fat Meat, 1 Starch/Bread, 4 Vegetable, 2 Fat
chow mein noodles	½ cup	1 Starch/Bread, 1 Fat
Pork chow mein with	1½ cups	3 Medium-Fat Meat, 1 Starch/Bread, 4 Vegetable, 4 Fat
chow mein noodles	½ cup	1 Starch/Bread, 1 Fat

Eggdrop soup	1 cup	Negligible
Egg foo yung (shrimp)	2 patties with sauce	3 Medium-Fat Meat, 3 Fat
Egg roll	1	1 Medium-Fat Meat 1 Vegetable, 1 Fat
Ham-and-egg fried rice	1 cup	1 Medium-Fat Meat, 2 Fat
Moo goo gai pan	1½ cups	3 Medium-Fat Meat, 1 Vegetable, 2 Fat
Pepper steak	¾ cup	3 Medium-Fat Meat, 1 Vegetable, 1 Fat
Sweet-and-sour pork*	1 cup	2 Medium-Fat Meat, 2 Vegetable, 2 Fruit, 3 Fat
Wonton soup	2 wontons and 1 cup broth	1 Starch/Bread

*Part of the carbohydrate in this recipe, although called fruit exchanges, is derived from sugar (approximately 12 grams and 50 calories of sugar per serving).

MEXICAN

Guacamole	2 Tablespoons	1 Fat
Taco (meat, cheese, lettuce, tomato)	1	2 Medium-Fat Meat, 1 Starch/Bread
Tostada with refried beans	1 small	2 Starch/Bread
with meat	1 small	1 Medium-Fat Meat, 1 Starch/Bread
Tostada, beef	1 large	2 Medium-Fat Meat, 1½ Starch/Bread, 1 Fat
Burrito, bean	1 small	2 Starch/Bread
	1 large	1 Medium-Fat Meat, 3 Starch/Bread, 2 Fat

beef	1 small	1 Medium-Fat Meat, 2½ Starch/Bread,
Chili	1 cup	1 Fat
Chili sauce	2 teaspoons	2 Medium-Fat Meat, 2 Starch/Bread, 1 Fat
Corn chips	1 cup (1 ounce)	1 Fruit
Enchilada	1 small	1 Starch/Bread, 2 Fat
Meat or cheese	(6-inch tortilla)	1 Medium-Fat Meat, 1 Starch/Bread
Refried beans	½ cup	
Spanish rice	1 cup	1 Starch/Bread, 1 Fat
Spanish sauce	½ cups	2 Starch/Bread, 1 Fat
Tamale with sauce	1	1 Fruit, 1 Fat
		1 Medium-Fat Meat, 1 Starch/Bread

APPENDIX III: METRIC CONVERSION MADE EASY

	To Change	to	Multiply by
W **E** **I** **G** **H** **T**	Ounces	Grams	30*
	Pounds	Kilograms	0.45
	Grams	Ounces	0.035
	Kilograms	Pounds	2.2
V **O** **L** **U** **M** **E**	Teaspoons	Milliliters	5
	Tablespoons	Milliliters	15
	Fluid ounces	Milliliters	30
	Cups	Liters	0.24
	Pints	Liters	0.47
	Quarts	Liters	0.95
	Gallons	Liters	3.8
	Milliliters	Fluid ounces	0.03
	Liters	Pints	2.1
	Liters	Quarts	1.06
	Liters	Gallons	0.26
L **E** **N** **G** **T** **H**	Inches	Centimeters	2.5
	Feet	Centimeters	30
	Yards	Meters	0.9
	Millimeters	Inches	0.04
	Centimeters	Inches	0.4

| Meters | Feet | 3.3 |
| Meters | Yards | 1.1 |

*The precise figure is 28.25. However, some dietitians find it more convenient to use 30.

□ INDEX